OUR THEATRES IN THE NINETIES

PUBLISHED BY

Constable & Company Limited
London W.C.2

.

BOMBAY
CALCUTTA   MADRAS

Oxford University
Press

.

TORONTO

The Macmillan Company
of Canada, Limited

.

OUR THEATRES IN THE NINETIES BY BERNARD SHAW

IN THREE VOLUMES

VOLUME I

LONDON

CONSTABLE AND COMPANY

LIMITED

Revised and reprinted for this Standard Edition 1932

PRINTED IN GREAT BRITAIN
BY R. & R. CLARK, LIMITED, EDINBURGH

THE AUTHOR'S APOLOGY

In justice to many well-known public persons who are handled rather recklessly in the following pages, I beg my readers not to mistake my journalistic utterances for final estimates of their worth and achievements as dramatic artists and authors. It is not so much that the utterances are unjust; for I have never claimed for myself the divine attribute of justice. But as some of them are hardly even reasonably fair I must honestly warn the reader that what he is about to study is not a series of judgments aiming at impartiality, but a siege laid to the theatre of the XIXth Century by an author who had to cut his own way into it at the point of the pen, and throw some of its defenders into the moat.

Pray do not conclude from this that the things hereinafter written were not true, or not the deepest and best things I knew how to say. Only, they must be construed in the light of the fact that all through I was accusing my opponents of failure because they were not doing what I wanted, whereas they were often succeeding very brilliantly in doing what they themselves wanted. I postulated as desirable a certain kind of play in which I was destined ten years later to make my mark (as I very well foreknew in the depth of my own unconsciousness); and I brought everybody: authors, actors, managers and all, to the one test: were they coming my way or staying in the old grooves?

Sometimes I made allowances for the difference in aim, especially in the case of personal friends. But as a rule I set up my own standard of what the drama should be and how it should be presented; and I used all my art to make every deviation in aiming at this standard, every recalcitrance in approaching it, every refusal to accept it seem ridiculous and old-fashioned. In this, however, I only did what all critics do who are worth their salt. The critics who attacked Ibsen and defended Shakespear whilst I was defending Ibsen and attacking Shakespear; or who were acclaiming the reign of Irving at the Lyceum Theatre as the Antonine age of the Shakespearean drama whilst I was battering at it in open preparation for its subsequent downfall, were no more impartial than I. And when my own turn came to be criticized, I also was attacked because I produced what I wanted to produce and not what some of my critics wanted me to produce.

Dismissing, then, the figment of impartiality as attainable only through an indifference which would have prevented me from writing about the theatre at all, or even visiting it, what merit have these essays to justify their republication? Well, they contain something like a body of doctrine, because when I criticized I really did know definitely what I wanted. Very few journalistic critics do. When they attack a new man as Ibsen was attacked, they are for the most part only resisting a change which upsets their habits, the proof being that when they get the sort of play they blame the innovator for not producing, they turn up their noses at it, yawn over it, even recommend the unfortunate author to learn from the newcomer how to open his eyes and use his brains. Weariness of the theatre is the prevailing note of London criticism. Only the ablest critics believe that the theatre is really important: in my time none of them would claim for it, as I claimed for it, that it is as important as the Church was in the Middle Ages and much more important than the Church was in London in the years under review. A theatre to me is a place "where two or three are gathered together." The apostolic succession from Eschylus to myself is as serious and as continuously inspired as that younger institution, the apostolic succession of the Christian Church.

Unfortunately this Christian Church, founded gaily with a pun, has been so largely corrupted by rank Satanism that it has become the Church where you must not laugh; and so it is giving way to that older and greater Church to which I belong: the Church where the oftener you laugh the better, because by laughter only can you destroy evil without malice, and affirm good fellowship without mawkishness. When I wrote, I was well aware of what an unofficial census of Sunday worshippers presently proved: that churchgoing in London has been largely replaced by playgoing. This would be a very good thing if the theatre took itself seriously as a factory of thought, a prompter of conscience, an elucidator of social conduct, an armory against despair and dullness, and a temple of the Ascent of Man. I took it seriously in that way, and preached about it instead of merely chronicling its news and alternately petting and snubbing it as a licentious but privileged form of public entertainment. This, I believe, is why my sermons gave so little offence, and created so much interest. The artists of the theatre, led by Sir Henry Irving, were winning their struggle to be considered ladies and gentlemen, qualified for official honors. Now for their gentility and knighthoods I cared very little: what lay at the root of my criticism was their deeper claim to be considered, not merely actors and actresses, but men and women, not hired buffoons and posturers, however indulged, but hierophants of a cult as eternal and sacred as any professed religion in the world. And so, consciously or unconsciously, I was forgiven when many of my colleagues, less severe because less in earnest on the subject, gave deadly offence.

1906.

POSTSCRIPT, 1931. The foregoing was prefaced to a reprint of a selection from my criticisms entitled Dramatic Opinions and Essays, edited in America by the late James Huneker. Let me add now what I should have added then: that a certain correction should be made, especially in reading my onslaught on Shakespear, but also in valuing my vigorous slating of my contemporaries, for the devastating effect produced in the nineties by the impact of Ibsen on the European theatre. Until then Shakespear had been conventionally ranked as a giant among psychologists and philosophers. Ibsen dwarfed him so absurdly in those aspects that it became impossible for the moment to take him seriously as an intellectual force. And if this was Shakespear's fate what could the others expect? The appearance of a genius of the first order is always hard on his competitors. Salieri said of Mozart "If this young man goes on what is to become of us?"

and was actually accused of poisoning him. And certainly no one has since been just to Salieri. If my head had not been full of Ibsen and Wagner in the nineties I should have been kinder and more reasonable in my demands. Also, perhaps, less amusing. So forgive; but make the necessary allowances.   G. B. S.

These criticisms were contributed week
by week to THE SATURDAY REVIEW from
January 1895 to May 1898

OUR THEATRES IN THE NINETIES

SLAVES OF THE RING

SLAVES OF THE RING. A new and original play in three acts. By
Sydney Grundy. Garrick Theatre, 29 December 1894.

[5 *January* 1895]

OF all wonderful scenes that the modern theatre knows, com-
mend me to that in the first act of Wagner's Tristan, where Tristan and Isolde drink the death draught. There is nothing else for
them to do; since Tristan, loving Isolde and being beloved by
her, is nevertheless bringing her across the sea to be the bride of
his friend King Mark. Believing themselves delivered by death
from all bonds and duties and other terrestrial fates, they enter
into an elysium of love in perfect happiness and freedom, and remain there until their brief eternity is cut short by the shouts of
the sailors and the letting go of the anchor, and they find themselves still on earth, with all secrets told and barriers cast down
between them, and King Mark waiting to receive his bride. The
poison had been exchanged by a friendly hand for a love potion.

At what period Mr Sydney Grundy came under the spell of
this situation, and resolved that he, too, would have a "new and
original" turn at it, I do not know. It may be, since these dramatic
imaginings are really the common heritage of the human imagination, and belong to no individual genius, however grandly he may
have shaped them into a masterpiece of his art, that Mr Grundy
may have found the situation in the air, and not at Bayreuth. Howbeit he conceived it somehow, and proceeded to make out of it
the play entitled Slaves of the Ring, which differs from Wagner's
Tristan in this very essential respect, that whereas Tristan is the
greatest work of its kind of the century, Slaves of the Ring is not
sufficiently typical or classical to deserve being cited even as the
worst. It is not a work of art at all: it is a mere contrivance for
filling a theatre bill, and not, I am bound to say, a very apt contrivance even at that.

Here was the problem as it presented itself to Mr Grundy. Wanted, a married lady declaring her love for a man other than her husband under the impression that she and he are both dead, and consequently released from all moral obligations (this, observe, is the indispensable condition which appears to lie at the back of the popular conception of Paradise in all countries). The lady's conviction that she has passed the gates of death preserves her innocence as an English heroine. But what about the gentleman? Wagner made the gentleman believe himself dead also, and so preserved his innocence. But the English stage gentleman is as frail as the English stage lady is pure: therefore Mr Grundy's Tristan, though perfectly alive and well aware of it, takes the deluded lady to his bosom. Hereupon Mr Grundy owes it to his character as a master of drama that Tristan's wife should overhear these proceedings; and he owes it to his reputation as a master of stage technique that she should announce her presence by turning up a lamp, which the other lady has previously had turned down for that express purpose (as every experienced playgoer in the house plainly foresees) on the somewhat emaciated pretext that she prefers to sit in the dark. But it is of course possible that this also is a reminiscence of Tristan and Isolde's love of night and death. At all events, Miss Rorke turns up the lamp with the expertness due to long practice; and then, the dramatic possibilities of the theme being exhausted, the parties get off the stage as best they can.

Here you have the whole play. Once this scene was invented, nothing remained for the author to do except to prepare for it in a first act, and to use up its backwash in a third. And concerning that first act, I can only say that my utter lack of any sort of relish for Mr Grundy's school of theatrical art must be my excuse if I fail, without some appearance of malice, adequately to convey my sense of the mathematic lifelessness and intricacy of his preliminaries. I am not alluding to the inevitable opening explanations on the subject of "the old Earl" and "the late Countess," which Mrs Boucicault industriously offers to Miss Kate Phillips, who replies with much *aplomb*, "I see your point." Even if I

2

could follow such explanations, I could not remember them. Often as I have sat them out, I have never listened to them, and I never will; though I am far from objecting to a device which gives me leisure to look at the scenery and dresses, and helps to attune the ear of the pit to the conversational pitch of the house. But I do expect the author to get through the task of introducing the persons of the drama to the audience in a lucid and easily memorable way, and not to leave me at the end of half an hour feeling like a boy on his first day at a new school, or a stranger at an At-Home in a new set. Mr Grundy somehow managed to plunge me into the densest confusion as to who was who, a confusion which almost touched aberration when I saw a double leading lady walk on to the stage, both of her in full wedding dress. Like the dying Mousquetaire in the Ingoldsby Legends, when his friends tried to cure him of seeing a ghost by dressing up a nurse exactly like it, I exclaimed

"Mon Dieu! V'là deux!
By the Pope, *there are two!*"

The spectacular effect alone of so much white silk was sufficiently unhingeing. But when the two brides proceeded solemnly to marry one another with a wedding ring, I really did feel for a moment a horrible misgiving that I had at last broken through that "thin partition" which divides great wits from madness. It was only afterwards, when we came to the Tristan scene, for which all this was mere preparation, that I realized how Mr Grundy's imagination, excited solely by that one situation, and unhappily not fertilized by it sufficiently to bring its figures to life as created characters, was inert during this first act; so that in elaborating a tissue of artificialities to lead us to accept a situation which we would willingly have taken for granted without any explanations at all, he was unable to visualize the stage, even with two brides on it in full fig. Well was it for Mr Grundy that that act was under the wing of Mr Hare at the Garrick Theatre. Even as it was, there were moments when even the firmest faith that

3

something must be coming presently showed signs of breaking down.

The third act was better. There were no explanations, because, the murder being out, there was nothing more to explain. Unfortunately, though the plot was over, it was too late to begin the play. Further, the scene was in a conservatory, lit with so many lamps that Miss Rorke could not have made any particular difference by turning down one of them; so she jumped through a palm-tree instead, and cried, "Aha! Ive caught you at last," just as the other lady, though now convalescent and in her right mind, was relapsing into her dream with Tristan. In spite of this and a few other claptraps, there was a certain force at work in this act, a force which finally revealed itself as a burning conviction in Mr Grundy that our law and custom of making marriage indissoluble and irrevocable except by the disgrace of either party, is a cruel social evil. Under the stimulus of this, the only definite "view" anywhere discoverable in his works, he does manage to get some driving weight of indignant discontent into the end of the play, though even in the very heat of it he remains so captivated by worn-out French stage conventions that he makes one of his characters strike the supposed lover of his wife across the face with a white glove. Whereat it is really impossible to do anything but laugh and fish out one's hat to go. Being safely at home, well-disposed to Mr Grundy, and desirous above all things to slip gently over the staring fact that the play might be a better one, let me note gratefully that there is no villain, no hero, a quadrille of lovers instead of a pair, and that Mr Grundy's imagination, stretched and tortured as it is on the Procrustean framework of "the well-made play," yet bursts fitfully into activity—though not, alas! into rebellion—with angry vigor.

As to the acting, it is, on the whole, much worse than the play. Miss Kate Rorke, comely, ladylike and self-possessed, turns her emotion on and off by her well-established method with a business-like promptitude that makes the operation as certain as the turning up and down of the lamp. I feel sure that Miss Rorke would regard what I call acting as mere hysteria; and indeed I

4

should be loth to recommend it to her, as she is no doubt quite as popular, and perhaps a good deal happier, without it. Miss Calhoun, equally experienced, also obliged with whatever was wanted at the right moment. Her outcries in the first act, and again in the last, were discordant and unconvincing; and she should have made the Tristan scene at least six times as effective. Mr Brandon Thomas, as a broken-hearted personage charged with the duty of accompanying the play by an explanatory lecture in the manner of Dumas *fils*, was in a deplorable situation throughout. It happens that the plot devised by Mr Grundy to bring off his one scene has all the potentialities of a capital comedy plot. Mr Brandon Thomas divined this, and knew in his soul (as I read him) that if only he might be allowed the smallest twinkle of humor, he could make the play go like wildfire. Under these circumstances his enforced gravity had a baffled quality which was the more ludicrous because it looked as if he were killing the play, whereas the play was really killing him. Mr Gilbert Hare had a more important part than he would have been cast for in any other theatre; but as he played it with great care and thoroughness to the very best of his ability, it would be churlish to grudge him his advantage. Mr Bourchier had nothing to act, though, fundamentally, this observation is perhaps hardly more true of him than of the rest. Some comic relief gave an opportunity to Mr Hare and Miss Kate Phillips. Mr Hare, to be quite frank, had a very cheap job; but he got the last inch of effect out of it. He, also, was provided with a patent broken heart, though he happily kept it to himself until a moment before his final exit. Miss Phillips was hampered in the first two acts by that sort of comic part which is almost as much a nuisance as a relief; but she played a little scene with Mr Hare in the last act very cleverly, and was, it seemed to me, the only lady in the cast whose artistic sensitiveness had survived the case-hardening of professional routine. The stage-mounting and coloring were solidly and expensively Philistine, the dresses in the last act, and the style of domestic decoration in the first, epitomizing the whole history of plutocracy in England during the expiring century.

5

TWO NEW PLAYS

GUY DOMVILLE. A play in three acts. By Henry James. St James's
Theatre, 5 January 1895.
AN IDEAL HUSBAND. A new and original play of modern life. By
Oscar Wilde. Haymarket Theatre, 3 January 1895.

[12 *January* 1895]

THE truth about Mr James's play is no worse than that it is out of
fashion. Any dramatically disposed young gentleman who, cultivating sentiment on a little alcohol, and gaining an insight to the
mysteries of the eternal feminine by a couple of squalid intrigues,
meanwhile keeps well aloof from art and philosophy, and thus
preserves his innocence of the higher life of the senses and of the
intellect, can patch up a play tomorrow which will pass as real
drama with the gentlemen who deny that distinction to the works
of Mr Henry James. No doubt, if the literary world were as completely dominated by the admirers of Mr Rider Haggard as the
dramatic world is by their first cousins, we should be told that
Mr James cannot write a novel. That is not criticism: it is a mere
begging of the question. There is no reason why life as we find it
in Mr James's novels—life, that is, in which passion is subordinate
to intellect and to fastidious artistic taste—should not be represented on the stage. If it is real to Mr James, it must be real to
others; and why should not these others have their drama instead
of being banished from the theatre (to the theatre's great loss) by
the monotony and vulgarity of drama in which passion is everything, intellect nothing, and art only brought in by the incidental
outrages upon it. As it happens, I am not myself in Mr James's
camp: in all the life that has energy enough to be interesting to me,
subjective volition, passion, will, make intellect the merest tool.
But there is in the centre of that cyclone a certain calm spot where
cultivated ladies and gentlemen live on independent incomes or
by pleasant artistic occupations. It is there that Mr James's art
touches life, selecting whatever is graceful, exquisite, or dignified
in its serenity. It is not life as imagined by the pit or gallery, or

6

even by the stalls: it is, let us say, the ideal of the balcony; but that is no reason why the pit and gallery should excommunicate it on the ground that it has no blood and entrails in it, and have its sentence formulated for it by the fiercely ambitious and wilful professional man in the stalls. The whole case against its adequacy really rests on its violation of the cardinal stage convention that love is the most irresistible of all the passions. Since most people go to the theatre to escape from reality, this convention is naturally dear to a world in which love, all powerful in the secret, unreal, day-dreaming life of the imagination, is in the real active life the abject slave of every trifling habit, prejudice, and cowardice, easily stifled by shyness, class feeling, and pecuniary prudence, or diverted from what is theatrically assumed to be its hurricane course by such obstacles as a thick ankle, a cockney accent, or an unfashionable hat. In the face of this, is it good sense to accuse Mr Henry James of a want of grip of the realities of life because he gives us a hero who sacrifices his love to a strong and noble vocation for the Church? And yet when some unmannerly play-goer, untouched by either love or religion, chooses to send a derisive howl from the gallery at such a situation, we are to sorrowfully admit, if you please, that Mr James is no dramatist, on the general ground that "the drama's laws the drama's patrons give." Pray, which of its patrons?—the cultivated majority who, like myself and all the ablest of my colleagues, applauded Mr James on Saturday, or the handful of rowdies who brawled at him? It is the business of the dramatic critic to educate these dunces, not to echo them.

Admitting, then, that Mr James's dramatic authorship is valid, and that his plays are *du théâtre* when the right people are in the theatre, what are the qualities and faults of Guy Domville? First among the qualities, a rare charm of speech. Line after line comes with such a delicate turn and fall that I unhesitatingly challenge any of our popular dramatists to write a scene in verse with half the beauty of Mr James's prose. I am not now speaking of the verbal fitness, which is a matter of careful workmanship merely. I am speaking of the delicate inflexions of feeling conveyed by

7

the cadences of the line, inflexions and cadences which, after so long a course of the ordinary theatrical splashes and daubs of passion and emphasis, are as grateful to my ear as the music of Mozart's Entführung aus dem Serail would be after a year of Ernani and Il Trovatore. Second, Guy Domville is a story, and not a mere situation hung out on a gallows of plot. And it is a story of fine sentiment and delicate manners, with an entirely worthy and touching ending. Third, it relies on the performers, not for the brute force of their personalities and popularities, but for their finest accomplishments in grace of manner, delicacy of diction, and dignity of style. It is pleasant to be able to add that this reliance, rash as it undeniably is in these days, was not disappointed. Mr Alexander, having been treated little better than a tailor's dummy by Mr Wilde, Mr Pinero, and Mr Henry Arthur Jones successively, found himself treated as an artist by Mr James, and repaid the compliment, not only, as his manager, by charming eighteenth-century stage setting of the piece, but, as actor, by his fine execution of the principal part, which he touched with great skill and judgment. Miss Marion Terry, as Mrs Peveril, was altogether charming, every movement, every tone, harmonized perfectly with the dainty grace and feeling of her lines. In fact, had the second act been equal to the first and third, and the acting as fine throughout as in the scenes between Mr Alexander and Miss Terry (in which, by the way, they were well supported by Mr Waring), the result would have been less doubtful. It will be a deplorable misfortune if Guy Domville does not hold the stage long enough to justify Mr Alexander's enterprise in producing it.

Unfortunately, the second act dissolved the charm rather badly; and what was more, the actors felt it. The Falstaffian make-up of Mrs Saker, and the senseless drunken scene, which Mr Alexander played with the sobriety of desperation, made fuss instead of drama; and the dialogue, except for a brief and very pretty episode in which Miss Millard and Mr Esmond took part, fell off into mere rococo. Little of this act can be remembered with pleasure except Miss Millard's "Forgive me a little," and a few cognate scraps of dialogue. It had better have been left out, and the wanderings of the prodigal taken for granted. And, to weight it still further, it contained a great deal of the gentleman who played Lord Devenish, and played him just as he might have played an elderly marquis in a comic opera, grimacing over a snuff-box, and withering all sense and music out of Mr James's lines with a diction which I forbear to describe. He was very largely responsible for the irritation which subsequently vented itself on the author; and I am far from sure that I ought not to borrow a weapon from the Speaker of the House of Commons, and go to the extreme length of naming him.

Guy Domville is preceded by a farce (called in the bill a comedy) by Julian Field, entitled Too Happy by Half. It is deftly turned out from old and seasoned materials, and is capital fun for the audience and for Mr Esmond and Miss Millard. Miss Millard is not yet quite experienced enough to do very easy work quite well: she is the least bit crude occasionally.

Mr Oscar Wilde's new play at the Haymarket is a dangerous subject, because he has the property of making his critics dull. They laugh angrily at his epigrams, like a child who is coaxed into being amused in the very act of setting up a yell of rage and agony. They protest that the trick is obvious, and that such epigrams can be turned out by the score by any one lightminded enough to condescend to such frivolity. As far as I can ascertain, I am the only person in London who cannot sit down and write an Oscar Wilde play at will. The fact that his plays, though apparently lucrative, remain unique under these circumstances, says much for the self-denial of our scribes. In a certain sense Mr Wilde is to me our only thorough playwright. He plays with everything: with wit, with philosophy, with drama, with actors and audience, with the whole theatre. Such a feat scandalizes the Englishman, who can no more play with wit and philosophy than he can with a football or a cricket bat. He works at both, and has the consolation, if he cannot make people laugh, of being the best cricketer and footballer in the world. Now it is the mark of the artist that he will not work. Just as people with social ambitions will practise the meanest economies in order to live expensively;

9

so the artist will starve his way through incredible toil and discouragement sooner than go and earn a week's honest wages. Mr Wilde, an arch-artist, is so colossally lazy that he trifles even with the work by which an artist escapes work. He distils the very quintessence, and gets as product plays which are so unapproachably playful that they are the delight of every playgoer with twopenn'orth of brains. The English critic, always protesting that the drama should not be didactic, and yet always complaining if the dramatist does not find sermons in stones and good in everything, will be conscious of a subtle and pervading levity in An Ideal Husband. All the literary dignity of the play, all the imperturbable good sense and good manners with which Mr Wilde makes his wit pleasant to his comparatively stupid audience, cannot quite overcome the fact that Ireland is of all countries the most foreign to England, and that to the Irishman (and Mr Wilde is almost as acutely Irish an Irishman as the Iron Duke of Wellington) there is nothing in the world quite so exquisitely comic as an Englishman's seriousness. It becomes tragic, perhaps, when the Englishman acts on it; but that occurs too seldom to be taken into account, a fact which intensifies the humor of the situation, the total result being the Englishman utterly unconscious of his real self, Mr Wilde keenly observant of it and playing on the self-unconsciousness with irresistible humor, and finally, of course, the Englishman annoyed with himself for being amused at his own expense, and for being unable to convict Mr Wilde of what seems an obvious misunderstanding of human nature. He is shocked, too, at the danger to the foundations of society when seriousness is publicly laughed at. And to complete the oddity of the situation, Mr Wilde, touching what he himself reverences, is absolutely the most sentimental dramatist of the day.

It is useless to describe a play which has no thesis: which is, in the purest integrity, a play and nothing less. The six worst epigrams are mere alms handed with a kind smile to the average suburban playgoer; the three best remain secrets between Mr Wilde and a few choice spirits. The modern note is struck in Sir Robert Chiltern's assertion of the individuality and courage of his wrongdoing as against the mechanical idealism of his stupidly good wife, and in his bitter criticism of a love that is only the reward of merit. It is from the philosophy on which this scene is based that the most pregnant epigrams in the play have been condensed. Indeed, this is the only philosophy that ever has produced epigrams. In contriving the stage expedients by which the action of the piece is kept going, Mr Wilde has been once or twice a little too careless of stage illusion: for example, why on earth should Mrs Cheveley, hiding in Lord Goring's room, knock down a chair? That is my sole criticism.

The performance is very amusing. The audience laughs conscientiously: each person comes to the theatre prepared, like a special artist, with the background of a laugh ready sketched in on his or her features. Some of the performers labor intensely at being epigrammatic. I am sure Miss Vane Featherstone and Miss Forsyth could play Lady Macbeth and Medea with less effort than Lady Basildon and Mrs Marchmont, who have nothing to do but sit on a sofa and be politely silly for ten minutes. There is no doubt that these glimpses of expensive receptions in Park Lane, with the servants announcing titles *ad libitum*, are enormously attractive to social outsiders (say ninety-nine hundredths of us); but the stage reproduction is not convincing: everybody has an outrageous air of being at a party; of not being used to it; and, worst of all, of enjoying themselves immensely. Mr Charles Hawtrey has the best of the fun among the principals. As everyone's guide, philosopher, and friend, he has moments in which he is, I think, intended to be deep, strong, and tender. These moments, to say the least, do not quite come off; but his lighter serious episodes are excellent, and his drollery conquers without effort. When Miss Neilson sits still and lets her gifts of beauty and grace be eloquent for her, she is highly satisfying; but I cannot say the same for the passages in which she has to take the stage herself and try to act. She becomes merely artificial and superficially imitative. Miss Fanny Brough makes Lady Markby, an eminently possible person, quite impossible; and Miss Maude Millet, playing very well indeed as Mabel Chiltern, nevertheless occasionally spoils a word by certain vowel sounds which are only permissible to actresses of the second rank. As an adventuress who, like the real and unlike the stage adventuress, is not in love with any one, and is simply selfish, dishonest, and third rate, Miss Florence West is kinetoscopically realistic. The portrait is true to nature; but it has no artistic character: Miss West has not the art of being agreeably disagreeable. Mr Brookfield, a great artist in small things, makes the valet in the third act one of the heroes of the performance. And Mr Waller is handsome and dignified as the ideal husband, a part easily within his means. His management could not have been more auspiciously inaugurated.

KING ARTHUR

KING ARTHUR. A drama in a prologue and four acts. By J. Comyns Carr. Lyceum Theatre, 12 January 1895.

[19 *January* 1895]

MR IRVING is to be congratulated on the impulse which has led him to exclaim, on this occasion, "Let us get rid of that insufferably ignorant specialist, the dramatist, and try whether something fresh cannot be done by a man equipped with all the culture of the age." It was an inevitable step in the movement which is bringing the stage more and more into contact with life. When I was young, the banquets on the stage were made by the property man: his goblets and pasties, and epergnes laden with grapes, regaled guests who walked off and on through illusory wainscoting simulated by the precarious perspective of the wings. The scene-painter built the rooms; the costumier made the dresses; the armor was made apparently by dipping the legs of the knights in a solution of salt of spangles and precipitating the metal on their calves by some electro-process; the leader of the band made the music; and the author wrote the verse and invented the law, the morals, the religion, the art, the jurisprudence, and whatever else might be needed in the abstract department of the play. Since then we have seen great changes. Real walls, ceilings, and doors are made by real carpenters; real tailors and dressmakers

12

clothe the performers; real armorers harness them; and real musicians write the music and have it performed with full orchestral honors at the Crystal Palace and the Philharmonic. All that remains is to get a real poet to write the verse, a real philosopher to do the morals, a real divine to put in the religion, a real lawyer to adjust the law, and a real painter to design the pictorial effects. This is too much to achieve at one blow; but Mr Irving made a brave step towards it when he resolved to get rid of the author and put in his place his dear old friend Comyns Carr as an encyclopædic gentleman well up to date in most of these matters. And Mr Comyns Carr, of course, was at once able to tell him that there was an immense mass of artistic and poetic tradition, accumulated by generations of poets and painters, lying at hand all ready for exploitation by any experienced dealer with ingenuity and literary faculty enough to focus it in a stage entertainment. Such a man would have to know, for instance, that educated people have ceased to believe that architecture means "ruins by moonlight" (style, ecclesiastical Gothic); that the once fashionable admiration of the Renascence and "the old masters" of the sixteenth and seventeenth centuries has been swept away by the growth of a genuine sense of the naïve dignity and charm of thirteenth-century work, and a passionate affection for the exquisite beauty of fifteenth-century work, so that nowadays ten acres of Carracci, Giulio Romano, Guido, Domenichino, and Pietro di Cortona will not buy an inch of Botticelli, or Lippi, or John Bellini— no, not even with a few yards of Raphael thrown in; and that the whole rhetorical school in English literature, from Shakespear to Byron, appears to us in our present mood only another side of the terrible *degringolade* from Michael Angelo to Canova and Thorwaldsen, all of whose works would not now tempt us to part with a single fragment by Donatello, or even a pretty foundling baby by Della Robbia. And yet this, which is the real art culture of England today, is only dimly known to our dramatic authors as a momentary bygone craze out of which a couple of successful pieces, Patience, and The Colonel, made some money in their day. Mr Comyns Carr knows better. He knows that Burne-Jones has made himself the greatest among English decorative painters by picking up the tradition of his art where Lippi left it, and utterly ignoring "their Raphaels, Correggios, and stuff." He knows that William Morris has made himself the greatest living master of the English language, both in prose and verse, by picking up the tradition of the literary art where Chaucer left it, and that Morris and Burne-Jones, close friends and co-operators in many a masterpiece, form the highest aristocracy of English art today. And he knows exactly how far their culture has spread and penetrated, and how much simply noble beauty of Romanesque architecture, what touching loveliness and delicate splendor of fifteenth-century Italian dresses and armor, what blue from the hills round Florence and what sunset gloom deepening into splendid black shadow from the horizons of Giorgione will be recognized with delight on the stage if they be well counterfeited there; also what stories we long to have as the subject of these deeply desired pictures. Foremost among such stories stands that of King Arthur, Lancelot, and Guinevere; and what Mr Comyns Carr has done is to contrive a play in which we have our heart's wish, and see these figures come to life, and move through halls and colonnades that might have been raised by the master-builders of San Zeno or San Ambrogio, out into the eternal beauty of the woodland spring acting their legend just as we know it, in just such vestures and against just such backgrounds of blue hill and fiery sunset. No mere dramatic author could have wrought this miracle. Mr Comyns Carr has done it with ease, by simply knowing whom to send for. His long business experience as a man of art and letters, and the contact with artists and poets which it has involved, have equipped him completely for the work. In Mr Irving's theatre, with Burne-Jones to design for him, Harker and Hawes Craven to paint for him, and Malory and Tennyson and many another on his bookshelves, he has put out his hand cleverly on a ready-made success, and tasted the joy of victory without the terror of battle.

But how am I to praise this deed when my own art, the art of literature, is left shabby and ashamed amid the triumph of the arts of the painter and the actor? I sometimes wonder where Mr Irving will go to when he dies—whether he will dare to claim, as a master artist, to walk where he may any day meet Shakespear whom he has mutilated, Goethe whom he has travestied, and the nameless creator of the hero-king out of whose mouth he has uttered jobbing verses. For in poetry Mr Comyns Carr is frankly a jobber and nothing else. There is one scene in the play in which Mr Irving rises to the height of his art, and impersonates, with the noblest feeling, and the most sensitive refinement of execution, the King Arthur of all our imaginations in the moment when he learns that his wife loves his friend instead of himself. And all the time, whilst the voice, the gesture, the emotion expressed are those of the hero-king, the talk is the talk of an angry and jealous costermonger, exalted by the abject submission of the other parties to a transport of magnanimity in refraining from reviling his wife and punching her lover's head. I do not suppose that Mr Irving said to Mr Comyns Carr in so many words, "Write what trash you like: I'll play the real King Arthur over the head of your stuff"; but that was what it came to. And the end of it was that Mr Comyns Carr was too much for Mr Irving. When King Arthur, having broken down in an attempt to hit Lancelot with his sword, left Guinevere grovelling on the floor with her head within an inch of his toes, and stood plainly conveying to the numerous bystanders that this was the proper position for a female who had forgotten herself so far as to prefer another man to him, one's gorge rose at the Tappertitian vulgarity and infamy of the thing; and it was a relief when the scene ended with a fine old Richard the Third effect of Arthur leading his mail-clad knights off to battle. That vision of a fine figure of a woman, torn with sobs and remorse, stretched at the feet of a nobly superior and deeply wronged lord of creation, is no doubt still as popular with the men whose sentimental vanity it flatters as it was in the days of the Idylls of the King. But since then we have been learning that a woman is something more than a piece of sweetstuff to fatten a man's emotions; and our amateur King Arthurs are beginning to realize, with shocked surprise, that the more generous the race grows, the stronger becomes its disposition to bring them to their senses with a stinging dose of wholesome ridicule. Mr Comyns Carr miscalculated the spirit of the age on this point; and the result was that he dragged Mr Irving down from the height of the loftiest passage in his acting to the abyss of the lowest depth of the dialogue.

Whilst not sparing my protest against this unpardonable scene, I can hardly blame Mr Comyns Carr for the touch of human frailty which made him reserve to himself the honor of providing the "book of the words" for Burne-Jones's picture-opera. No doubt, since Mr Carr is no more a poet than I am, the consistent course would have been to call in Mr William Morris to provide the verse. Perhaps, if Mr Irving, in his black harness, with his visor down and Excalibur ready to hand and well in view, were to present himself at the Kelmscott Press fortified with a propitiatory appeal from the great painter, the poet might, without absolutely swearing, listen to a proposal that he should condescend to touch up those little rhymed acrostics in which Merlin utters his prophecies, leaving the blank verse padding to Mr Comyns Carr. For the blank verse is at all events accurately metrical, a fact which distinguishes the author sharply from most modern dramatists. The ideas are second-hand, and are dovetailed into a coherent structure instead of developing into one another by any life of their own; but they are sometimes very well chosen; and Mr Carr is often guided to his choice of them by the strength and sincerity of their effect on his own feelings. At such moments, if he does not create, he reflects so well, and sometimes reflects such fine rays too, that one gladly admits that there are men whose originality might have been worse than his receptivity. There are excellent moments in the love scenes: indeed, Lancelot's confession of his love to Guinevere all but earns for the author the poet's privilege of having his chain tested by its strongest link.

The only great bit of acting in the piece is that passage of Mr Irving's to which I have already alluded—a masterly fulfilment of the promise of one or two quiet but eloquent touches in his

16

scene with Guinevere in the second act. Popularly speaking, Mr Forbes Robertson as Lancelot is the hero of the piece. He has a beautiful costume, mostly of plate-armor of Burne-Jonesian design; and he wears it beautifully, like a fifteenth-century St George, the spiritual, interesting face completing a rarely attractive living picture. He was more than applauded on his entrance: he was positively adored. His voice is an organ with only one stop on it: to the musician it suggests a clarionet in A, played only in the chalumeau register; but then the chalumeau, sympathetically sounded, has a richly melancholy and noble effect. The one tune he had to play throughout suited it perfectly: its subdued passion, both in love and devotion, affected the house deeply; and the crowning moment of the drama for most of those present was his clasping of Guinevere's waist as he knelt at her feet when she intoxicated him by answering his confession with her own. As to Miss Ellen Terry, it was the old story, a born actress of real women's parts condemned to figure as a mere artist's model in costume plays which, from the woman's point of view, are foolish flatteries written by gentlemen for gentlemen. It is pathetic to see Miss Terry snatching at some fleeting touch of nature in her part, and playing it not only to perfection, but often with a parting caress that brings it beyond that for an instant as she relinquishes it, very loth, and passes on to the next length of arid sham-feminine twaddle in blank verse, which she pumps out in little rhythmic strokes in a desperate and all too obvious effort to make music of it. I should prove myself void of the true critic's passion if I could pass with polite commonplaces over what seems to me a heartless waste of an exquisite talent. What a theatre for a woman of genius to be attached to! Obsolete tomfooleries like Robert Macaire, schoolgirl charades like Nance Oldfield, blank verse by Wills, Comyns Carr, and Calmour, with intervals of hashed Shakespear; and all the time a stream of splendid women's parts pouring from the Ibsen volcano and minor craters, and being snapped up by the rising generation. Strange, under these circumstances, that it is Mr Irving and not Miss Terry who feels the want of a municipal theatre. He has certainly done his best to make everyone else feel it.

The rest of the acting is the merest stock company routine, there being only three real parts in the play. Sir Arthur Sullivan (who, in the playbill, drops his knighthood whilst Burne-Jones parades his baronetcy) sweetens the sentiment of the scenes here and there by penn'orths of orchestral sugarstick, for which the dramatic critics, in their soft-eared innocence, praise him above Wagner. The overture and the vocal pieces are pretty specimens of his best late work. Some awkwardness in the construction of the play towards the end has led the stage manager into a couple of absurdities. For instance, when the body of Elaine is done with, it should be taken off the stage and not put in the corner like a portmanteau at a railway station. I do not know what is supposed to happen in the last act—whether Guinevere is alive or a ghost when she comes in at Arthur's death (I understood she was being burnt behind the scenes), or what becomes of Lancelot and Mordred, or who on earth the two gentlemen are who come in successively to interview the dying Arthur, or why the funeral barge should leave Mr Irving lying on the stage and bear off to bliss an impostor with a strikingly different nose. In fact I understand nothing that happened after the sudden blossoming out of Arthur into Lohengrin, Guinevere into Elsa, Mordred into Telramund, and Morgan le Fay into Ortruda in the combat scene, in which, by the way, Mr Comyns Carr kills the wrong man, probably from having read Wagner carelessly. But I certainly think something might be done to relieve the shock of the whole court suddenly bolting and leaving the mortally wounded king floundering on the floor without a soul to look after him. These trifles are mere specks of dust on a splendid picture; but they could easily be brushed off.

THE INDEPENDENT THEATRE

THYRZA FLEMING. In four acts. By Miss Dorothy Leighton. The
Independent Theatre (Terry's), 4 January 1895.
THE FIRST STEP. A Dramatic Moment. By William Heinemann.
London: John Lane. 1895.   [26 *January* 1895]

Now that the fashionable productions at the Lyceum, the Haymarket, and the St James's have been attended to, the Independent Theatre claims a modest word for two plays, one which it
would have produced had the Queen's reader of plays permitted,
and another which it actually has produced. The Independent
Theatre is an excellent institution, simply because it is independent. Its disparagers ask what it is independent of, knowing well
that no question is so difficult to answer as that to which the
answer is obvious. It is, of course, independent of commercial
success. It can take a masterpiece of European dramatic literature, which, because it is a masterpiece, is above the level of
commercial practicability fixed by the average taste of a hundred
thousand playgoing Londoners, and produce it for at least a
night or two. What is more, it has done it. If Mr Grein had not
taken the dramatic critics of London and put them in a row before Ghosts and The Wild Duck, with a certain small but in-
quisitive and influential body of enthusiasts behind them, we
should be far less advanced today than we are. The real history
of the drama for the last ten years is not the history of the prosperous enterprises of Mr Hare, Mr Irving, and the established
West-end theatres, but of the forlorn hopes led by Mr Vernon,
Mr Charrington, Mr Grein, Messrs Henley and Stevenson, Miss
Achurch, Miss Robins and Miss Lea, Miss Farr, and the rest of the
Impossibilists. Their commercial defeat has been slaughterous:
each scaling party has gained the rampart only to be hurled
back into the moat with empty pockets, amid plentiful jeering
from the baser sort, with their opportunities of a share in the
ordinary lucrative routine of their profession considerably di-
minished, and their acquaintances, after the manner of acquaint-

ances, rather ashamed of them. For my part, I take off my hat to them. Besides, that is the way things get done in England; so, as a prudent man, I always make friends with able desperadoes, knowing that they will seize the citadel when the present garrison retires.

The special danger of the Independent Theatre is its liability to its subscribers for the production of half a dozen new plays every season. No author whose play strikes, or is aimed at, the commercially successful pitch will give it to Mr Grein. Until, for one reason or another, the author has come to the conclusion that his play is either too good or too bad or too new for the regular theatres, his manuscript does not come Mr Grein's way. Now Nature is lavish of plays that are too bad for the ordinary theatre, and niggard of plays that are too good—much more niggard than Mr Grein dare be of new plays if he wishes to give his subscribers enough performances to make them feel that they are having some sort of value for their subscriptions. It lies, therefore, in the very nature of the case that the majority of the performances of the Independent Theatre, taken by themselves, will not justify its existence; and the late reconstitution of the enterprise as The Independent Theatre, Limited, in no way modifies this rather hard condition. We must make up our minds to accept one really remarkable play a year as a sufficient excuse for half a dozen in-different ones, including perhaps an occasional dismal failure. And I think our London managers, if they were wise, would help and cherish the Independent Theatre as a sort of laboratory in which they can have experiments tried on the public from time to time without the cost and responsibility incurred by, for ex-ample, Mr Beerbohm Tree in the experiments he made at the Haymarket with Beau Austin and An Enemy of the People.

Thyrza Fleming, with which Mr Grein has inaugurated the *régime* under which he divides the responsibilities of managing director with Miss Dorothy Leighton, is a courageous attempt at a counterblast to The Heavenly Twins, sometimes sinking to the level of a mere skit, as in the schoolgirlish caricature of Ideala as Theophila, and sometimes rising into tolerable drama, or swerving into mere abstract discussion. The contest between Miss Leighton's talent and Sarah Grand's genius is an unequal one; and the play evades the challenged issue in a sufficiently ridiculous way. Sarah Grand's heroine married a gentleman with "a past"; discovered it on her wedding day; and promptly went home, treating him exactly as he would have been conventionally expected to treat her under like circumstances. To this Miss Leighton says, in effect: "Let me shew you what a frightful mistake it is for a woman to take such a step." She accordingly creates a heroine who leaves her husband on their wedding day, and presently returns repentant to confess that she was wrong, the proof being that her husband is really a blameless gentleman with no past at all. It is exactly as if Shakespear had written Othello as a confutation of the Tue-la of Dumas *fils*. Leaving this aspect of the play out of the question, one may say that it shews a promising turn on Miss Leighton's part for the theatre. Its main fault is that at the height of her argument she has not written the play at all, but simply stated its intellectual basis in the style proper to the Royal Institution. If she will translate these passages into the idiomatic, vernacular language by which feeling, which is for her the true material of drama, leaps into expression; and if she will allow her characters, when they are no longer wanted, to simply walk off the stage without making far-fetched excuses, her play will do very well. Even as it is, it would have carried off its shortcomings if the title part had been better presented. Miss Esther Palliser, who a year ago was a slender and attractive young lady making a place for herself in the front rank of our oratorio singers, has taken as little heed to her physical training as any German *prima donna*; and her performance can only be described as a fairly intelligent reading aloud of the part by rote. It was just a degree better than having it read from the book by the prompter. As to the blameless Colonel, the incorrigibly good-natured Mr Bernard Gould, talented, handsome, and proof (thanks to a rare soundness of head and heart) against all the crazy illusions of stageland, lent his engaging personality for the part, and shewed us what it was like with his usual cleverness. The considerateness and adroitness with which he steered Miss Palliser among the smaller shipping was delightful; but between them the scenes on which Miss Leighton's play chiefly depended for its success left the imagination inexpressibly untouched. Mr Gould's only real chance, in fact, was in the scenes with Miss Winifred Frazer, whose charm in sympathetic and rather fragile parts is becoming sufficiently well known to render it unnecessary to compliment her on her success in the important but not very exacting character of the victim of the Heavenly Twins. Mr Bonney was rather interesting; and Miss Beaugarde, as Jones the maid, managed, perhaps through inexperience, to put the real female domestic servant on the stage for the first time within my experience.

So much for the play which has been produced. The other, frustrated by that insane institution for the taxation of authors, the Censorship of the Lord Chamberlain, is Mr William Heinemann's First Step. In this instance Mr Pigott has been the instrument of the irony of fate, the flavor of which can be fully relished only in view of the following facts, not hitherto publicly collated. A few years ago certain matters in Central America required the presence of a plenipotentiary from the Colonial Office. This mission was entrusted to Mr Sidney Olivier, a gentleman who, having an esoteric reputation as a sort of lucid George Meredith, is at present, no doubt, awaiting discovery by Mr Le Gallienne in the dignified security of Downing Street. Last year Mr Olivier wrote a play entitled, A Freedom in Fetters, embodying his observations of human nature as developed in the British colonist by a tropical climate. The Censor, after one horrified glimpse into this strange region, refused to allow the play to be performed. The spectacle of a subordinate court official appointed by patronage, arbitrarily suppressing an upper division civil servant appointed by strenuous competitive examination, and one moreover of Mr Olivier's standing and personal character, was an exceptionally piquant addition to the scandals of the Censorship; and Mr Olivier sought the usual remedy—publication. But the first publisher approached sided with the Censor, and refused to publish the play on moral grounds. That publisher was Mr William Heinemann, who thereupon proceeded to write a play himself, and was immediately suppressed by Mr Pigott, to the accompaniment, one fancies, of a hollow laugh from the Colonial Office. Mr Heinemann, with admirable consistency, refused to publish his own play, and sent it on to Mr John Lane of the Bodley Head, who has duly issued five hundred copies of it to clear Mr Heinemann from the imputation of having written something worse than the intentional and gross indecencies which Mr Pigott has licensed from time to time, as I, an old musical critic, well know from my experience of comic-opera books. Of course there is nothing of that sort in Mr Heinemann's work any more than there was in Mr Olivier's; only the hero and heroine are living together without being legally married, which is against Mr Pigott's rule-of-thumb for determining whether a play is "moral" or not.

In Mr Heinemann's play, the grounds on which it is assumed that this unconventional arrangement is beneficial to the hero are so inadequately conveyed that if the pair were married, the play would gain rather than lose in verisimilitude, though, no doubt, the heroine would tumble out of her place in Mr Heinemann's imagination as a woman with certain noble qualities which have led her to sacrifice her reputation for the sake of helping a man of genius. In such an error of the feminine imagination, and in its fearfully real consequences, there is material for a tragedy. And there is always drama to be got out of a man who is on with the new love before he is off with the old, particularly when, as Mr Heinemann begins by suggesting, the man has character and temperament enough to be interesting. But all this slips through Mr Heinemann's fingers on the introduction of a couple of good-for-nothings in the second act. In drawing these Mr Heinemann discovered that he could do that sort of sketching rather well; and immediately he abandoned his attempt at the higher manner, and turned his hero and heroine into a pair of loose-lived Bohemians of the commonest clay. Consequently, after having taken the trouble to conceive the man as a great dramatic poet, and the woman as having sufficient generosity and force of character to make a compact with him involving a heavy sacrifice on her part, we are put off with a drunken squabble which might have been better carried on by the most dissolute couple picked from the gallery of a third-rate music-hall. This is worse than Rossini's lazy way of beginning with a Te Deum and finishing with a galop; for he at least gave us the Te Deum, whereas Mr Heinemann only gives us the exordium, and then tails off at once into his galop. I would not stand such trifling from an author, much less from my natural enemy, a publisher. The opening of the First Step is an abandoned and derelict fragment; and I invite Mr Heinemann to turn to again like a man and rescue it.

POOR SHAKESPEAR!

ALL'S WELL THAT ENDS WELL. Performance by the Irving Dramatic Club at St George's Hall, 22 and 24 January 1895.
[2 *February* 1895]

WHAT a pity it is that the people who love the sound of Shakespear so seldom go on the stage! The ear is the sure clue to him: only a musician can understand the play of feeling which is the real rarity in his early plays. In a deaf nation these plays would have died long ago. The moral attitude in them is conventional and secondhand: the borrowed ideas, however finely expressed, have not the overpowering human interest of those original criticisms of life which supply the rhetorical element in his later works. Even the individualization which produces that old-established British speciality, the Shakespearean "delineation of character," owes all its magic to the turn of the line, which lets you into the secret of its utterer's mood and temperament, not by its commonplace meaning, but by some subtle exaltation, or stultification, or slyness, or delicacy, or hesitancy, or what not in the sound of it. In short, it is the score and not the libretto that keeps the work alive and fresh; and this is why only musical critics should be allowed to meddle with Shakespear—especially early Shakespear. Unhappily, though the nation still retains

24

its ears, the players and playgoers of this generation are for the most part deaf as adders. Their appreciation of Shakespear is sheer hypocrisy, the proof being that where an early play of his is revived, they take the utmost pains to suppress as much of it as possible, and disguise the rest past recognition, relying for success on extraordinary scenic attractions; on very popular performers, including, if possible, a famously beautiful actress in the leading part; and, above all, on Shakespear's reputation and the consequent submission of the British public to be mercilessly bored by each of his plays once in their lives, for the sake of being able to say they have seen it. And not a soul has the hardihood to yawn in the face of the imposture. The manager is praised; the bard is praised; the beautiful actress is praised; and the free list comes early and comes often, not without a distinct sense of conferring a handsome compliment on the acting manager. And it certainly is hard to face such a disappointment without being paid for it. For the more enchanting the play is at home by the fireside in winter, or out on the heather of a summer evening—the more the manager, in his efforts to realize this enchantment by reckless expenditure on incidental music, colored lights, dances, dresses, and elaborate rearrangements and dislocations of the play—the more, in fact, he departs from the old platform with its curtains and its placards inscribed "A street in Mantua," and so forth, the more hopelessly and vulgarly does he miss his mark. Such crown jewels of dramatic poetry as Twelfth Night and A Midsummer Night's Dream, fade into shabby colored glass in his purse; and sincere people who do not know what the matter is, begin to babble insufferably about plays that are meant for the study and not for the stage.

Yet once in a blue moon or so there wanders on to the stage some happy fair whose eyes are lodestars and whose tongue's sweet air's more tunable than lark to shepherd's ear. And the moment she strikes up the true Shakespearean music, and feels her way to her part altogether by her sense of that music, the play returns to life and all the magic is there. She may make nonsense of the verses by wrong conjunctions and misplaced commas,

25

which shew that she has never worked out the logical construction of a single sentence in her part; but if her heart is in the song, the protesting commentator-critic may save his breath to cool his porridge: the soul of the play is there, no matter where the sense of it may be. We have all heard Miss Rehan perform this miracle with Twelfth Night, and turn it, in spite of the impossible Mr Daly, from a hopelessly ineffective actress show into something like the exquisite poem its author left it. All I can remember of the last performance I witnessed of A Midsummer Night's Dream is that Miss Kate Rorke got on the stage somehow and began to make some music with Helena's lines, with the result that Shakespear, who had up to that moment lain without sense or motion, immediately began to stir uneasily and shew signs of quickening, which lasted until the others took up the word and struck him dead.

Powerful among the enemies of Shakespear are the commentator and the elocutionist: the commentator because, not knowing Shakespear's language, he sharpens his reasoning faculty to examine propositions advanced by an eminent lecturer from the Midlands, instead of sensitizing his artistic faculty to receive the impression of moods and inflexions of feeling conveyed by word-music; the elocutionist because he is a born fool, in which capacity, observing with pain that poets have a weakness for imparting to their dramatic dialogue a quality which he describes and deplores as "sing-song," he devotes his life to the art of breaking up verse in such a way as to make it sound like insanely pompous prose. The effect of this on Shakespear's earlier verse, which is full of the naïve delight of pure oscillation, to be enjoyed as an Italian enjoys a barcarolle, or a child a swing, or a baby a rocking-cradle, is destructively stupid. In the later plays, where the barcarolle measure has evolved into much more varied and complex rhythms, it does not matter so much, since the work is no longer simple enough for a fool to pick to pieces. But in every play from Love's Labour Lost to Henry V, the elocutionist meddles simply as a murderer, and ought to be dealt with as such without benefit of clergy. To our young people studying for the stage I say, with all solemnity, learn how to pronounce the English alphabet clearly and beautifully from some person who is at once an artist and a phonetic expert. And then leave blank verse patiently alone until you have experienced emotion deep enough to crave for poetic expression, at which point verse will seem an absolutely natural and real form of speech to you. Meanwhile, if any pedant, with an uncultivated heart and a theoretic ear, proposes to teach you to recite, send instantly for the police.

Among Shakespear's earlier plays, All's Well that Ends Well stands out artistically by the sovereign charm of the young Helena and the old Countess of Rousillon, and intellectually by the experiment, repeated nearly three hundred years later in A Doll's House, of making the hero a perfectly ordinary young man, whose unimaginative prejudices and selfish conventionality make him cut a very fine mean figure in the atmosphere created by the nobler nature of his wife. That is what gives a certain plausibility to the otherwise doubtful tradition that Shakespear did not succeed in getting his play produced (founded on the absence of any record of a performance of it during his lifetime). It certainly explains why Phelps, the only modern actor-manager tempted by it, was attracted by the part of Parolles, a capital study of the adventurous yarn-spinning society-struck coward, who also crops up again in modern fiction as the hero of Charles Lever's underrated novel, A Day's Ride: a Life's Romance. When I saw All's Well announced for performance by the Irving Dramatic Club, I was highly interested, especially as the performers were free, for once, to play Shakespear for Shakespear's sake. Alas! at this amateur performance, at which there need have been none of the miserable commercialization compulsory at the regular theatres, I suffered all the vulgarity and absurdity of that commercialism without its efficiency. We all know the stock objection of the Brixton Family Shakespear to All's Well—that the heroine is a lady doctor, and that no lady of any delicacy could possibly adopt a profession which involves the possibility of her having to attend cases such as that of the

king in this play, who suffers from a fistula. How any sensible
and humane person can have ever read this sort of thing without
a deep sense of its insult to every charitable woman's humanity
and every sick man's suffering is, fortunately, getting harder to
understand nowadays than it once was. Nevertheless All's Well
was minced with strict deference to it for the members of the
Irving Dramatic Club. The rule for expurgation was to omit
everything that the most pestiferously prurient person could
find improper. For example, when the non-commissioned officer,
with quite becoming earnestness and force, says to the disgraced
Parolles: "If you could find out a country where but women
were that had received so much shame, you might begin an impudent nation," the speech was suppressed as if it were on all
fours with the obsolete Elizabethan badinage which is and should
be cut out as a matter of course. And to save Helena from anything so shocking as a reference to her virginity, she was robbed
of that rapturous outburst beginning

> There shall your master have a thousand loves—
> A mother and a mistress and a friend, etc.

But perhaps this was sacrificed in deference to the opinion of the
editor of those pretty and handy little books called the Temple
Shakespear, who compares the passage to "the nonsense of some
foolish conceited player"—a criticism which only a commentator could hope to live down.

The play was, of course, pulled to pieces in order that some
bad scenery, totally unconnected with Florence or Rousillon,
might destroy all the illusion which the simple stage directions
in the book create, and which they would equally have created
had they been printed on a placard and hung up on a curtain.
The passage of the Florentine army beneath the walls of the city
was managed in the manner of the end of the first act of Robertson's Ours, the widow and the girls looking out of their sitting-
room window, whilst a few of the band gave a precarious selection from the orchestral parts of Berlioz's version of the Rack-
oczy March. The dresses were the usual fancy ball odds and ends,

Helena especially distinguishing herself by playing the first scene partly in the costume of Hamlet and partly in that of a waitress in an Aerated Bread shop, set off by a monstrous auburn wig which could by no stretch of imagination be taken for her own hair. Briefly, the whole play was vivisected, and the fragments mutilated, for the sake of accessories which were in every particular silly and ridiculous. If they were meant to heighten the illusion, they were worse than failures, since they rendered illusion almost impossible. If they were intended as illustrations of place and period, they were ignorant impostures. I have seen poetic plays performed without costumes before a pair of curtains by ladies and gentlemen in evening dress with twenty times the effect: nay, I will pledge my reputation that if the members of the Irving Dramatic Club will take their books in their hands, sit in a Christy Minstrel semicircle, and read the play decently as it was written, the result will be a vast improvement on this St George's Hall travesty.

Perhaps it would not be altogether kind to leave these misguided but no doubt well-intentioned ladies and gentlemen without a word of appreciation from their own point of view. Only, there is not much to be said for them even from that point of view. Few living actresses could throw themselves into the sustained transport of exquisite tenderness and impulsive courage which makes poetry the natural speech of Helena. The cool young woman, with a superior understanding, excellent manners, and a habit of reciting Shakespear, presented before us by Miss Olive Kennett, could not conceivably have been even Helena's thirty-second cousin. Miss Lena Heinekey, with the most beautiful old woman's part ever written in her hands, discovered none of its wonderfully pleasant good sense, humanity, and originality: she grieved stagily all through in the manner of the Duchess of York in Cibber's Richard III. Mr Lewin-Mannering did not for any instant make it possible to believe that Parolles was a real person to him. They all insisted on calling him *parole*, instead of Parolles, in three syllables, with the *s* sounded at the end, as Shakespear intended: consequently, when he came to the couplet which cannot be negotiated on any other terms:

> Rust, sword; cool, blushes; and, Parolles, thrive;
> Theres place and means for every man alive,

he made a desperate effort to get even with it by saying:

> Rust, rapier; cool, blushes; and, *parole*, thrive,

and seemed quite disconcerted when he found that it would not do. Lafeu is hardly a part that can be acted: it comes right if the right man is available: if not, no acting can conceal the makeshift. Mr Herbert Everitt was not the right man; but he made the best of it. The clown was evidently willing to relish his own humor if only he could have seen it; but there are few actors who would not have gone that far. Bertram (Mr Patrick Munro), if not the most intelligent of Bertrams, played the love scene with Diana with some passion. The rest of the parts, not being character studies, are tolerably straightforward and easy of execution; and they were creditably played, the king (Mr Ernest Meads) carrying off the honors, and Diana (Mrs Herbert Morris) acquitting herself with comparative distinction. But I should not like to see another such performance of All's Well or any other play that is equally rooted in my deeper affections.

WHY NOT SIR HENRY IRVING?

[9 *February* 1895]

In an old-fashioned play revived the other day by Mr Terry, a kitchen discussion of literature leads to the question, "Who wrote Shakespear?" Let me put a cognate question. Who writes Mr Irving's lectures? Of course, I must not altogether exclude the hypothesis that he writes them himself; but I had rather flatter him by assuming that he contents himself with jotting down a scenario, and orders some literary retainer to write the dialogue, enjoining him especially to put in plenty of art and learning, and not to forget some good declamatory passages, in the manner of the late Mr Wills, for elocutionary display. At all events, this is

what is suggested by the report of his recent discourse at the
Royal Institution. Dr Johnson—"Punch, sir, has no feelings"
—Homer—"poetry, music, sculpture, painting"—Hamlet—
Shakespear—"the poor player of Wittenberg"—Hogarth—
Edmund Kean—Raphael and Michael Angelo—Praxiteles and
Phidias—the Colosseum and the Parthenon—"Roscius a name
that lives in history": who could not deliver the lecture verbatim
from these notes as easily as Mr Percy Fitzgerald could write a
book from them? And would we stand it from anybody but
Henry Irving? Some years ago Mr William Archer lectured on
the drama at the Royal Institution. What would the directors
have said to Mr Archer had he put them off with stuff which any
sufficiently old-fashioned auctioneer could improvise at a sale of
theatrical prints? No: let us deal faithfully with Mr Irving in this
matter, and not treat him like a spoiled child. The other evening,
after King Arthur, he wished us all a happy new year. He wished
it heartily, respectfully, and so on; and then, with a friendly impulse to get on more intimate terms with us, he asked whether
he might wish it to us "affectionately." Naturally, the house immediately shook hands with him, so to speak—I among the rest.
Consequently I hold myself privileged now to drop all insincere
ceremony, and tell Mr Irving bluntly what every competent person thinks of his lecture. Their opinion may not seem consistent
with their applause; but Mr Irving must remember that we now
applaud him, not critically, but affectionately, and that we allow
him to play like a child at being a learned lecturer, just as we
indulge him, every evening at the Lyceum, with a broadsword
combat the solemn absurdity of which quite baffles my powers
of description. If we treat his orations as lectures, do we not
also treat Mr Gladstone's tree-felling exploits as acts of states-
manship? No one can say that we are not indulgent to our
favorites.

Mr Irving, however, began his lecture seriously and well, by
putting forward "a formal claim to have acting classified *officially*
among the fine arts." We all know what official recognition of a
fine art means; but for the benefit of the millions of persons who

never know anything, and therefore are not included in such general expressions as "we all," Mr Irving explicitly said, "Official recognition of anything worthy is a good, or at least a useful thing. It is a part, and an important part, of the economy of the State: if it is not, of what use are titles and distinctions, names, badges, offices, in fact all the titular and sumptuary ways of distinction?" Here the "formal claim" is put as precisely as Mr Irving himself feels he can decorously put it. I, who am not an actor, and am therefore not hampered by any personal interest in the claim, can put it much more definitely. What Mr Irving means us to answer is this question: "The artist who composed the music for King Arthur is Sir Arthur Sullivan; the artist who composed the poem which made King Arthur known to this generation died Lord Tennyson; the artist who designed the suit of armor worn by King Arthur is Sir Edward Burne-Jones: why should the artist who plays King Arthur be only Mister Henry Irving?" That is clearly Mr Irving's meaning, since his art lacks no other sort of recognition or advancement than this.

Here let me plead against any envious and base-minded view of this claim. Mr Irving is entitled to an entirely honorable construction: we owe him an unhesitating assumption that his jealousy is for the dignity of his art and not of himself, and that it would never have been advanced if the friend of Sir Joshua Reynolds had been Sir David Garrick, and if every successive P.R.A. had had for his officially recognized peer the leading actor of his day. The theatre at present only boasts one title, that of Sir Augustus Harris, who was knighted, not on the excellent ground of his public services as opera impresario, but through the perfectly irrelevant accident of his having been sheriff when the Emperor of Germany visited the City. Who can deny that the actor is regarded as less worthy of official honors than the musician, the painter, or the poet? We have Sir Arthur Sullivan, Sir A. C. Mackenzie, and Sir Charles Hallé (a purely "executive" artist); and we have Sir Edward Burne-Jones, Sir John Millais, and Sir Frederick Leighton. No one questions the social position of these gentlemen; and an expression of any doubt as to whether it was right to go to a concert or to the Royal Academy Exhibition would be considered an un-heard-of eccentricity. But numbers of respectable English people still regard a visit to the theatre as a sin; and numbers more, including most of those who have become accustomed to meet-ing even rank-and-file actors and actresses in society where thirty years ago they would as soon have expected to meet an acrobat, would receive a proposal from an actor for the hand of their daughter with a sense of *mésalliance* which they would certainly not have if the suitor were a lawyer, a doctor, a clergyman, or a painter. Such people, being intellectually and socially mere sheep, are very much influenced by titles—indeed, that influence is the *raison d'être* of titles; and there can be no doubt that if the next list of birthday honors were to include the names of Sir Henry Irving, Sir John Hare, and Sir Charles Wyndham, the boycott would lose half its force and all its credit at one stroke. On this account it is tenable, not only that Mr Irving might with perfect propriety and dignity accept an official honor which we should expect a great poet, for instance, to refuse just as a great com-moner is expected to refuse a peerage, but that he is quite right, on behalf of his profession, to claim it as his due before it is offered. His lecture is such a claim; and in advancing it, he has done worthily and courageously—worthily, because a title can add nothing to his personal eminence, and courageously, because many unworthy persons will wound him by seeing nothing in the act but a vain man grasping at a handle for his name.

But since this was Mr Irving's meaning, why was he too shy to say so in plain words, with the i's dotted and the t's crossed? Why observe that "the philologists define the word Art, as we have it, as coming through the Latin from the Greek. In this language the root-word means etc. etc. etc."? In the Royal Insti-tution an actor should not meddle with philology, for precisely the same reason as a philologist should not meddle with acting. And even when an actor exercises his right as an artist to talk about art, he should be careful to speak from his knowledge and not from his imagination, lest he unknowingly fall into the style of a Cabinet Minister proposing the health of the President of the Royal Academy, and be received by irreverent Slade scholars with the thumb to the nose. For example:

"What is there in works of genius, howsoever they may be represented, which touches the heart with emotion? We feel it as we gaze on the beauty which Canova wrought in marble, which Raphael and Velasquez and Vandyke and Reynolds and Gainsborough depicted on canvas, which Michael Angelo piled up to the dome of St Peter's or as we listen to the tender strains of Mozart, the sad witchery of Mendelssohn, or the tempestuous force of Wagner."

I have no doubt Mr Irving, reading this over, and not for the life of him being able to see what I have to complain of in it, will think me nothing short of a wizard when I tell him that I have discovered from it that he does not know Arnolfo from Brunelleschi in architecture, nor Carpaccio from Guido in painting, nor Rossini from Rubinstein in music. One does not illustrate Michael Angelo's genius from the dome of St Peter's, which was another man's affair; nor do you lump Canova with Velasquez or Raphael with Gainsborough, any more than you lump Blondin and the late Mr Spurgeon with Henry Irving. As to the "sad witchery" put forward as Mendelssohn's general characteristic, I can only wish Mr Irving better luck next time. Never did man make a worse shot in the dark. And yet Mr Irving has a fine ear; for he hears the music of Mozart, Mendelssohn, and Wagner, as aforesaid, "in Nature's choral forces—that mighty gamut of creation which rises from the tiniest whisper of whirring wings in the insect world, through the sighing of the night wind, the crackle of swaying corn, the roar of falling water, and the mighty voice of the sounding sea, up to the hiss of the lightning flash and the crash of the thunderbolt."

This quotation, by the way, also proves that Mr Irving does not know fine literature from penny-a-liner's fustian—though that, alas! we have known ever since we heard him, as Mephistopheles, threatening to do all manner of horrible things to Faust in a passage not at all unlike the above.

34

Here I can imagine some good-natured reader asking me why I go on like this at our favorite actor—whether I deliberately wish to be disagreeable. My answer is, yes. I do deliberately want to make it impossible for Mr Irving, or any other member of his profession, ever hereafter to get on the Royal Institution or any other platform, and, with stores of first-hand experience to draw on for a sincere and authoritative, and consequently enormously interesting and valuable lecture on his art, to put us off with two columns of stereo concerning which I can tell Mr Irving with the utmost exactitude, and without fear of contradiction, that if he wrote it himself he wasted his time, and that if—as I prefer to believe—he got it written for him, he need not have paid the writer a farthing more than one-and-sixpence an hour, at which rate I will undertake to procure him, in the reading-room of the British Museum and at the shortest notice, as much literary matter to match his sample as he wants. And of all the critics who paid Mr Irving flowery little compliments on his exhibition next day, there is not one who does not know this as well as I know it. Some day, no doubt, I, too, shall succumb to Mr Irving's charm and prestige. But for the present I prefer to say what I think. I can well understand that it is natural for an actor to resort to his art on the platform, and to *act* the lecturer from a written part rather than venture, without experience, to be the lecturer. But surely, if Mr Irving could so happily come before the curtain at the Lyceum, and wish an audience of friends that affectionate happy new year, he could equally come before a still more select circle of friends in Albemarle Street, and, having told them frankly what he knew about his own art, plead that whether it be ranked as a creative art, like Sir Frederick Leighton's (or like Liszt's playing of Beethoven's sonatas, according to a memorable and luminous criticism of Wagner's), or an executive art like Sir Charles Hallé's, it is no less worthy than theirs of a recognition which, though it could make no personal difference to him, would make all the difference in the world to the status of his profession. Of course, that would not be acting; but then acting is the one thing that is intolerable in a lecturer.

35

Even on the stage it is a habit that only the finest actors get rid of completely.

A PURIFIED PLAY

A LEADER OF MEN. A new and original comedy. By Charles E. D. Ward. Comedy Theatre, 9 February 1895.

[16 *February* 1895]

AFTER all, things begin to march a little at the theatre. Here is Mr Comyns Carr accepting and producing a play by an untried author who is apparently a literate person, conversant with politics and society, capable of intellectual interests, and even of recognizing a certain degree of delicacy of manner and feeling as an enhancement of human intercourse. If "Mr Ward" were a celebrated novelist like Mr Henry James, or a noted wit like Mr Oscar Wilde, one could understand a manager consenting to overlook his education in consideration of his reputation; but as nobody ever heard of the author of A Leader of Men until his play was announced, it is difficult to avoid the conclusion that Mr Comyns Carr is so far an innovator that he does not regard even an unknown author as being any the worse for a little cultivation, or even a good deal of it. The significance of this can only be appreciated by those who know the theatrical world well enough to understand how strongly it is still dominated by the tradition that crudity, vulgarity, and profligacy, no further disguised than "evening dress" can disguise any wastrel, are the natural characteristics of playhouse entertainments. The force of this insane faith in blackguardism is apparent enough in the huge sums lavished by managers and syndicates on stage shows with nothing to redeem their obvious silliness but a promise of as much lewdness as the audience will stand, even with all public sense of responsibility relieved by that sanction which the Lord Chamberlain never seems to withhold from anything that is openly and intentionally vile. Where it is less apparent, but far more mischievous, is in the timidity of the managers who are struggling against it, and who are, of course, heavily handicapped by the determination of the same official to thrust the drama back into the gutter whenever an attempt is made to deal seriously with social questions on the stage.

I have not dragged this public grievance of the censorship in here merely to ventilate it out of season as well as in season. It is true that no question of censorship arises on the play Mr Ward has written. But it arises very pointedly indeed on the much better play he did not write, but evidently would have written but for the certainty of seeing it strangled at its birth by Mr Pigott. Mr Ward, like all dramatic authors, has had to choose between infanticide and abortion; and he has chosen abortion. What he meant to put on the stage was that most dramatic page of our political history in which Mr Gladstone, the late Charles Stewart Parnell, and the lady who was then Mrs O'Shea were the principal figures. Lord Killarney, Mr Llewellyn, M.P., and Mrs Dundas are as clearly stage-names for these three as Morton Stone, M.P., is a stage-name for Mr Timothy Healy. We all know their story as it was played out on the larger stage which Mr Pigott, doubtless to his own great scandal, is not empowered to purify—how the issue of a bitter political conflict became suddenly bound up with that of an intensely exciting and tragic personal struggle between the two political leaders, in which it was at once apparent that the fiercer, younger, more terrible, least popular of the combatants, trapped between the compulsive force of his affections on the one side, and, on the other, of the stubborn resistance of that unnatural deficiency in our law which makes a mistaken marriage indissoluble except at the cost of social disgrace to the woman and political ruin to the man, was going down, and his cause with it, beneath a well-timed blow from his opponent, driven home with the colossal weight of our public hypocrisy and the Nonconformist Conscience. Probably there is not a playwright in the country who has not thought of giving artistic life and form to that drama, only to relinquish the project at the thought of Mr Pigott, and to pass on, possibly, to some farcical comedy theme sufficiently salacious to be sure of a licence.

Mr Ward, being a young hand, did not wholly submit to the

despot. But neither did he defy him, being still sufficiently modest to content himself with an expurgated version of the tragedy. Accordingly, we have Mr Llewellyn, a "labor leader" rejoicing in the novelty of a following in the House of Commons, on the eve of forcing a crucial division—presumably concerning the unemployed—on the Prime Minister, a grand old man called Lord Killarney. Both leaders, in an amative and parental way respectively, flirt with a Mrs Dundas, who has positively declined to live with an exceedingly objectionable husband. Llewellyn declares his love; and Mrs Dundas, ladylike, bids him begone. This he is maladroit enough to do, whereupon it becomes necessary for the lady to explain that what she meant was that she returns his love. People thereupon begin to talk; and Mr Timothy Healy, *alias* Morton Stone, M.P., rebels, and is bullied by his leader in the most trenchant Committee Room 15 style. Lord Killarney, also disquieted by the talking, goes to the lady and suggests that she shall go back to her husband in order to place herself above suspicion. She instantly overwhelms him with a tirade in which she recites the horrors of her marriage one by one, fitting each instance with the biting anti-climax, "therefore I must go back to him." She then goes to Llewellyn's house, and is about, by taking up her quarters there, to save the Government, ruin the labor leader, and bring down Mr Pigott's blue pencil on the whole play, when another lady, also enamored of the labor leader, persuades her to think better of it. This ending, however moral, being most discouragingly unhappy, as purely moral endings usually are, Mr Dundas considerately expires behind the scenes, and thereby enables the play to comply not only with Mr Pigott's ethical code, but also with the public demand that virtue shall cost nothing.

It is a public duty to point out here that the process of adapting the play to Mr Pigott has consisted in taking a real episode which made a profound moral impression on the nation, and ruthlessly demoralizing it. Suppose Mr Ward had been permitted to dramatize the famous case with the utmost exactitude! Suppose he had introduced his hero in the second act as Mr Fox, and in

the third as Mr Preston; suppose he had made him descend from
the window of Mrs Dundas's house by a fire escape at the sound
of Mr Dundas's latchkey, and immediately reappear at the front
door in the character of a casual visitor delighted to see his old
friend back again, still he could have gone no further than he
actually has gone: that is, represented a married woman as
deliberately transferring her declared affection from her husband
to another man. The difference in point of adultery would have
been a mere technical difference of no moral significance whatever.
But there would have been the very serious difference that in
the real story the adultery brought tragic consequences which
may yet nerve us to bring our marriage law into harmony with
those of most other highly civilized communities, whereas in the
perversion made for Mr Pigott the consequences are that the
lady and her lover live happily ever after, the husband being
slaughtered by Providence like a Chicago pig for their convenience. Such are the results of handing over the drama to be
purified by a respectable householder at a guinea an act or two
guineas for three.

Allowing for the shackles in which the author had to work,
the play is by no means an unwelcome one, though how far its
simplicity and refinement of feeling and its chivalrous idealism
of sentiment are qualities of the author's youth, and how far of
his genius, remains to be seen. The character-drawing has hardly
any individualization. The young women, a little etherealized, are
feminine enough, and very sympathetically and tenderly handled;
but then they are all the same young woman with different names.
It is much the same with the men: one fails to catch any idio-
syncrasy. Even the attempt, made for the sake of comic relief,
to make one of them a bounder and another an idiot, came off
very faintly, though it was, one must admit, powerfully reinforced
by the artists entrusted with the two parts in question. The
flashes of wit in the play, brilliant enough in themselves, made
no effect, because they did not illuminate either the character of
the utterers or any irony in the dramatic situation. And the persons of the drama belong rather to the world of imagination than

39

of reality. Even the feeling, which is the author's most effective quality so far, is imaginative feeling, and never has quite the conviction that experience alone brings; but it is fine and intellectual as well as abundant. Every act was saved by some stroke of it: indeed the play was triumphantly rescued, act by act, rather than carried safely and surely through; yet the total result was a very considerable success for a young author making his first attempt with a difficult and ambitious theme.

The acting, as far as the gentlemen in the cast were concerned, several times touched the point of making me think it the very worst I had ever seen. I will not venture to criticize Mr Fred Terry; for, frankly, I did not understand his proceedings. It did not seem to me that any person, labor leader or other, would have spoken the author's words as Mr Terry spoke them, or accompanied them with the gestures he used. Nor did his tones and gestures strike me as having that beauty and grace which one looks for as the differentia between a skilled actor and an ordinary gentleman who has not specialized himself in these directions. I do not for a moment accuse Mr Fred Terry of being a bad actor. The position he occupies is, I presume, hardly to be won without considerable professional competence. Neither is mine. And yet I could see neither appropriateness in the design, nor skill and elegance in the execution of his impersonation of Robert Llewellyn. If the fault is with me, I can only express my regret. Mr H. B. Irving was not good as Louis Farquhar: he was gratuitously tragic, and introduced the heroics of facial expression into drawing room comedy in a way that he will not dream of five years hence; but he is industriously and successfully learning to act; and that is for him at present the whole duty of man. If Mr Dennis's Lord Killarney was not a very remarkable performance, that was perhaps as much the author's fault as the actor's. Something was supposed to be wrong with Mr Carne's acting as the Archdeacon. The defect was really in his wig, which was a powdered servant's wig, and gave him an irresistible air of being his own coachman.

Fortunately for Mr Ward, the women's parts, on which the

play chiefly depends, were in capable hands. Miss Marion Terry and Miss Alma Murray not only know the technical routine of their business—which is really saying a good deal nowadays— but their execution has a cultivated artistic character throughout; and each has an original and completely formed style. The two styles—Miss Murray's carefully guarded, and a little reticent and fastidious; Miss Terry's delicately frank and sympathetic—con- trast very happily, making the scene between the two women in the last act a very pretty piece of work indeed. Unfortunately the public, accustomed to tolerate any sort of bumptious bungling, provided a big effect is pulled off now and then by some actor or actress for whom it has a purely personal admiration, did not shew half as much appreciation of this scene as of Miss Terry's big curtain points, which, to be sure, were admirably done, but which would have been just as loudly applauded had they been crudely thrown at our heads by the youngest and rawest of our leading ladies. When, in this third act, Miss Murray and Miss Terry left the stage, and the men came on, it was as if we had suddenly passed from a first-rate theatre to a country-house infested with amateurs. Miss May Harvey, with a pretty but rather colorless part, was too strong for it: her opportunities evidently lie in tragi-comic parts of a much more forcible kind. Still, that is more her griev- ance than the author's: one does not complain of receiving over- weight.

AN OLD NEW PLAY AND A NEW OLD ONE

THE IMPORTANCE OF BEING EARNEST. A trivial comedy for serious people. By Oscar Wilde. St James's Theatre, 14 February 1895.

? A play in ? acts. By ?. Opera Comique, 16 February 1895.

THE SECOND MRS TANQUERAY. A play in four acts. By Arthur W. Pinero. London: W. Heinemann. 1895.

[23 *February* 1895]

IT is somewhat surprising to find Mr Oscar Wilde, who does not usually model himself on Mr Henry Arthur Jones, giving his latest play a five-chambered title like The Case of Rebellious Susan. So I suggest with some confidence that The Importance of Being Earnest dates from a period long anterior to Susan. However it may have been retouched immediately before its production, it must certainly have been written before Lady Windermere's Fan. I do not suppose it to be Mr Wilde's first play: he is too susceptible to fine art to have begun otherwise than with a strenuous imitation of a great dramatic poem, Greek or Shakespearean; but it was perhaps the first which he designed for practical commercial use at the West End theatres. The evidence of this is abundant. The play has a plot—a gross anachronism; there is a scene between the two girls in the second act quite in the literary style of Mr Gilbert, and almost inhuman enough to have been conceived by him; the humor is adulterated by stock mechanical fun to an extent that absolutely scandalizes one in a play with such an author's name to it; and the punning title and several of the more farcical passages recall the epoch of the late H. J. Byron. The whole has been varnished, and here and there veneered, by the author of A Woman of no Importance; but the general effect is that of a farcical comedy dating from the seventies, unplayed during that period because it was too clever and too decent, and brought up to date as far as possible by Mr Wilde in his now completely formed style. Such is the impression left by the play on me. But I find other critics, equally entitled to respect, declaring that The Importance of Being Earnest is a strained effort of Mr Wilde's at ultra-modernity, and that it could never have been written but for the opening up of entirely new paths in drama last year by Arms and the Man. At which I confess to a chuckle.

I cannot say that I greatly cared for The Importance of Being Earnest. It amused me, of course; but unless comedy touches me as well as amuses me, it leaves me with a sense of having wasted my evening. I go to the theatre to be moved to laughter, not to be tickled or bustled into it; and that is why, though I laugh as much as anybody at a farcical comedy, I am out of spirits before the end of the second act, and out of temper before the end of the third, my miserable mechanical laughter intensifying these symptoms at every outburst. If the public ever becomes intelligent enough to know when it is really enjoying itself and when it is not, there will be an end of farcical comedy. Now in The Importance of Being Earnest there is plenty of this rib-tickling: for instance, the lies, the deceptions, the cross purposes, the sham mourning, the christening of the two grown-up men, the muffin eating, and so forth. These could only have been raised from the farcical plane by making them occur to characters who had, like Don Quixote, convinced us of their reality and obtained some hold on our sympathy. But that unfortunate moment of Gilbertism breaks our belief in the humanity of the play. Thus we are thrown back on the force and daintiness of its wit, brought home by an exquisitely grave, natural, and unconscious execution on the part of the actors. Alas! the latter is not forthcoming. Mr Kinsey Peile as a man-servant, and Miss Irene Vanbrugh as Gwendolen Fairfax, alone escaped from a devastating consciousness of Mr Wilde's reputation, which more or less preoccupied all the rest, except perhaps Miss Millard, with whom all comedy is a preoccupation, since she is essentially a sentimental actress. In such passages as the Gilbertian quarrel with Gwendolen, her charm rebuked the scene instead of enhancing it. The older ladies were, if they will excuse my saying so, quite maddening. The violence of their affectation, the insufferable low comedy soars and swoops of the voice, the rigid shivers of elbow, shoulder, and neck, which are supposed on the stage to characterize the behavior of ladies after the age of forty, played havoc with the piece. In Miss Rose Leclerq a good deal of this sort of thing is only the mannerism of a genuine if somewhat impossible style; but Miss Leclerq was absent through indisposition on the night of my visit; so that I had not her style to console me. Mr Aynesworth's easy-going Our Boys style of play suited his part rather happily; and Mr Alexander's graver and more refined manner made the right contrast with it. But Mr Alexander, after playing with very nearly if not quite perfect conviction in the first two acts, suddenly lost confidence in the third, and began to spur up

43

for a rattling finish. From the moment that began, the play was done with. The speech in which Worthing forgives his supposed mother, and the business of searching the army lists, which should have been conducted with subdued earnestness, was bustled through to the destruction of all verisimilitude and consequently all interest. That is the worst of having anyone who is not an inveterate and hardened comedian in a leading comedy part. His faith, patience, and relish begin to give out after a time; and he finally commits the unpardonable sin against the author of giving the signal that the play is over ten minutes before the fall of the curtain, instead of speaking the last line as if the whole evening were still before the audience. Mr Alexander does not throw himself genuinely into comedy: he condescends to amuse himself with it; and in the end he finds that he cannot condescend enough. On the whole I must decline to accept The Importance of Being Earnest as a day less than ten years old; and I am altogether unable to perceive any uncommon excellence in its presentation.

I am in a somewhat foolish position concerning a play at the Opera Comique, whither I was bidden this day week. For some reason I was not supplied with a program; so that I never learnt the name of the play. I believe I recognized some of the members of the company—generally a very difficult thing to do in a country where, with a few talented exceptions, every actor is just like every other actor—but they have now faded from my memory. At the end of the second act the play had advanced about as far as an ordinary dramatist would have brought it five minutes after the first rising of the curtain; or, say, as far as Ibsen would have brought it ten years before that event. Taking advantage of the second interval to stroll out into the Strand for a little exercise, I unfortunately forgot all about my business, and actually reached home before it occurred to me that I had not seen the end of the play. Under these circumstances it would ill become me to dogmatize on the merits of the work or its performance. I can only offer the management my apologies.

I am indebted to Mr Heinemann for a copy of The Second

Mrs Tanqueray, which he has just published in a five-shilling volume, with an excellent photographic portrait of the author by Mr Hollyer. Those who did not see the play at the St James's Theatre can now examine the literary basis of the work that so immoderately fascinated playgoing London in 1893. But they must not expect the play to be as imposing in the library as it was on the stage. Its merit there was relative to the culture of the playgoing public. Paula Tanqueray is an astonishingly well-drawn figure as stage figures go nowadays, even allowing for the fact that there is no cheaper subject for the character draughts-man than the ill-tempered sensual woman seen from the point of view of the conventional man. But off the stage her distinction vanishes. The novels of Anthony Trollope, Charles Lever, Bulwer Lytton, Charles Reade, and many other novelists, whom nobody praised thirty years ago in the terms in which Mr Pinero is praised now, are full of feats of character-drawing in no way inferior— to say the least—to Mr Pinero's. The theatre was not ready for that class of work then: it is now; and accordingly Mr Pinero, who in literature is a humble and somewhat belated follower of the novelists of the middle of the nineteenth century, and who has never written a line from which it could be guessed that he is a contemporary of Ibsen, Tolstoi, Meredith, or Sarah Grand, finds himself at the dawn of the twentieth hailed as a man of new ideas, of daring originality, of supreme literary distinction, and even —which is perhaps oddest—of consummate stage craft. Stage craft, after all, is very narrowly limited by the physical conditions of stage representation; but when one turns over the pages of The Second Mrs Tanqueray, and notes the naïve machinery of the exposition in the first act, in which two whole actors are wasted on sham parts, and the hero, at his own dinner party, is compelled to get up and go ignominiously into the next room "to write some letters" when something has to be said behind his back; when one follows Cayley Drummle, the confidant to whom both Paula and her husband explain themselves for the benefit of the audience; when one counts the number of doors which Mr Pinero needs to get his characters on and off the stage, and how they have finally to be supplemented by the inevitable "French windows" (two of them); and when the activity of the postman is taken into consideration, it is impossible to avoid the conclusion that what most of our critics mean by mastery of stage craft is recklessness in the substitution of dead machinery and lay figures for vital action and real characters. I do not deny that an author may be driven by his own limitations to ingenuities which Shakespear had no occasion to cultivate, just as a painter without hands or feet learns to surpass Michael Angelo in the art of drawing with the brush held in the mouth; but I regard such ingenuity as an extremity to be deplored, not as an art to be admired. In the Second Mrs Tanqueray I find little except a scaffold for the situation of a step-daughter and step-mother finding themselves in the positions respectively of affianced wife and discarded mistress to the same man. Obviously, the only necessary conditions of this situation are that the persons concerned shall be respectable enough to be shocked by it, and that the step-mother shall be an improper person. Mr Pinero has not got above this minimum. He is, of course, sufficiently skilled in fiction to give Ellean, Mrs Cortelyon, Ardale, Tanqueray, and Cayley Drummle a passable air of being human beings. He has even touched up Cayley into a Thackerayan *flâneur* in order to secure toleration of his intrusiveness. But who will pretend that any of these figures are more than the barest accessories to the main situation? To compare them with the characters in Robertson's Caste would be almost as ridiculous as to compare Caste with A Doll's House. The two vulgar characters produce the requisite jar—a pitilessly disagreeable jar—and that is all. Still, all the seven seem good as far as they go; and that very little way may suggest that Mr Pinero might have done good creative work if he had carried them further. Unfortunately for this surmise, he has carried Paula further; and with what result? The moment the point is reached at which the comparatively common gift of "an eye for character" has to be supplemented by the higher dramatic gift of sympathy with character—of the power of seeing the world from the point of view of others instead of merely describing or judging them

46

from one's own point of view in terms of the conventional systems of morals, Mr Pinero breaks down. I remember that when I saw the play acted I sat up very attentively when Tanqueray said to Paula, "I know what you were at Ellean's age. You hadnt a thought that wasnt a wholesome one; you hadnt an impulse that didnt tend towards good; you never harbored a notion you couldnt have gossiped about to a parcel of children. And this was a very few years back, etc. etc." On the reply to that fatuous but not unnatural speech depended the whole question of Mr Pinero's rank as a dramatist. One can imagine how, in a play by a master-hand, Paula's reply would have opened Tanqueray's foolish eyes to the fact that a woman of that sort is already the same at three as she is at thirty-three, and that however she may have found by experience that her nature is in conflict with the ideals of differently constituted people, she remains perfectly valid to herself, and despises herself, if she sincerely does so at all, for the hypocrisy that the world forces on her instead of for being what she is. What reply does Mr Pinero put into her mouth? Here it is, with the stage directions: "A few—years ago! (*She walks slowly towards the door, then suddenly drops upon the ottoman in a paroxysm of weeping.*) O God! A few years ago!" That is to say, she makes her reply from the Tanqueray-Ellean-Pinero point of view, and thus betrays the fact that she is a work of prejudiced observation instead of comprehension, and that the other characters only owe their faint humanity to the fact that they are projections of Mr Pinero's own personal amiabilities and beliefs and conventions. Mr Pinero, then, is no interpreter of character, but simply an adroit describer of people as the ordinary man sees and judges them. Add to this a clear head, a love of the stage, and a fair talent for fiction, all highly cultivated by hard and honorable work as a writer of effective stage plays for the modern commercial theatre; and you have him on his real level. On that level he is entitled to all the praise The Second Mrs Tanqueray has won him; and I very heartily regret that the glamor which Mrs Patrick Campbell cast round the play has forced me to examine pretensions which Mr Pinero himself never put forward rather than to acknowledge the merits with which his work is so concisely packed.

THE LATE CENSOR

[2 *March* 1895]

MR E. F. SMYTH PIGOTT, for twenty years examiner of stage plays to the Lord Chamberlain's department, has joined the majority. It is a great pity that the Censorship cannot be abolished before the appointment of a successor to Mr Pigott creates a fresh vested interest in one of the most mischievous of our institutions.

The justification of the Censorship is to be found in the assumption, repeatedly and explicitly advanced by the late holder of the office, that, if the stage were freed, managers would immediately produce licentious plays; actresses would leave off clothing themselves decently; and the public would sit nightly wallowing in the obscenity which the Censor now sternly withholds from them. This assumption evidently involves the further one, that the Examiner of Plays is so much better than his neighbors, as to be untainted by their assumed love of filth. This is where the theory of the Censorship breaks down in practice. The Lord Chamberlain's reader is not selected by examination either in literature or morals. His emoluments, estimated at about £800 a year, will fetch nothing more in the market than well connected mediocrity. Therefore it is necessary to give him absolute power, so that there may be no appeal from his blunders. If he vetoes serious plays and licenses nasty ones, which is exactly what the late Mr Pigott did, there is no remedy. He is the Tsar of the theatres, able to do things that no prime minister dare do. And he has the great advantage that in ninety-eight out of every hundred plays submitted to him (this is an official estimate), no question of morals is raised. He has nothing to do but read the play, pocket his two guineas, license the performance, and leave the manager and the author under the impression that he is a very agreeable, unobjectionable person, whose licence is cheap at the price since it relieves every one of responsibility and makes things

48

pleasant all round. It is not until the two per cent of plays in which received opinions and hardened prejudices are called in question, and offered for testing under the searching rays of the footlights—in other words, the plays on which the whole growth and continued vitality of the theatre depend—that the Censor has his opportunity of shewing how much better he is than the public by saying, "You should listen to these plays, however much they may shock you. I have read them, and can certify that they will interest really cultivated people and help to set everybody thinking." But as the Censor never is any better than the average public, he does exactly the reverse of this. He shares its ignorant intolerance and its petulance under criticism, and uses his official authority to forbid the performance of the exceptional plays. The late Mr Pigott is declared on all hands to have been the best reader of plays we have ever had; and yet he was a walking compendium of vulgar insular prejudice, who, after wallowing all his life in the cheapest theatrical sentiment (he was a confirmed playgoer), had at last brought himself to a pitch of incompetence which, outside the circle of those unfortunate persons who have had to try and reason with him personally, can only be measured by reading his evidence before the Commission of 1892, and the various letters of his which are just now finding their way into print. He had French immorality on the brain; he had American indecency on the brain; he had the womanly woman on the brain; he had the Divorce Court on the brain; he had "not before a mixed audience" on the brain; his official career in relation to the higher drama was one long folly and panic, in which the only thing definitely discernible in a welter of intellectual confusion was his conception of the English people rushing towards an abyss of national degeneration in morals and manners, and only held back on the edge of the precipice by the grasp of his strong hand.

In the Daily Telegraph of Monday last there was an obituary notice of Mr Pigott from the sympathetic pen of Mr Clement Scott, who is far too kind-hearted to tell the truth on so sad an occasion, and who, I am afraid, will characterize my remarks, in his very ownest style, as "a cowardly attack on a dead man." Mr Scott tells us of Mr Pigott's "difficult and delicate duties," of his "admirable discretion," his "determination to persist in the path that seemed right to him," his conscientiousness, zeal, efficiency, tact, and so on. I do not question Mr Pigott's personal character: I have no doubt he was as excellent a man for all private purposes as Charles I. But when Mr Scott's benevolence to Mr Pigott leads him to discredit my protests against the Censorship as "allegations that are as coarse as they are untrue," I must open Mr Scott's eyes a little. Not that I deny the coarseness. To accuse anyone of encouraging lewd farce at the expense of fine drama is to bring a coarse charge against him; but Mr Scott will admit that the policeman must not be put out of court because he has a coarse charge to prefer. The question is, Is the charge true? Mr Scott says no. I produce my evidence, and leave the public to judge.

Not very many seasons ago, in the exercise of my duties as a musical critic, I went to an opera at a certain West End theatre. (Mr Scott, not having enjoyed the advantage of a training as musical critic, misses these things.) There were two heroines, one a princess. The hero had to marry the princess, though he loved the other heroine. In the second act, the stage represented an antechamber in the palace of the bride's father on the night of the wedding. The door of the nuptial chamber appeared on the stage. It was guarded by an elderly duenna. The reluctant bridegroom arrived on his way to join his bride. The duenna presented him with the golden key of the chamber. Suddenly it occurred to him that if he were to criminally assault this lady, who was renowned at court for her austerity, her screams would rouse the court, and he would be consigned by the outraged monarch to a dungeon, thereby escaping his conjugal obligations. On proceeding to carry out this stratagem, he was taken aback by finding the old lady, far from raising an alarm, receive his advances with the utmost ardour. In desperation he threw her to the ground, and was about to escape when she, making no effort to rise, said, with archly affectionate reproach, "Dont you see where youve left me, duckie?" On this he fled; and presently a young man and a young woman entered and flirted until they were interrupted by the king. He, overhearing a kiss, supposed it to proceed from the bridal chamber of his daughter. He immediately went to the door; listened at the keyhole; and, hearing another kiss, remarked with an ecstatic shiver that it made him feel young again. If that scene had not been presented to the public under the authority of the Lord Chamberlain, it would be impossible for me to describe it in these columns. The sole justification for the Censorship is that, without its restraining hand, the scene would have been worse than it was. Pray how much worse could it have been?

Take another instance, this time of a well-known farcical comedy which Mr Scott must have witnessed. I spare the details: suffice it to say that the piece contained three or four "laughs" which could not possibly have been explained or described at a dinner party, which is, if I mistake not, Mr Scott's test of propriety. I did not see the piece until, finding myself at Northampton on the eve of a political meeting in which I had to take part, I went into the theatre, and found this comedy "on tour" there. Now Northampton is not like London: it is not large enough to support one theatre where improper jests are permitted, and another guaranteed safe for clergymen and their daughters. What was the result? The Censorship of public opinion—of that Monsieur Tout le Monde who is admitted to be wiser than everyone except the Lord Chamberlain—acted spontaneously. The questionable points were either omitted or slurred over in such a way that nobody could possibly catch their intention. Everything that Mr Pigott might have done, and did not do, to make the play decent was done without compulsion by the management in order to avoid offending that section of the public which does not relish smoking-room facetiousness.

These two typical cases, which, as Mr Scott knows better than anyone else, I can easily multiply if he puts me to it, will, I hope, convince him that my statement that the Censorship does not withhold its approval from blackguardism on the stage is much better considered than his counter-statement that I have simply said the thing that is not. But if he demands equally direct proof of my statement that the Censorship suppresses fine work, he has me at a disadvantage; for I naturally cannot produce the plays that the Censorship has prevented from existing. And yet this is the very statement I chiefly desire to establish; for I do not in the least object to the licensing of plays which disgust me, if there are people who are entertained by them: what I object to is the suppression, because they disgust other people, of plays that entertain me. All I can do is to offer to produce a staggering list of authors who have not written for the stage since the evil day when Walpole established the Censorship to prevent Fielding from exposing the corruption of Parliament on the stage. Fielding never wrote another play; and from his time to that of Dickens, who was once very fond of the stage, a comparison of our literature with our drama shews a relative poverty and inferiority on the part of the latter not to be paralleled in any of the countries where the Censor only interferes on political grounds. May I ask Mr Scott whether he thinks that Mr Grant Allen's The Woman who Did would have been licensed by Mr Pigott if it had been a play, or whether The Heavenly Twins could have been written under the thumb of a Censor? Or, to come to actual plays, would Ibsen's Ghosts have been licensed had Mr Grein risked subjecting himself to a £50 penalty by making the attempt? Is Tolstoi's Dominion of Darkness likely to be produced here as it has been elsewhere? Would Die Walküre be licensed as a spoken play? Would Shakespear, or the great Greek dramatists, have stood a chance with Mr Pigott? Mr Scott may reply that Mr Pigott actually did license Ibsen's plays. Fortunately, I am in a position to give both Mr Pigott's opinion of Ibsen's plays and his reason for licensing them. Here are his own words, uttered on one of the most responsible occasions of his official career:

"I have studied Ibsen's plays pretty carefully; and all the characters in Ibsen's plays appear to me morally deranged. All the heroines are dissatisfied spinsters who look on marriage as a monopoly, or dissatisfied married women in a chronic state of rebellion against not only the conditions which nature has imposed on their sex, but against all the duties and obligations of mothers and wives. As for the men, they are all rascals or imbeciles."

Not unnaturally, Mr Woodall asked Mr Pigott on this why he did not think the plays sufficiently injurious to public morals to be suppressed. Mr Pigott replied that they were too absurd to do any harm. Thus the one great writer who has escaped what Mr Scott has called "the kindly blue pencil," was let pass, not because he was a great writer, but because Mr Pigott was so stupendously incompetent as to think him beneath contempt. I have suggested that Shakespear would have been vetoed by him; but he has anticipated that misgiving in the following remarkable utterance: "Shakespear himself was a member, I believe, at one time, of the Lord Chamberlain's company; but that did not prevent his plays being written." Imagine Mr Pigott, who refused to license The Cenci, confronted with the relationship between the king and queen in Hamlet, or with the closet scene in that play.

Let me add a few more touches to the sketch of Mr Pigott's mind. First, as to his notion of morality in an audience, of vice and virtue, of fine sentiment:

"The further east you go, the more moral your audience is. You may get a gallery full of roughs in which every other boy is a pickpocket, and yet their collective sympathy is in favor of self-sacrifice; collectively they have a horror of vice and a love of virtue. A boy might pick your pocket as you left the theatre, but have his reserve of fine sentiment in his heart."

This is immoral balderdash, nothing more and nothing less; and yet poor Mr Pigott believed it as firmly as he believed that Browning and George Meredith and James Russell Lowell, in attending the Shelley Society's unlicensed performance of The Cenci, were indulging a vicious taste for immoral exhibitions.

Mr Pigott's highly praised tact, both as a critic and a controversialist, may be judged from the following *obiter dicta*:

"Managers' backers are in most cases men who do not care to keep a theatre—I will not say for the elevation of dramatic art, or for the public edification—but for purposes which can be openly avowed."

"Absolute free trade in theatres and theatrical representation may be left to the advocacy of disciples of Jack Cade, whose political economy is a sort of Benthamism burlesqued. These purveyors of theatrical scandals are equally in favor of absolute free trade in disorderly houses and houses of ill-fame."

I must say I wish Mr Scott had not trifled so outrageously as he has with this great public question. It is a frightful thing to see the greatest thinkers, poets, and authors of modern Europe—men like Ibsen, Wagner, Tolstoi, and the leaders of our own literature —delivered helpless into the vulgar hands of such a noodle as this amiable old gentleman—this despised and incapable old official— most notoriously was. And just such a man as he was his successor is likely to be too, because a capable man means a known man; and a known man means one whose faults have become as public as his qualities. The appointment of Mr Archer, for instance, would awaken Mr Scott to the infamy of the Censorship as effectually as the appointment of Mr Scott himself would fortify Mr Archer's case against the institution. Yet the Lord Chamberlain cannot possibly find a better man than either one or other of these gentlemen. He will therefore have to appoint a nobody whose qualifications, being unknown, can be imagined by foolish people to be infinite. Is this, then, the time for Mr Scott to announce that "the dramatic world is well content with the control now vested in the Lord Chamberlain and his staff?" Who constitute the dramatic world?! take the first handful of names that comes to hand. Do Messrs Oscar Wilde, Sydney Grundy, Robert Buchanan, Henry Arthur Jones belong to it? Do Mr Hermann Vezin, Mr Lewis Waller, Mr Charles Charrington, Miss Alma Murray, Mrs Theodore Wright, Miss Janet Achurch, Miss Elizabeth Robins belong to it? Does Mr Scott himself belong to it? and, if so, do I?—does Mr Archer?—does Mr Walkley?—do the numerous critics who never refer to the Censorship except in terms of impatient contempt at such an anomaly? Would one of the managers who pay the Lord Chamberlain compliments now that they are in his power, waste a word on him if they were out of it? No: the dramatic world, Mr Scott may depend on it, wants the same freedom that exists in America and—oddly enough—

in Ireland. Not, mind, a stage controlled by the County Council or any such seventy-seven times worse evil than the present, but a stage free as the Press is free and as speech is free. When Mr Scott has dropped his tear over the lost friend whom he has forced me to handle so roughly, I shall thank him to come back to his own side and fight for that freedom. Abominations like the Censorship have quite enough flatterers without him.

MR ARTHUR ROBERTS AS A GENTLEMAN

GENTLEMAN JOE. A New Musical Farce. Words and Lyrics by
    Basil Hood. Music by Walter Slaughter. Prince of Wales
    Theatre, 2 March 1895.   [9 *March* 1895]

IT is impossible to sit out an entertainment like Gentleman Joe without reflecting on the enormous part played in the theatre by hypnotic suggestion. At what point I fall a victim to it myself I, of course, do not know. No "professor" in the world can persuade me that a glass of paraffin oil is a bumper of Imperial Tokay. But as I look back on my earliest impressions of certain performances which completely dominated my imagination, I have to admit that my view of them was very far from being a sane and objective one. And now that it is my business as a critic to gain such a sane and objective view over the whole field of art, I sometimes find myself at the theatre in a state of distressingly complete sanity among neighbors who are in the wildest ecstasies at nothing. This was my predicament at Gentleman Joe. A variety of causes have produced a powerful hypnotic suggestion that Mr Arthur Roberts is a buffoon of almost superhuman powers, and that the musical farces "written round him," as the technical phrase goes, are immensely exhilarating, racy, up-to-date, and necessary to complete the experience of every dashing young undergraduate in the joy of life. The spell is undeniably successful, though nothing but the fear of seeming to pose as a superior person prevents me from adding that the weakness of its subjects has a great deal to do with its apparently irresistible strength. At any rate, it did not operate on me. When Mr Roberts, on the sands at Margate, turned to a gentleman who was about to annihilate a sand castle, and told him not to sit down on the Christmas pudding, I sat patiently enduring whilst all around me roared with merriment. And again, when, wishing to convey to the audience that one of the persons on the stage was beside himself, he tapped his forehead and said, "Balmy on the crumpet," I, having long ago exhausted such delight as lurks in that fantastic expression, heaved a sigh amid the general laughter. I do not deny that these sallies are funny in comparison with absolute vacuity; but surely, since private life supplies rather more than enough of them free of charge, one need not go to the trouble and expense of a visit to the theatre to procure them. Then there were certain humors which probably made a majority of the audience uneasy, and were not witty enough to excuse the company for condescending to them. For example, Mr Roberts, as Gentleman Joe, the hansom cabby, comes to see his sweetheart. He says to the butler, "Where's Emma?" The butler replies, "Emma is getting ready to see you, and is taking off her things." Mr Roberts receives this in such a way as to shew that the line may be construed to mean that the young lady is undressing herself completely; and the house, pleased at its own cleverness in finding this out, and at Mr Roberts' artfulness in suggesting it, laughs at the schoolboy indecency for fully half a minute. Again, Mr Roberts is conversing with Miss Kitty Loftus, the sweetheart aforesaid, who has a piece of frilling in her hand. He asks her what it is. "That," she tells him, "is frilling for me to wear." "Where?" he asks; and as "where" and "wear" make a sort of pun, there is a faint laugh from the quicker wits present. "In my hat," is Miss Loftus's answer. Whereupon Mr Roberts, by appropriate pantomime, makes it appear that he had supposed the frilling to belong to her undergarments; and there is again a huge guffaw. Now this sort of thing is to me mere silly misbehavior, and I want to have it banished from the stage. The question is, how is it to be done? The Censorship, even if there were no larger grounds for condemning it, is worse than useless here; for in the two instances given above, the first arose on a line which no Censor could possibly object to without exposing himself to the charge of having an intolerably prurient imagination; whilst the second enjoys the licence of the Lord Chamberlain, although the incident of the frilling is dragged in by the ears, for the express purpose of Mr Roberts' ribaldry, with an obviousness which even the most angelically innocent Censor could not possibly miss if he did his duty with any sort of intelligent vigilance. The Censorship of the public is of no use either, because part of any audience is sure to laugh—even the people who are annoyed cannot all help laughing; and the others will put up with an offensive passage or two for the sake of the rest of the entertainment sooner than make a fuss about an unpleasant matter. As for the critics, they must either complain of Mr Roberts' coarseness in general terms, thereby leaving the extent of the evil to the imagination, or else they must do what I have been compelled to do: that is, describe the objectionable passages with an exactitude which jars disagreeably on my readers and myself. There is, fortunately, another power to appeal to—the self-respect of the artist. Although the qualities found in Mr Roberts' performances by the hypnotized young gentlemen in the stalls of the Prince of Wales Theatre are nine-tenths imaginary, none the less must an actor possess a great deal of merit to outstrip all his competitors in the struggle to be rated as the most entertaining performer of his class in London. Granted that the Arthur Roberts of the popular imagination has no objective existence; that dozens of artists at the music-halls and in the provincial pantomimes can sing a comic song as well as he; that London is familiar with better dancers and pantomimists; and that his popularity is widest among people whose admiration is not worth having, still he has intense comic force, an eye for characteristic London street and shop types hardly inferior to Mr Phil May's, much shrewdness and tact, and great skill and experience. Some day, when his younger admirers outgrow their taste for him, and the coming generations find him as old-fashioned as Mr Toole, he will take to acting, and probably earn a distinguished place as a low comedian. Mr Roberts, in short, has plenty of dignity as an artist if he will only stand on it. He dare not carry indecorum far enough to satisfy the people who like it, though he can and does go quite far enough to disgust the people who do not like it. When he says to Miss Jenoure, "May I take you on one side for a moment?" in such a way as to make the speech an insult, he simply throws away his own respectability and that of his art for nothing, since nobody can possibly be so feeble-minded as to see any wit in the perception of such a point or any cleverness in the execution of it. I strongly recommend Mr Roberts to drop it; and I suggest to the author, Mr Basil Hood, who must be aware of the turn given to his lines, and to the management, who are equally responsible with the author and performer, that they should immediately signify to Mr Roberts that they would prefer not to have the three points I have mentioned made in future.

At the same time, I am of opinion that these entertainments would be far more enjoyable if they were not so depressingly moral. Let them be courageously written from the point of view of the devil's advocate; and then there will be conviction in them, interest in them, and wit in them. For example, I have not the slightest objection to Yvette Guilbert singing Les Vierges. In that song you hear virtue attacked with bitter irony by a poet who does not believe in it and—I must not say by an artist who does not believe in it either, but at all events by one who has the power of throwing herself with mordant intensity into the poet's attitude for the moment. Let us by all means have whole plays written like Les Vierges, in which the votaries of pleasure can religiously put forward their creed against the idealists and the Puritans. There would be life in that—purpose, honesty, reality, and the decency which arises spontaneously beside them. But a timidly conventional play like Gentleman Joe, with its abject little naughtinesses furtively slipped in under cover of the tamest propriety, and with a pitiful whoop at the end about a debauched clergyman riding in a cab with a lady, of whom Mr Roberts sings

> Perhaps she was his aunt,
> Or another Mrs Chant,

—all this is about as lively as the performances of the children who make faces at their teachers in Sunday-school. The nearest approach to a witty line in Gentleman Joe is Mrs Ralli-Carr's reply to the question, "Why dont you divorce your husband?" "I cant prove the cruelty"; but this faint attempt to say something scandalous with piquant indirectness was too subtle for the audience.

As usual in such entertainments, there is a tedious preliminary "exposition" of the relations between the characters. Nobody listens to it. Mr Roberts is a hansom cabman who is mistaken most impossibly for a lord. He has his moments of clever mimicry, as well as one good passage of acting, where he becomes respectful to the lady whom he has mistaken for a servant. The quaint line, "Excuse me keeping my hat off," is the only one in the piece which shews the artist under the buffoon and caricaturist. A touch of cheap "John Anderson my jo" sentiment in the duet with Miss Kitty Loftus in the last act was a huge relief after all the dead galvanized vivacity that preceded it. Miss Sadie Jerome, a dashing American lady, made a huge effect by launching her name "Potts" in one enormous consonantal convulsion at the end of her song. Miss Kate Cutler sang nicely; and Mr Philp, a rather throaty tenorino, just at the age at which throaty tenorinos are agreeable, delivered himself acceptably of a ballad. Miss Jenoure, as Mrs Ralli-Carr, had a part in which she saw no harm. Possibly the author found her innocuousness disappointing. I did not.

The music, by Mr Walter Slaughter, does not contain a single novel or even passably fresh point either in melody, harmony, or orchestration. The song in the "old English" style, sung by Miss Cutler, was almost the only passage which Mr Slaughter seemed to have composed with any feeling or enjoyment.

MR PINERO'S NEW PLAY

THE NOTORIOUS MRS EBBSMITH. An original play in four acts. By A. W. Pinero. Garrick Theatre, 13 March 1895.

[16 *March* 1895]

MR PINERO's new play is an attempt to reproduce that peculiar stage effect of intellectual drama, of social problem, of subtle

59

psychological study of character, in short, of a great play, with which he was so successful in The Profligate and The Second Mrs Tanqueray. In the two earlier plays, it will be remembered, he was careful to support this stage effect with a substantial basis of ordinary dramatic material, consisting of a well worked-up and well worn situation which would have secured the success of a conventional Adelphi piece. In this way he conquered the public by the exquisite flattery of giving them plays that they really liked, whilst persuading them that such appreciation was only possible from persons of great culture and intellectual acuteness. The vogue of The Second Mrs Tanqueray was due to the fact that the commonplace playgoer, as he admired Mrs Patrick Campbell, and was moved for the twentieth time by the conventional wicked woman with a past, consumed with remorse at the recollection of her innocent girlhood, and unable to look her pure step-daughter (from a convent) in the face, believed that he was one of the select few for whom "the literary drama" exists, and thus combined the delights of an evening at a play which would not have puzzled Madame Celeste with a sense of being immensely in the modern movement. Mr Pinero, in effect, invented a new sort of play by taking the ordinary article and giving it an air of novel, profound, and original thought. This he was able to do because he was an inveterate "character actor" (a technical term denoting a clever stage performer who cannot act, and therefore makes an elaborate study of the disguises and stage tricks by which acting can be grotesquely simulated) as well as a competent dramatist on customary lines. His performance as a thinker and social philosopher is simply character acting in the domain of authorship, and can impose only on those who are taken in by character acting on the stage. It is only the make-up of an actor who does not understand his part, but who knows—because he shares—the popular notion of its externals. As such, it can never be the governing factor in his success, which must always depend on the commonplace but real substratum of ordinary drama in his works. Thus his power to provide Mrs Tanqueray with equally popular successors depends on his freedom from the illusion he has himself created as to his real strength lying in his acuteness as a critic of life. Given a good play, the stage effect of philosophy will pass with those who are no better philosophers than he; but when the play is bad, the air of philosophy can only add to its insufferableness. In the case of The Notorious Mrs Ebbsmith, the play is bad. But one of its defects: to wit, the unreality of the chief female character, who is fully as artificial as Mrs Tanqueray herself, has the lucky effect of setting Mrs Patrick Campbell free to do as she pleases in it, the result being an irresistible projection of that lady's personal genius, a projection which sweeps the play aside and imperiously becomes the play itself. Mrs Patrick Campbell, in fact, pulls her author through by playing him clean off the stage. She creates all sorts of illusions, and gives one all sorts of searching sensations. It is impossible not to feel that those haunting eyes are brooding on a momentous past, and the parted lips anticipating a thrilling imminent future, whilst some enigmatic present must no less surely be working underneath all that subtle play of limb and stealthy intensity of tone. Clearly there must be a great tragedy somewhere in the immediate neighborhood; and most of my colleagues will no doubt tell us that this imaginary masterpiece is Mr Pinero's Notorious Mrs Ebbsmith. But Mr Pinero has hardly anything to do with it. When the curtain comes down, you are compelled to admit that, after all, nothing has come of it except your conviction that Mrs Patrick Campbell is a wonderful woman. Let us put her out of the question for a moment and take a look at Mrs Ebbsmith.

To begin with, she is what has been called "a platform woman." She is the daughter of a secularist agitator—say a minor Bradlaugh. After eight years of married life, during which she was for one year her husband's sultana, and for the other seven his housekeeper, she has emerged into widowhood and an active career as an agitator, speaking from the platforms formerly occupied by her father. Although educated, well conducted, beautiful, and a sufficiently powerful speaker to produce a great effect in Trafalgar Square, she loses her voice from starvation, and has to fall back on nursing—a piece of fiction which shews that Mr

Pinero has not the faintest idea of what such a woman's career is
in reality. He may take my word for it that a lady with such
qualifications would be very much better off than a nurse; and
that the plinth of the Nelson column, the "pitch" in the park, and
the little meeting halls in poor parishes, all of which he speaks of
with such an exquisitely suburban sense of their being the dark
places of the earth, enter nowadays very largely into the political
education of almost all publicly active men and women; so that
the Duke of St Olpherts, when he went to that iron building in
St Luke's, and saw "Mad Agnes" on the platform, might much
more probably have found there a future Cabinet Minister, a
lady of his own ducal family, or even a dramatic critic. However,
the mistakes into which Mr Pinero has been led by his want of
practical acquaintance with the business of political agitation are
of no great dramatic moment. We may forgive a modern British
dramatist for supposing that Mrs Besant, for example, was an
outcast on the brink of starvation in the days when she gradu-
ated on the platform, although we should certainly not tolerate
such nonsense from any intellectually responsible person. But
Mr Pinero has made a deeper mistake. He has fallen into the
common error of supposing that the woman who speaks in public
and takes an interest in wider concerns than those of her own
household is a special variety of the human species; that she
"Trafalgar Squares" aristocratic visitors in her drawing room;
and that there is something dramatic in her discovery that she
has the common passions of humanity.

Mrs Ebbsmith, in the course of her nursing, finds a patient
who falls in love with her. He is married to a shrew; and he proposes to spend the rest of his life with his nurse, preaching the
horrors of marriage. Off the stage it is not customary for a man
and woman to assume that they cannot co-operate in bringing
about social reform without living together as man and wife: on
the stage, this is considered inevitable. Mrs Ebbsmith rebels
against the stage so far as to propose that they shall prove their
disinterestedness by making the partnership a friendly business
one only. She then finds out that he does not really care a rap

about her ideas, and that his attachment to her is simply sexual. Here we start with a dramatic theme capable of interesting development. Mr Pinero, unable to develop it, lets it slip through his fingers after one feeble clutch at it, and proceeds to degrade his drama below the ordinary level by making the woman declare that her discovery of the nature of the man's feelings puts within her reach "the only one hour in a woman's life," in pursuance of which detestable view she puts on an indecent dress and utterly abandons herself to him. A clergyman appears at this crisis, and offers her a Bible. She promptly pitches it into the stove; and a thrill of horror runs through the audience as they see, in imagination, the whole Christian Church tottering before their eyes. Suddenly, with a wild scream, she plunges her hand into the glowing stove and pulls out the Bible again. The Church is saved; and the curtain descends amid thunders of applause. In that applause I hope I need not say I did not join. A less sensible and less courageous stage effect I have never witnessed. If Mr Pinero had created for us a woman whose childhood had been made miserable by the gloomy terrorism which vulgar, fanatical parents extract from the Bible, then he might fitly have given some of the public a very wholesome lesson by making the woman thrust the Bible into the stove and leave it there. Many of the most devoted clergymen of the Church of England would, I can assure him, have publicly thanked him for such a lesson. But to introduce a woman as to whom we are carefully assured that she was educated as a secularist, and whose one misfortune —her unhappy marriage—can hardly by any stretch of casuistry be laid to the charge of St Paul's teaching; to make this woman senselessly say that all her misfortunes are due to the Bible; to make her throw it into the stove, and then injure herself horribly in pulling it out again: this, I submit, is a piece of claptrap so gross that it absolves me from all obligation to treat Mr Pinero's art as anything higher than the barest art of theatrical sensation. As in The Profligate, as in The Second Mrs Tanqueray, he has had no idea beyond that of doing something daring and bringing down the house by running away from the consequences.

I must confess that I have no criticism for all this stuff. Mr Pinero is quite right to try his hand at the higher drama; only he will never succeed on his present method of trusting to his imagination, which seems to me to have been fed originally on the novels and American humor of forty years ago, and of late to have been entirely starved. I strongly recommend him to air his ideas a little in Hyde Park or "the Iron Hall, St Luke's," before he writes his next play. I shall be happy to take the chair for him.

I should, by the way, like to know the truth about the great stage effect at the end of the second act, where Mrs Patrick Campbell enters with her plain and very becoming dress changed for a horrifying confection apparently made of Japanese bronze wall-paper with a bold pattern of stamped gold. Lest the maker should take an action against me and obtain ruinous damages, I hasten to say that the garment was well made, the skirt and train perfectly hung, and the bodice, or rather waistband, fitting flawlessly. But, as I know nothing of the fashion in evening dresses, it was cut rather lower in the pectoral region than I expected; and it was, to my taste, appallingly ugly. So I fully believed that the effect intended was a terrible rebuke to the man's complaint that Mrs Ebbsmith's previous dress was only fit for "a dowdy demagogue." Conceive my feelings when everyone on the stage went into ecstasies of admiration. Can Mr Pinero have shared that admiration? As the hero of a recent play observes, "That is the question that torments me."

A great deal of the performance is extremely tedious. The first twenty minutes, with its intolerable, unnecessary, and unintelligible explanations about the relationships of the characters, should be ruthlessly cut out. Half the stage business is only Mr Pinero's old "character actor" nonsense; and much of the other half might be executed during the dialogue, and not between the sentences. The company need to be reminded that the Garrick is a theatre in which very distinct utterance is desirable. The worrying from time to time about the stove should be dropped, as it does not in the least fulfil its purpose of making the Bible incident—which is badly stage managed—seem more natural when it comes.

Mr Hare, in the stalest of parts, gives us a perfect piece of acting, not only executed with extraordinary fineness, but conceived so as to produce a strong illusion that there is a real character there, whereas there is really nothing but that hackneyed simulacrum of a cynical and epigrammatic old libertine who has helped to carry on so many plots. Mr Forbes Robertson lent himself to the hero, and so enabled him to become interesting on credit. Miss Jeffreys, miraculously ill fitted with her part, was pleasant for the first five minutes, during which she was suggesting a perfectly different sort of person to that which she afterwards vainly pretended to become. The other characters were the merest stock figures, convincing us that Mr Pinero either never meets anybody now, or else that he has lost the power of observation. Many passages in the play, of course, have all the qualities which have gained Mr Pinero his position as a dramatist; but I shall not dwell on them, as, to tell the truth, I disliked the play so much that nothing would induce me to say anything good of it. And here let me warn the reader to carefully discount my opinion in view of the fact that I write plays myself, and that my school is in violent reaction against that of Mr Pinero. But my criticism has not, I hope, any other fault than the inevitable one of extreme unfairness.

I must change the subject here to say that Mr Clement Scott has been kind enough to let me know that he did not write the obituary notice which I ascribed to him throughout my recent utterance on the subject of the Censorship in these columns. Not that Mr Scott has at all changed his views on that subject. The continuity of his policy was strictly maintained by the actual writer of the article; so that the argument between us on that point remains, I am sorry to say, where it was. But as I have incidentally made it appear that Mr Scott wrote an anonymous obituary notice of his late friend, and made it the occasion for a defence of him against certain strictures of mine, I am bound not only to comply with Mr Scott's request to make it known that he did not write the article, but to express my sense of the very considerate terms in which he has pointed out my mistake, and to beg him to excuse it.

THE INDEPENDENT THEATRE REPENTS

A MAN'S LOVE, a Play in three acts, from the Dutch of J. C. de Vos; and SALVÊ, a Dramatic Fragment in one act, by Mrs Oscar Beringer. The Independent Theatre (Opéra Comique), 15 March 1895. [23 *March* 1895]

THE Independent Theatre is becoming wretchedly respectable. Nobody now clamors for the prosecution of Mr Grein under Lord Campbell's Act, or denounces myself and the other frequenters of the performances as neurotic, cretinous degenerates. This is not as it should be. In my barbarous youth, when one of the pleasures of theatre-going was the fierce struggle at the pit-door, I learnt a lesson which I have never forgotten: namely, that the secret of getting in was to wedge myself into the worst of the crush. When ribs and breastbone were on the verge of collapse, and the stout lady in front, after passionately calling on her escort to take her out of it if he considered himself a man, had resigned herself to death, my hopes of a place in the front row ran high. If the pressure slackened I knew I was being extruded into the side eddies where the feeble and half-hearted were throwing away their chance of a good seat for such paltry indulgences as freedom to breathe and a fully expanded skeleton. The progressive man goes through life on the same principle, instinctively making for the focus of struggle and resisting the tendency to edge him out into the place of ease. When the Independent Theatre was started, its supporters all made for it, I presume— certainly I did—because it was being heavily squeezed. There was one crowded moment when, after the first performance of Ghosts, the atmosphere of London was black with vituperation, with threats, with clamor for suppression and extinction, with everything that makes life worth living in modern society. I have myself stood before the Independent footlights in obedience to my

66

vocation (literally) as dramatic author, drinking in the rapture of such a hooting from the outraged conventional first-nighter as even Mr Henry James might have envied. But now that glory has departed to the regular theatres. My poor little audacity of a heroine who lost her temper and shook her housemaid has been eclipsed by heroines who throw the Bible into the fire. Mr Grein, no longer a revolutionist, is modestly bidding for the position left vacant by the death of German Reed, and will shortly be consecrated by public opinion as the manager of the one theatre in London that is not a real wicked Pinerotic theatre, and is, consequently, the only theatre in London that it is not wrong for good people to go to. His latest playbill is conclusive on this point. It begins with A Man's Love, from the Dutch of J. C. de Vos, and ends with Salvê, by Mrs Oscar Beringer. The first would be contemptuously rejected by Mr Hare as a snivelling, pietistic insult to the spirit of the age; and the second might without the least incongruity be played as a curtain-raiser before Green Bushes or The Wreck Ashore.

The defence to this grave disparagement will probably be that, in A Man's Love, the hero makes advances to his undeceased wife's sister, and that Salvê ends unhappily. I cannot allow the excuse. Any man, on the stage or off it, may make love to his sister-in-law without rousing the faintest sense of unexpectedness in the spectator. And when, as in Mr de Vos's play, the young lady tells him he ought to be ashamed of himself, and leaves the house without making her sister miserable by telling her why, the situation becomes positively triter than if he had not made love to her at all. There is only one Independent Theatre drama to be got out of such a theme; and that is the drama of the discovery by the man that he has married the wrong sister, and that the most earnest desire on the part of all concerned to do their duty does not avail against that solid fact. Such a drama occurred in the life of one of the greatest English writers of the nineteenth century, one who was never accused by his worst enemies of being a loose liver. But Mr de Vos has not written that drama, or even pretended to write it. As to the unhappy ending of Salvê, unhappy endings are not a new development in the theatre, but a reversion to an older stage phase. I take it that the recently defunct happy ending, which is merely a means of sending the audience away in good humor, was brought in by the disappearance of the farce. Formerly you had The Gamester to begin with; and then, when Beverley had expired yelling from the effects of swallowing some powerful mineral irritant, there was a screaming farce to finish with. When it suddenly occurred to the managers that for twenty-five years or so no experienced playgoer had ever been known to wait for the farce, it was dropped; and nothing was left in the bill except the play of the evening and a curtain-raiser to keep the gallery amused whilst waiting for the plutocracy to finish their dinners and get down to their reserved seats. Still the idea of sending away the audience in a cheerful temper survived, and led to the incorporation of that function of the farce into the end of the play. Hence the happy ending. But in course of time this produced the same effect as the farce. The people got up and made for the doors the moment they saw it coming; and managers were reduced to the abject expedient of publishing in the program a request to the audience not to rise until the fall of the curtain. When even this appeal *ad misericordiam* failed, there was nothing for it but to abolish the happy ending, and venture on the wild innovation of ringing down the curtain the moment the play was really over. This brought back the old tragic ending of the farce days, which was of course immediately hailed, as the custom is whenever some particularly ghastly antiquity is trotted out, as the newest feature of the new drama.

So much then for the novelty of Mrs Beringer's idea of ending her little play by making the mother slay her long-lost cheeyild, and go mad then and there like Lucia di Lammermoor. Indeed, if Mrs Theodore Wright had struck up Spargi d' amaro pianto, with flute obbligato and variations, my old Italian operatic training would have saved me from the least feeling of surprise, though the younger generation would certainly have thought us both mad. The variations would have been quite in keeping with the bags of gold poured out on the table, and with the spectacle of a mother taking up the breadknife and transfixing her healthy young son full in the public view. Is it possible that Mrs Beringer has not yet realized that these mock butcheries belong to the babyhood of the drama? She may depend on it there is a solid reason for Hedda Gabler shooting herself behind the scenes instead of stabbing herself before them. In that, Ibsen shakes hands with the Greek dramatic poets just as clearly as Mrs Beringer, with her gory breadknife, shakes hands with the most infantile melodramatists of the Donizettian epoch. Salvê is not at all a bad piece of work of its naïve kind: indeed, except for a few unactable little bits here and there, it would merit high praise at the Pavilion or Marylebone theatres; but what, in the name of all thats Independent, has it to do with the aims of Mr Grein's society?

To find any sort of justification for the performance I must turn to the acting—for let me say that I should consider Mr Grein quite in order in giving a performance of Robertson's Caste, followed by Box and Cox, if he could handle them so as to suggest fresh developments in stage art. Unfortunately, the management made an incomprehensible mistake in casting A Man's Love. It had at its disposal Miss Winifred Fraser and Miss Mary Keegan; and the two women's parts in the play were well suited to their strongly contrasted personalities. Accordingly, it put Miss Keegan into the part which suited Miss Fraser, and Miss Fraser into the part which suited Miss Keegan. The two ladies did what they could under the circumstances; but their predicament was hopeless from the outset. The resultant awkwardness made the worst of the very clumsy devices by which the action of the play is maintained—impossible soliloquies, incidents off the stage described by people on it as they stare at them through the wings, and the like: all, by the way, reasons why the Independent Theatre should not have produced the work unless these crudities were atoned for by boldness or novelty in some other direction.

The two ladies being practically out of the question, the burden of the play fell upon Mr Herbert Flemming, whose work presénted a striking contrast to the sort of thing we are accustomed to from our popular "leading men." We all know the faultlessly dressed, funereally wooden, carefully phrased walking negation who is so careful not to do anything that could help or hinder our imaginations in mending him into a hero. His great secret is to keep quiet, look serious, and, above all, not act. To this day you see Mr Lewis Waller and Mr George Alexander struggling, even in the freedom of management, with the habits of the days when they were expected to supply this particular style of article, and to live under the unwritten law: "Be a nonentity, or you will get cast for villains," a fate which has actually overtaken Mr Waring because his efforts to suppress himself stopped short of absolute inanity. Only for certain attractive individual peculiarities which have enabled Mr Forbes Robertson to place himself above this law occasionally as a personal privilege, our stage heroes would be as little distinguishable from one another as bricks in a wall. Under these circumstances, I was quite staggered to find Mr Flemming, though neither a comic actor nor a "character actor," acting—positively acting—in a sentimental leading part. He was all initiative, life, expression, with the unhesitating certainty of execution which stamps an actor as perfectly safe for every effect within his range. This amounted to a combination of the proficiency and positive power (as distinguished from negative discretion) of the old stock actor, with the spontaneity, sensitiveness, and touch with the cultivated non-professional world which the latest developments of the drama demand. Mr Flemming first made his mark here by his performances in certain Ibsen parts, and by his playing of the hero in Voss's Alexandra, Stuttgart's pet tragedy. Yet when he appeared recently in such an absurd melodrama as Robbery Under Arms, he was as equal to the occasion as the veteran Mr Clarance Holt; and his return without effort to the new style in A Man's Love is interesting as a sign that the new drama is at last beginning to bring in its harvest of technically efficient actors, instead of being, as it was at first, thrown into hands which were, with one or two brilliant exceptions, comparatively unskilled.

The occasion was not a favorable one for Mr Flemming—quite the contrary. He was not on his mettle; he was in the unmistakeable attitude of an experienced actor towards a play which he knows to be beyond saving; the extent to which he fell back on his mere stage habits shewed that he had refused to waste much time in useless study of a dramatically worthless character, and was simply using his professional skill to get through his part without damage to his reputation; and he was sometimes taken out of the character by his very free recourse to that frankly feminine style of play which is up to a certain point the secret, and beyond it the mere stage trick, of modern acting, and which is enormously effective in a man who, like Mr Flemming, is virile enough to be feminine without risk of effeminacy. None the less this half-studied performance in a third-rate play at a depressing matinée (I was not present at the first performance) was striking enough to demand, at the present moment, all the attention I have given to it.

Mrs Theodore Wright, as the mother in Salvê, had no difficulty in touching and harrowing the audience to the necessary degree. Her acting, also, has the imaginative quality which the reviving drama requires. She made a mistake or two over Mrs Beringer's unactable bits, trying to worry some acting into them instead of letting them quietly slip by; but that was a fault on the right side; and one felt sorry for her sake when the breadknife reduced the little play to absurdity, and half spoiled the admirable effect of her playing in the scenes just before and after her journey of intercession. Happily, the audience did not mind the breadknife at all, and made her an ovation.

I must somewhat tardily acknowledge an invitation to witness a performance at the Royalty Theatre by a Miss Hope Booth, a young lady who cannot sing, act, dance, or speak, but whose appearance suggests that she might profitably spend three or four years in learning these arts, which are useful on the stage. I watched her performance critically for ten minutes, and then went on to the Comedy Theatre, where I found Mr Grundy's Sowing the Wind resuming its career. Miss Millard freshened the

piece wonderfully: she did not, like Miss Emery, rise from a somewhat stolid average level to a forcible climax at one or two fixed
points; but she was finer, swifter and more responsive in feeling
and utterance, and very like the ideal *ingénue* of the period indicated. Miss Millard is clearly a young lady with a future—a Mary
Anderson without that lady's solitary fault of being no actress.
Mr Brandon Thomas repeated his old success by playing with
genuine feeling as the father, and was forgiven accordingly for
his Grundeian lecture on the sex question, "Sex against sex, etc."
—the greatest nonsense possible. Mr Grundy can no more be
cured of his tendency to hold forth in this fashion than of his
habit of writing a play round a "situation," instead of developing
a situation into a play; but in Sowing the Wind, the human interest of the old gentleman's heart and the young lady's good
character, which is not the usual stage shoddy but a very real and
worthy ladylikeness, keeps the piece alive. As to the rest of the
acting, Miss Phillips plays excellently and refrains from caricature, in which all the rest indulge remorselessly. The only member of the original cast who shewed signs of staleness was Mr
Sidney Brough, who was possibly not in the vein on that particular evening.

L'ŒUVRE

Théâtre de l'Œuvre de Paris. Performances at the Opéra
Comique, London, of Ibsen's Rosmersholm and Master
Builder, and of Maeterlinck's L'Intruse and Pelléas et Méli-
sande, 25-30 March 1895.   [30 *March* 1895]

M. Lugné-Poë and his dramatic company called L'Œuvre came
to us with the reputation of having made Ibsen cry by their performance of one of his works. There was not much in that: I have
seen performances by English players which would have driven
him to suicide. But the first act of Rosmersholm had hardly
begun on Monday night, when I recognized, with something like
excitement, the true atmosphere of this most enthralling of all
Ibsen's works rising like an enchanted mist for the first time on
an English stage. There were drawbacks, of course. The shabbi-

ness of the scenery did not trouble me; but the library of Pastor Rosmer got on my nerves a little. What on earth did he want, for instance, with Sell's World's Press? That he should have provided himself with a volume of my own dramatic works I thought right and natural enough, though when he took that particular volume down and opened it, I began to speculate rather uneasily on the chances of his presently becoming so absorbed as to forget all about his part. I was surprised, too, when it appeared that the Conservative paper which attacked the Pastor for his conversion to Radicalism was none other than our own Globe; and the thrill which passed through the house when Rebecca West contemptuously tore it across and flung it down, far exceeded that which Mrs Ebbsmith sends nightly through the Garrick audiences. Then I was heavily taken aback by Mortensgard. He, in his determination to be modern and original, had entrusted the making-up of his face to an ultra-Impressionist painter who had recklessly abused his opportunity. Kroll, too, had a frankly incredible wig, and a costume of which every detail was a mistake. We know Kroll perfectly well in this country: he is one out of many instances of that essential and consequently universal knowledge of mankind which enables Ibsen to make his pictures of social and political life in outlandish little Norwegian parishes instantly recognizable in London and Chicago (where Mr Beerbohm Tree, by the way, has just made a remarkable sensation with An Enemy of the People). For saying this I may be asked whether I am aware that many of our critical authorities have pointed out how absurdly irrelevant the petty parochial squabblings which stand for public life in Ibsen's prose comedies are to the complex greatness of public affairs in our huge cities. I reply that I am. And if I am further pressed to declare straightforwardly whether I mean to disparage these authorities, I reply, pointedly, that I do. I affirm that such criticisms are written by men who know as much of political life as I know of navigation. Any person who has helped to "nurse" an English constituency, local or parliamentary, and organized the election from the inside, or served for a year on a vestry, or attempted to set on foot a movement for broadening the religious and social views of an English village, will not only vouch for it that The League of Youth, An Enemy of the People, and Rosmersholm, are as true to English as they can possibly be to Norwegian society, but will probably offer to supply from his own acquaintances originals for all the public characters in these plays.

I took exception, then, to Kroll, because I know Kroll by sight perfectly well (was he not for a long time chairman of the London School Board?); and I am certain he would die sooner than pay a visit to the rector in a coat and trousers which would make a superannuated coffee-stall keeper feel apologetic, and with his haircutting and shampooing considerably more than three months overdue.

I take a further exception which goes a good deal deeper than this. Mdlle Marthe Mellot, the clever actress who appeared as Rebecca West, Pelléas, and Kaia, played Rebecca in the manner of Sarah Bernhardt, the least appropriate of all manners for the part. Rebecca's passion is not the cold passion of the North—that essentially human passion which embodies itself in objective purposes and interests, and in attachments which again embody themselves in objective purposes and interests on behalf of others —that fruitful, contained, governed, instinctively utilized passion which makes nations and individuals great, as distinguished from the explosive, hysterical, wasteful passion which makes nothing but a scene. Now in the third and fourth acts of Rosmersholm, Mdlle Mellot, who had played excellently in the first and second, suddenly let the part slip through her fingers by turning to the wrong sort of passion. Take, for example, the situation in the third act. Rosmer, who has hitherto believed that his wife was mad when she committed suicide, is now convinced (by Mortensgard) that she did it because he transferred his affection to Rebecca West. Rebecca, seeing that Rosmer will be utterly broken by his own conscience if he is left to believe that he is almost a murderer, confesses that it was she who drove the unfortunate wife to suicide by telling her certain lies. The deliberate character of this self-sacrifice is carefully marked by Ibsen both in Rebecca's cold rebuke to Kroll's attempt to improve the occasion by a gaol chaplain's homily, and in the scene with Madame Helseth in which she calmly arranges for her departure after the men have left her in horror. It was here that Mdlle Mellot yielded to the temptation to have a tearing finish in the Bernhardt style. The confession became the mere hysterical incontinence of a guilty and worthless woman; the scene with Madame Helseth had to be spiced with gasps and sobs and clutches; and the curtain fell on applause that belonged not to Rosmersholm, but to Frou-frou. Rebecca West, therefore, still remains to be created in England. Her vicissitudes have already been curious enough to the student of acting. Miss Farr, the first to attempt the part here, played it as the New Woman, fascinated by Rebecca's unscrupulousness, asking amazed interviewers why such a useless Old Woman as Mrs Rosmer should not have been cleared out of Rosmer's way into the millrace, and generally combining an admirable clearness as to the logic of the situation with an exasperating insensibility to the gravity, or even the reality, of the issues. The result was that the point which Mdlle Mellot has just missed was hit by Miss Farr, who, in spite of failures in whole sections of the play through want of faith in Rebecca's final phase of development, and in various details through the awkwardness of a somewhat amateurish attempt to find a new stage method for a new style of play, yet succeeded on the whole in leaving an impression of at least one side of Rebecca—and that the side which was then strangest—which has not been obliterated by any subsequent performance. A second attempt was made by Miss Elizabeth Robins; and from this a great deal was expected, Miss Robins having been remarkably successful in The Master Builder as Hilda Wangel, who is clearly the earlier Rebecca West of the "free fearless will." But that devastating stage pathos which is Miss Robins's most formidable professional speciality, and which made her so heartrending in Alan's Wife, and so touching as Agnes in Brand, suddenly rose in Rosmersholm and submerged Rebecca in an ocean of grief. So that opportunity, too, was lost; and we still wait the perfect Rebecca, leaving Miss

Farr with the honors of having at least done most to make us curious about her.

The performance of Maeterlinck's Pelléas and Mélisande, in which Mdlle Mellot, who was altogether charming as Pelléas, brought down the house in the Rapunzel scene, settled the artistic superiority of M. Lugné-Poë's company to the Comédie Française. When I recall the last evening I spent at that institution, looking at its laboriously drilled upper-housemaid queens and flunkey heroes, and listening to the insensate, inhuman delivery by which every half Alexandrine is made to sound exactly like a street cry—when I compare this depressing experience with last Tuesday evening at the Théâtre de l'Œuvre, I can hardly believe that the same city has produced the two. In the Comédie Française there is nothing but costly and highly organized routine, deliberately used, like the ceremonial of a court, to make second-rate human material presentable. In the Théâtre de l'Œuvre there is not merely the ordinary theatrical intention, but a vigilant artistic conscience in the diction, the stage action, and the stage picture, producing a true poetic atmosphere, and triumphing easily over shabby appointments and ridiculous incidents. Of course, this is so much the worse for the Théâtre de l'Œuvre from the point of view of the critics who represent the Philistinism against which all genuinely artistic enterprises are crusades. It is a stinging criticism on our theatre that ten years of constant playgoing in London seem to reduce all but the strongest men to a condition in which any attempt to secure in stage-work the higher qualities of artistic execution—qualities which have been familiar for thousands of years to all art students —appears an aberration absurd enough to justify reputable newspapers in publishing as criticism stuff which is mere streetboy guying. I am not here quarrelling with dispraise of the Théâtre de l'Œuvre and M. Maeterlinck. I set the highest value on a strong Opposition both in art and politics; and if Herr Max Nordau were made critic of the Standard (for instance) I should rejoice exceedingly. But when I find players speaking with such skill and delicacy that they can deliver M. Maeterlinck's fragile

76

word-music throughout five acts without one harsh or strained note, and with remarkable subtlety and conviction of expression; and when I see these artists, simply because their wigs are not up to Mr Clarkson's English standard, and the curtain accidentally goes up at the wrong time, denounced as "amateurs" by gentlemen who go into obedient raptures when M. Mounet Sully plasters his cheeks with white and his lips with vermilion, and positively howls his lines at them for a whole evening with a meaningless and discordant violence which would secure his dismissal from M. Lugné-Poë's company at the end of the first act, then—Well, what then? Shall I violate the sacredness of professional etiquette, and confess to a foreigner that the distinction some of our critics make between the amateur and the expert is really a distinction between a rich enterprise and a poor one, and has nothing in the world to do with the distinction made by the trained senses of the critic who recognizes art directly through his eyes and ears, and not by its business associations? Never! Besides, it would not be fair; no man, be he ever so accomplished a critic, can effectively look at or listen to plays that he really does not want to see or hear.

The interest taken in the performances culminated at that of The Master Builder on Wednesday. At first it seemed as if M. Lugné-Poë's elaborate and completely realized study of a self-made man breaking up, was going to carry all before it, a hope raised to the highest by the delightful boldness and youthfulness of Mdlle Suzanne Despres in the earlier scenes of Hilda. Unfortunately, Madam Gay as Mrs Solness was quite impossible; Miss Florence St John as Lady MacBeth would have been better suited. And in the second act, where Solness, the dominator and mesmerizer of Kaia, becomes himself dominated and mesmerized by the impulsive, irresponsible, abounding youth and force of Hilda, Mdlle Despres lost ground, and actually began to play Kaia— Kaia prettily mutinous, perhaps, but still Kaia. The last act, with a subjugated Hilda, and a Mrs Solness, who was visibly struggling with a natural propensity to cheerful common sense, all but failed; and it was perhaps just as well that an offensive Frenchman in the pit circle, by attempting to guy Mdlle Despres, provoked a sympathetic demonstration from the decent members of the audience at the fall of the curtain. Probably he had been reading the English papers.

Comparing the performance with those which we have achieved in England, it must be admitted that neither Mr Waring nor Mr Waller were in a position to play Solness as M. Lugné-Poë played him. They would never have got another engagement in genteel comedy if they had worn those vulgar trousers, painted that red eruption on their faces, and given life to that portrait which, in every stroke, from its domineering energy, talent, and covetousness, to its half witted egotism and crazy philandering sentiment, is so amazingly true to life. Mr Waring and Mr Waller failed because they were under the spell of Ibsen's fame as a dramatic magician, and grasped at his poetic treatment of the man instead of at the man himself. M. Lugné-Poë succeeded because he recognized Solness as a person he had met a dozen times in ordinary life, and just reddened his nose and played him without preoccupation.

With Hilda it was a different matter. Except for the first five minutes, in which she was so bright and girlish, Mdlle Despres could not touch Miss Robins as Hilda Wangel. Whether Miss Robins would know Hilda if she met her in the street, any more than Mr Waring would know Solness, I doubt; but Miss Robins *was* Hilda; and it is an essential part of Hilda that she does not realize her own humanity, much less that of the poor wretch whom she destroys, or the woman whom she widows both before and after his actual bodily death. This merciless insensibility, which gives such appalling force to youth, and which, when combined with vivid imagination, high brain power, and personal fascination, makes the young person in search of the "frightfully thrilling" more dangerous than a lion in the path, was presented by Miss Robins with such reality that she made The Master Builder seem almost a one-part play. It was a great achievement, the danger of which was realized here for the first time perhaps, on Wednesday last, when Mdlle Despres failed to hold the house at the critical moment. Had there been the most trifling bereavement in the part to call forth the tear-deluge which swamped Rebecca and Mrs Lessingham, Heaven only knows what would have happened to Miss Robins's Hilda. Happily the part is grief proof; and a Hilda who can even approach Miss Robins has not yet been seen in London.

Many thanks to the Independent Theatre for its share in bringing about the visit of the Théâtre de l'Œuvre to this country. Mr Grein could have rendered no better service to English art.

THE LIVING PICTURES

[6 *April* 1895]

I HAVE been to see the Living Pictures at the Palace Theatre. The moment Lady Henry Somerset called public attention to the fact that they were obnoxious to the National Vigilance Association, I resolved to try whether they would offend me. But this, like many other good resolutions of mine, remained unfulfilled until I was reminded of it by the address recently delivered by Mr William Alexander Coote, the secretary of the Association, to the Church and Stage Guild, as reported verbatim in that excellent little paper the Church Reformer. In this address, Mr Coote said that he considered the Living Pictures "the ideal form of indecency." I at first supposed this to mean an ideally desirable form of indecency; but later on I found Mr Coote denouncing the pictures as "shameful productions, deserving the condemnation of all right-thinking people." That cured my procrastination, and incidentally brought five shillings into the till of the Palace Theatre. For I hurried off to see the Living Pictures at once, not because I wanted to wallow in indecency—no man in his senses would go to a public theatre with that object even in the most abandoned condition of public taste, privacy being a necessary condition of thorough-going indecency—but because, as a critic, I at once perceived that Mr Coote had placed before the public an issue of considerable moment: namely, whether Mr Coote's opinion is worth anything or not. For Mr Coote is a person of real importance, active, useful, convinced, thoroughly respectable, able to point to achievements which we must all admit honorable to him, and backed by an Association strong enough to enable him to bring his convictions to bear effectively on our licensing authorities. But all this is quite compatible with Mr Coote being in artistic matters a most intensely stupid man, and on sexual questions something of a monomaniac.

I sat out the entire list of sixteen Living Pictures. Half a dozen represented naiads, mountain sprites, peris, and Lady Godiva, all practically undraped, and all, except perhaps Lady Godiva, who was posed after a well-known picture by Van Lerius (who should have read Landor's imaginary conversation between Lady Godiva and her husband), very pretty. I need hardly say that the ladies who impersonated the figures in these pictures were not actually braving our climate without any protection. It was only too obvious to a practised art critic's eye that what was presented as flesh was really spun silk. But the illusion produced on the ordinary music-hall frequenter was that of the undraped human figure, exquisitely clean, graceful, and, in striking contrast to many of the completely draped and elaborately dressed ladies who were looking at them, perfectly modest. Many of the younger and poorer girls in the audience must have gone away with a greater respect for their own persons, a greater regard for the virtues of the bath, and a quickened sense of the repulsiveness of that personal slovenliness and gluttony which are the real indecencies of popular life, in addition to the valuable recreation of an escape for a moment into the enchanted land to which naiads and peris belong. In short, the living pictures are not only works of art: they are excellent practical sermons; and I urge every father of a family who cannot afford to send his daughters the round of the picture galleries in the Haymarket and Bond Street, to take them all (with their brothers) to the Palace Theatre.

This is how they struck me. Now let Mr Coote explain how they struck him.

"What cant to talk about 'Art' in connection with these living picture exhibitions! They are so obviously 'living.' Human nature is so very much in evidence. The nude as represented by the true artist on canvas never has the slightest tendency to demoralize. The artist's soul so consciously pervades the work that the beauty of form and pose hides that which would mar or vulgarize the picture. The subject is spiritualized, and becomes an inspiration for good and lovely thoughts. It is very different with the 'living picture.' There is no art in it. Paradoxical as it may seem, there is no life in the living picture: it is even posed as a lifeless mass. There is a marked difference between the canvas or marble and the living picture, much to the disadvantage of the latter."

In discussing the above utterance, I do not want to take an unfair advantage of the fact that in writing about art I am a trained expert, and Mr Coote a novice. Mr Coote's object in undertaking a task so far beyond my powers as an explanation of the operation of the artist's soul is clearly to persuade us that he sees a distinction between an art that is false and an art that is true, and that it is his passionate devotion to the former that makes him so wroth with the latter. Let us see.

First, Mr Coote tells us that there is no art in the Palace pictures. Well, I can quite believe that Mr Coote conceives that the posing and lighting of the figures so as to throw the figure into the required light and shadow is pure accident. Let me therefore make a suggestion. Let Mr Morton, the manager of the Palace, request Mr Dando, the arranger of the pictures, to stand aside and entrust his functions for one night (on which a stall may be reserved for me at any price the management chooses to exact) to Mr William Alexander Coote. Let the entire resources of the establishment be placed absolutely under his direction; and let us then see whether he can take advantage of their being "no art in it" to produce a single tableau that will not be ludicrously and outrageously deficient in the artistic qualities without which Mr Dando's compositions would be hooted off the stage.

Now as to Mr Coote's assertion that the artist's soul spiritualizes his subject, and finds in it an inspiration for good and lovely thoughts. I can assure Mr Coote that he never made a greater mistake in his life. There are artists, and very able artists too, whose souls exactly resemble those of some members of the National Vigilance Association in debauching every subject, and finding in it an inspiration for obscene and unlovely thoughts. If Mr Coote, in the course of his next holiday, will travel from Padua to Mantua, and compare Giotto's pictorial decoration of the arena chapel with Giulio Romano's decoration of the Palazzo Té, he will learn that the artist's soul can commune with the satyrs as well as with the saints. He need go no further than our own National Gallery to see the work of great artists who, like Paul Veronese, or Rubens, materialize all their subjects and appeal to our love of physical splendor and vitality, exhibited under the same roof with those of the pre-Raphaelites (the real ones), whose works of art were also works of devotion. What is more, he will find the same artist expressing his devotional mood in one picture and his voluptuous mood in another; and if he will go as far as Venice—and the journey will be well worth his while—he can see there, in Titian's Virgin of the Assumption, a union of the flesh and the spirit so triumphantly beautiful, that he will return abashed to the Church and Stage Guild, and apologize to them very humbly for having mixed up his account of his Vigilance stewardship with a sham lecture on a subject of which he does not know enough to be even conscious of his own ignorance.

Let me now help Mr Coote out of his difficulty. He admits by implication that works of art are above the law, and should be tolerated at all hazards. He then attempts to shew that the works he objects to are not "true art," and that therefore his hostility to them does not imply any hostility to Phidias and Raphael and the Royal Academy and so on. No person who really understands Art would make any such admission. A work of art is no more above the law than anything else. An old bridge may be a beautiful work of mediaeval art; but if it obstructs navigation, causes the river to silt up, or becomes insufficient for the traffic, it must come down. A palace may be a gem of the builder's art; but if its site is imperatively required for a better lighted and drained modern building, however ugly, or for a new thoroughfare, down it must come too. And if the living pictures, or M. Jules Garnier's illustrations to Rabelais, can be proved to be doing more harm than good, then Mr Coote is quite right to demand their suppression, works of art or no works of art. Mr Coote is quite entitled to carry out all his aims, to forbid the circulation of cheap unexpurgated Shakespears; to make it a punishable offence for an artist to paint from a nude model; and to send the manager of the Palace Theatre to prison, if he can convince us that it is for the public interest that these things should be done. No plea as to the sacredness of art could in that case be admitted for a moment. If Mr Coote feels modest about claiming so much, let him consult the gentleman whom he describes as "that strange, peculiar, yet splendid man, Mr Stead." Mr Stead will, I think, as a matter of common sense, at once assure him that I am right.

Having now got rid of the Art question, and pulled Mr Coote out of that morass on to solid ground, I am almost tempted to begin by exhorting him to go to his Bible, and ponder the saying, "He which is filthy, let him be filthy still." But no public man in these islands ever believes that the Bible means what it says: he is always convinced that it says what he means; and I have no reason to hope that Mr Coote may be an exception to the rule. What, then, does Mr Coote found himself on? Apparently on this position, which I state in his own words: "Nothing in the management of our public entertainments can justify the exhibition of nude and semi-nude women as a means of amusement for a mixed audience." But why not, if the audience thinks the woman prettier and no less decent in that state than when fully draped, and she agrees with them; or if nudity or semi-nudity is appropriate to the character she is impersonating; or if she is performing athletic feats which skirts would hinder? Here is an instance which fulfils all three conditions. When Sir Augustus Harris first introduced at Covent Garden the Walpurgis ballet, which is one of the features of Gounod's Faust as performed at the Paris Grand Opéra, the dancer who impersonated Phryne dispensed with skirts altogether, and danced to the one exquisite tune that the ballet contains, in a costume which produced the illusion of nudity (I presume Mr Coote knows that it is only an illusion). She wore certain decorative ribbons, but no dress. She looked very graceful and quite modest; nobody in that huge theatre, which was crowded from floor to ceiling, objected in the least; it did not occur to us for a moment to complain of the absence of the ballet skirts and petticoats which make a woman look like an ostrich or a teetotum.

I will not pretend to misunderstand Mr Coote's objection to this. There are in the world a certain number of persons who, owing to morbid irritability in certain directions, are greatly incommoded by circumstances which are indifferent, or even agreeable, to the normal man. For instance, London is rather an ill-smelling place; and people with exceptionally acute noses suffer agonies on stagnant days when ordinary people notice nothing. Carlyle, even in the comparative quietude of Chelsea, had to take special measures to keep the noises of the streets from his irritable ears; people with tender eyes have to resort to blue spectacles; humane people are made miserable by the treatment of our beasts of burden; and we find people oppressed by a special susceptibility to the dread inspired by hydrophobia, cholera, the Jesuits, the possibility of being damned, and many other contingencies which only occur to normal persons when they are out of health. On the other hand, we find people who are deficient in certain faculties—blind people, deaf people, color-blind people, people with no musical faculty, callous people, unsocial people, and so on. And we also find people in whom a deficiency in one respect is associated with an excess of sensitiveness in others. Now, it is quite impossible to legislate and administer with a view to the comfort of these abnormal people, even though there may, in so large a population as ours, be enough of any one variety of them to form an association and make a vigorous agitation. For instance, the Church will not modify the rite of communion because certain deplorable cases are on record in which the taste of the sacramental wine has brought on a ruinous attack of drink craze in the communicant. We do

84

not suppress public meetings and abolish the right of free speech because people who are peculiarly susceptible to political excitement and the stimulus of platform oratory are led to behave foolishly and misuse their votes on such occasions. We do not prohibit "revivalist" prayer meetings because of the mischievously hysterical condition into which weak people are thrown by them, a condition which the ignorant preacher glories in producing. We shall not stop the performances of The Notorious Mrs Ebbsmith because it has produced a case of suicide. In short, we shall not lead the life of invalids for the sake of a handful of unfortunate people to whom such a life is the only safe one.

The application of all this to Mr Coote's position is obvious. We have among us a certain number of people who are morbidly sensitive to sexual impressions, and quite insensible to artistic ones. We have certain sects in which such a condition is artificially induced as a matter of religious duty. Children have their affections repressed, and their susceptibility to emotional excitement nursed on sin, wrath, terror, and vengeance, whilst they are forbidden to go to the theatre or to amuse themselves with stories or "profane" pictures. Naturally, when such people grow up, life becomes to them a prolonged temptation of St Anthony. You try to please them by a picture which appeals to their delight in graceful form and bright warm color, to their share in the romance which peoples the woods and streams with sylphs and water maidens, to the innocent and highly recreative love of personal beauty, which is one of the great advantages of having a sex at all. To your horror and discomposure, you are met by a shriek of "Nude woman: nude woman: police!" The one thing that the normal spectator overlooks in the picture is the one thing that St Anthony sees in it. Let me again put his protest in Mr Coote's own words: "Nothing can justify the exhibition of nude and semi-nude women as a means of amusement for a mixed audience. They are shameful productions, and deserve the condemnation of all right-thinking people. The manager deserves, and should have, the immediate attention of the County Council." You remonstrate, perhaps, from the point of view of the artist.

Mr Coote at once pleads: "They are so very obviously *living*. Human nature is so very much in evidence." And there you have the whole of Mr Coote's pessimistic, misanthropic philosophy in two sentences. Human nature and the human body are to him nasty things. Sex is a scourge. Woman is a walking temptation which should be covered up as much as possible. Well, let us be charitable to Mr Coote's infirmity, and ask him, as kindly as may be, what good covering women up will do. Carmencita is covered up; our skirt dancers are all petticoats; each of our serpentine dancers carries drapery enough to make skirts for a whole dozen schoolgirls. And yet they appeal far more to the sex instinct and far less to the artistic instinct than the Naiads and Phryne. There is only one solution of the difficulty; and that is for Mr Coote and those that sympathize with him to keep away from the Palace Theatre. Of course that will not protect them altogether. Every low-necked dress, every gust of wind that catches a skirt and reveals an ankle, perhaps every child in whom "human nature is in evidence" to the extent of a pair of sturdy little legs, may be a torment to the victims of this most pitiable of all obsessions. A quarrel with human nature admits of no fundamental remedy except the knife; and I should be sorry to see the members of the Vigilance Association cutting their own throats; they are useful and even necessary in keeping order among the people who suffer from morbid attractions instead of morbid repulsions. For it must not be forgotten that Mr Coote's error does not lie in his claim that the community shall suppress indecent exhibitions, but in his attempt to make nudity or semi-nudity the criterion of indecency. Perhaps I should qualify this statement of his position by limiting nudity to the female sex; for I notice that the semi-nudity which is quite a common spectacle in the case of male athletes is not complained of, though, if there were anything in the Vigilance Association's view of such exhibitions as demoralizing, our women ought by this time to be much more demoralized than our men.

MR WILLIAM ARCHER'S CRITICISMS

THE THEATRICAL WORLD OF 1894. By William Archer. With an Introduction by G. Bernard Shaw, and a synopsis of the playbills of the year by Henry George Hibbert. London: Walter Scott. 1895. [13 *April* 1895]

IT is well that the critic should be criticized occasionally, not only by wrathful protests made in the heat of the moment while his notices are still hot from the brain, but by a cool annual review of his whole year's work. This involves republication in volume form of the critic's yearly output, which can only pretend to such honor in virtue of being more interesting than the day-before-yesterday's newspaper. Unhappily, most of our theatre criticism is born stale: it is hardly sufferable as news even on the day of its birth; and its republication would almost justify the immediate abolition of the freedom of the press. This is due solely to the fact that newspapers do not want good criticism and will not pay for it. Criticisms are like boots: the low-priced ones are scamped, mechanical, and without individuality; the high-priced ones are sound, highly finished, and made by hand to the measure of their subject. Yet newspaper proprietors and editors who would not dream of walking down Bond Street in a pair of four-and-sixpenny boots, will buy criticism which would disgrace the humblest sort of old-fashioned police court reporter. I have known them do the work themselves for the sake of getting into the theatre for nothing, or even let their wives do it on the same ground. In the provinces, dramatic criticism is incredibly bad. The great newspapers of Bradford, Manchester, Liverpool, and Birmingham are, of course, exceptions; but in the ordinary local paper the "criticism" is simply an advertisement which is not up to the level of literacy reached in the commonest kind of commercial correspondence. Sometimes there is a perceptible striving after perfection: for instance, instead of the stereotyped "Miss Smith was good as Juliet," you find "Miss Smith shewed talent as Juliet"; but this is rare. When there is a facetious sally, it signifies that the writer is a local wit who expects to be employed, as such, to write the topical allusions for the pantomime, and is consequently hopelessly enslaved by the manager. And the manager does not hesitate to use his power as a good advertisement customer to threaten and dictate freely if the notices are not of the most abjectly complimentary character. But nobody minds. If I were to suggest that an editor or proprietor who tolerates this sort of thing ought to be cut, expelled from his club, erased from the Institute of Journalists, and treated generally like a runaway soldier, or a barrister who has sold his client, I should be poohpoohed for making an absurd fuss about nothing. Things are a little better in London; but even in London papers which ought to know better pay their critics meanly by the line, and make them feel that if they make themselves disagreeable to any person with the smallest influence (and the manager of a London theatre is always a person of some influence), they will probably be superseded by writers who may be depended on to give no trouble. I have repeatedly been urged by colleagues to call attention to some abuse which they themselves were not sufficiently strongly situated to mention; and I have twice had to resign very desirable positions on the critical staff of London papers of first-rate pretension—in one case because I was called upon as a recognized part of my duties to write corrupt puffs of the editor's personal friends, with full liberty, in return, to corruptly puff my own; and in the other, because my sense of style revolted against the interpolation in my articles of sentences written by the proprietor's wife to express her high opinion of artists, unknown to fame and me, who had won her heart by their hospitality. I mention these matters because the public has hardly any suspicion of the extreme rarity of the able editor who is loyal to his profession and to his staff. Without such an editor even moderately honest criticism is impossible; and that is why the average critic is a man (or woman) who, not being allowed to say what he thinks, has long ago given up the habit of thinking as useless and dangerous. And the worst of it, from my particular point of view, is that dramatic criticism is one of the last departments of conduct on which even a tolerably scrupulous editor's conscience can be awakened. The same man who is particular and even fastidious about political and literary criticism often cannot be induced to regard criticism of the theatre as anything but pure news, and expects to have the fact that Mr Irving has produced a new play chronicled in exactly the same spirit as the fact that Her Majesty has taken a drive accompanied by the Princess Beatrice.

For quite a different set of limitations imposed on the critic by the economic conditions of modern theatrical enterprise, I must refer the reader to my excellent preface to Mr Archer's book. Mr Archer and I campaigned together for several years under the editorship of the late Edmund Yates, who knew the value of genuine criticism, even musical criticism. We are intimate personal friends; and we roll each other's logs with a will. In my preface I imply that Mr Archer is the best of critics: in his epilogue he insists that there is nobody like G. B. S. If my judgment were not so exquisitely balanced that the slightest touch of personal bias upsets it, I should be a very poor critic: consequently my opinion as to Mr Archer's merits is flagrantly unjudicial. He has the reputation of being inflexible, impartial, rather cold but scrupulously just, and entirely incorruptible. I believe this impression is produced by his high cheek-bones, the ascetic outline of his chin and jaw, and his habit of wearing a collar which gives his head the appearance of being wedged by the neck into a jampot. In reality he is half a dozen different men, most of them Scotch ancestors, especially a very grim Calvinist with an intense belief in predestined damnation, who feels that it does the world good to be confronted with the hopelessness of its own doom. This particular Archer revels in La Tosca, in Alan's Wife, in Thérèse Raquin, in Ghosts, and in Mrs Lessingham. To see some harmless and preferably rather lovable and interesting person annihilated with the most ferocious cruelty by the mere blind stroke of Fate positively edifies and exalts him. Then there is the sentimental Archer, a snivelling personage with whom I quarrel furiously, who gushes over Sweet Lavender, weeps over Hedvig in The Wild Duck as "surely one of the loveliest characters in fiction," will blubber copiously (I prophesy) over Little Eyolf, and responds like an opening flower to the Amelia strain in his beloved Thackeray (an author I cannot abide). These are the two extremes of Archer; and I rejoice that 1894 did not produce a play capable of fully bringing out the qualities of either of them. There are several intermediate Archers, all of them in evidence in this volume: Archer the humorist; Archer the dialectician (another Scotch Archer), gravely and patiently straightening out the argument of A Bunch of Violets for Mr Grundy, as if the law of England for the next two centuries depended on the integrity of his logic; Archer the Cadi, sternly bastinadoing Mr Clement Scott for not seeing Ibsen's jokes; Archer the moralist, sermonizing me, in what I take to be the most shockingly bad criticism ever penned, for "dwelling on the seamy side of human nature to the exclusion of all else"; Archer the beglamored lover of literature and the theatre; and, finally, Archer the critic.

As I have said, I am no judge of Archer the critic, and can merely testify that he is honest, sober, careful, trustworthy, skilful, hardworking, and has been for many years in his present situation: all of which, though disgustingly prosaic, has more to do with the making of literary reputations than the public imagines. I shall confine myself here to the Archer whom I mentioned last but one, the Archer who describes himself as "born with an instinctive, unreasoning, unreasonable love for the theatre, the place of light and sound, of mystery and magic, where, at the stroke of the prompter's bell, a new world is revealed to the delighted sense." This is the Archer who has often told me that I have no real love of art, no enjoyment of it, only a faculty for observing performances, and an interest in the intellectual tendency of plays. At first I thought this ridiculous; but there is always something in what he says; and I cannot deny that though I was for years a keen professional critic of books, for years more of pictures, and for yet more years of music, I go to no picture galleries now in London, I attend no concerts, and I read no current literature. Put an end to my professional business in the theatre, and I shall stop going there. Put an end to Archer's, and he will still, as he says, "find a melancholy fascination in the glare of the footlights." For him there is illusion in the theatre: for me there is none. I can make imaginary assumptions readily enough; but for me the play is not the thing, but its thought, its purpose, its feeling, and its execution. And as most modern plays have no thought, and are absolutely vulgar in purpose and feeling, I am mainly interested in their execution. But in these criticisms by Mr Archer (I must really remember my manners) there is little that is memorable about the execution; and that little has reference solely to its effect on the illusion. Even those pages in which, because they deal with such famous executants as Duse, Bernhardt, Rehan, and Calvé, the critic is compelled to take the execution as his main theme, he still makes the congruity of the artist's performance with the illusion of the story his criterion of excellence in the acting. In a very interesting comparison of Duse's Santuzza in Cavalleria Rusticana with Calvé's, he declares that "the instinct of the world assigns a higher rank to pure mimetics than to even the highest so-called lyric acting." Now I confess that even to me the illusion created by Duse was so strong that the scene comes back to me almost as an event which I actually witnessed; whereas Calvé's performance was unmistakeably an opera at Covent Garden. Looking at Duse, I pitied Santuzza as I have often pitied a real woman in the streets miserably trying, without a single charm to aid her, to beg back the affection of some cockney Turiddu. But who has ever seen in the streets anything like Calvé's Santuzza, with her passion, her beauty, her intensity, her singing borne aloft by an orchestra? To Mr Archer, this is the condemnation of Calvé's performance and the justification of Duse's. Every element, even though it be an element of artistic force, which interferes with the credibility of the scene, wounds him, and is so much to the bad. To him acting, like scene-painting, is merely a means to an end, that end being to enable him to make believe. To me the play is only the means, the end being the expression of feeling by the arts of the actor, the poet, the musician. Anything that makes this expression more vivid, whether it be versification, or an orchestra, or a deliberately artificial delivery of the lines, is so much to the good for me, even though it may destroy all the verisimilitude of the scene. I do not for a moment set up this critical attitude of mine as standing to Mr Archer's in the relation of the right attitude to the wrong attitude. I only introduce it to make his more intelligible by contrast. Once his attitude is caught, and his sensitiveness to literature, which he calls "the divinest emanation of the human spirit" taken into account, his criticism becomes perfectly consistent, and its charm is seen to be a genuine imaginative quality which is quite independent of the adroit turn and fine intellectual texture of his sentences.

I had intended to devote this article almost entirely to my own preface; but I find myself with only space enough left to assure those gentlemen who are accusing me of advocating a *régime* of actress-manageresses, that I have advocated nothing at all. I have described the economic conditions of modern theatrical enterprise, with the results they have produced and seem likely to produce in the future. Among these last I enumerate the actress-manageress. I do not advocate her introduction, I simply announce her arrival. To state that she is "my remedy" for the state of things I have described is about as reasonable as to describe silence as Hamlet's remedy for death.

TWO BAD PLAYS

The Girl I Left Behind Me. A Drama in four acts. By Franklin Fyles and David Belasco. Adelphi Theatre, 13 April 1895.
Delia Harding. By Victorien Sardou. Adapted by J. Comyns Carr. Comedy Theatre, 17 April 1895.   [20 *April* 1895]

Last Saturday was made memorable to me by my first visit to the Adelphi Theatre. My frequent allusions to Adelphi melodrama were all founded on a knowledge so perfect that there was no need to verify it experimentally; and now that the experiment has been imposed on me in the course of my professional duty, it has confirmed my deductions to the minutest particular.

Should anyone rush to the conclusion hereupon that my attitude towards the Adelphi Theatre is that of a superior person, he will be quite right. It is precisely because I am able to visit all theatres as a superior person that I am entrusted with my present critical function. As a superior person, then, I hold Adelphi melodrama in high consideration. A really good Adelphi melodrama is of first-rate literary importance, because it only needs elaboration to become a masterpiece. Molière's Festin de Pierre and Mozart's Don Juan are elaborations of Punch and Judy, just as Hamlet, Faust, and Peer Gynt are elaborations of popular stories. Unfortunately, a really good Adelphi melodrama is very hard to get. It should be a simple and sincere drama of action and feeling, kept well within that vast tract of passion and motive which is common to the philosopher and the laborer, relieved by plenty of fun, and depending for variety of human character, not on the high comedy idiosyncrasies which individualize people in spite of the closest similarity of age, sex, and circumstances, but on broad contrasts between types of youth and age, sympathy and selfishness, the masculine and the feminine, the serious and the frivolous, the sublime and the ridiculous, and so on. The whole character of the piece must be allegorical, idealistic, full of generalizations and moral lessons; and it must represent conduct as producing swiftly and certainly on the individual the results which in actual life it only produces on the race in the course of many centuries. All of which, obviously, requires for its accomplishment rather greater heads and surer hands than we commonly find in the service of the playhouse.

The latest Adelphi melodrama, The Girl I Left Behind Me, is a very bad one. The only stroke in it that comes home is at the close of the second act, where the heroine sends her soldier lover, who has been accused of cowardice, off on a dangerous duty, and tells him that she loves him. The authors, I need hardly say, did not invent this situation, nor did they freshen it or add anything to it; but they at least brought it off without bungling it, and so saved the piece from the hostility of that sceptical spirit which is now growing among first-night audiences in a very marked degree. This is an inevitable reaction against the artificialities, insincerities, and impossibilities which form about three-fourths of the stock-in-trade of those playwrights who seek safety and success in the assumption that it is impossible to underrate the taste and intelligence of the British public. But there is a profound error in this policy. It is true that the public consists largely of people who are incapable of fully appreciating the best sort of artistic work. It is even true that in every audience, especially on first nights, there is an appreciable number of persons whose condition is such that—to turn Tennyson's shallow claptrap into a terrible truth—they needs must hate the highest when they see it. But why should we credit these unhappy persons with that attribute of the highest character, the power of liking what pleases them, of believing in it, of standing by those who give it to them? For the most part they never enjoy anything; they are always craving for stimulants, whereas the essence of art is recreation; let their flatterer slip, as he always does sooner or later, and they are at his throat mercilessly before he can recover himself. But if you speak in their hearing as the great men speak (which is easy enough if you happen to be a great man), then you will find that their speciality is self-torture, and that they are always hankering, in spite of themselves, after their own boredom and bewilderment, driven, probably, by some sort of uneasy hope that Ibsen or Wagner or some other gigantic bore may exorcise the devils which rend them. The fact is, there is nothing the public despises so much as an attempt to please it. Torment is its natural element: it is only the saint who has any capacity for happiness. There is no greater mistake in theology than to suppose that it is necessary to lock people into hell or out of heaven. You might as well suppose that it is necessary to lock a professional tramp into a public-house or out of a Monday popular concert, on the ground that the concert is the better and cheaper place of the two. The artist's rule must be Cromwell's: "Not what they want, but what is good for them." That rule, carried out in a kindly and sociable way, is the secret to success in the long run at the theatre as elsewhere.

My strong propensity for preaching is, I fear, leading me to deal with The Girl I Left Behind Me in rather too abstract a fashion. But it is only in its abstract bearings that the play provides interesting material to the critic. Instead of being natural and sincere, it is artificial and sanctimonious. The language, which should be vividly vernacular, is ineptly literary. Its fun runs too much on the underclothing of the ladies, which they tear up to make bandages for wounds, or offer, without detachment, to be used by gentlemen at a loss for towels after washing. The characters, instead of being consistent and typical, are patched and rickety, the author's grip constantly slipping from them. The villain and coward of the piece punches the hero's head with pluck and promptitude in the first act, lapses into abject poltroonery in the second, and in the third faces without concern a military emergency which drives all the rest into hysterical desperation. The hero, assaulted as aforesaid, ingloriously brings down the curtain with a stage villain's retort, "You shall rrepent—thiss —bblow," and subsequently becomes the sport of circumstances, which turn out happily for him without much aid from himself. As to Kennion, the sympathetic general, I cannot believe that even in the army so incapable a man could rise to high command. It is, of course, usual on the stage for all army commanders to be superseded at critical moments by their daughters; but still there is no good reason why they should not have moments of efficiency when nothing but routine business is in hand. Private Jones, who is cordially received by his officer when he describes, with an air of conscious merit, how he has just run away on being actually fired at by the enemy, and who calmly quits his post as sentry (at a stockade which may be surprised at any moment) to sit down beside his sleeping lady love, and is supported in that proceeding by the general against a not unnatural remonstrance from his lieutenant—Private Jones is certainly consistent; but what he is consistent with is not himself—for as an individual human being he has no credible existence—but the trained incapacity of the Adelphi audience to understand true military valor. Instead of being, as he should be in a popular melodrama, a typically good soldier, he is a mere folly of the ignorant civil imagination. There is also a medical man, an army surgeon, who makes love to a girl of sixteen by way of comic relief. He relaxed the tension of the third act very happily by a slight but astonishingly effective alteration of a single syllable in the author's text. In the agony of the siege, when all hope was gone, he sat down with heroic calmness to write two documents: one a prescription which there was no apparent means of getting compounded, and the other a farewell—I did not quite catch to whom—probably to his mother. The last touching words of this communication were prefaced by the author with the sentence, "I will add a postscript." The doctor, however, adroitly substituted, "I will add a postcard," and sent the audience, just at the moment when their feelings could bear no further harrowing, into shrieks of refreshing laughter.

The third act, by the way, is an adaptation of the Relief of Lucknow, which, as a dramatic situation, is so strong and familiar that it is hardly possible to spoil it, though the authors have done their best. The main difficulty is the foreknowledge of the hopelessly sophisticated audience that Mr Terriss will rush in at the last moment, sword in hand, and rescue everybody. The authors' business was to carry us on from incident to incident so convincingly and interestingly as to preoccupy us with the illusion of the situation sufficiently to put Mr Terriss out of our heads. Messrs Fyles and Belasco have not been equal to this. They have lamely staved off Mr Terriss for the necessary time by a flabbily commonplace treatment of the question of killing the women to save them from the Indians, and by bringing in the Indian chief's daughter to die in the stockade at the instant when the sound of her voice would have won quarter for the garrison. This is ill contrived, and only passes because the explanation is deferred until the last act, which is so transcendently imbecile that an absurdity more or less does not matter. As to the heroine, who had to kneel in the middle of the stage and rave her way through the burial service whilst her father, the general, hopped about, pulling horrible faces, and trying to make up his mind to shoot her, she was so completely out of the question from any rational human point of view, that I think the effort to impersonate her temporarily unhinged Miss Millward's reason; for when the rescue came, and she had to wave the American flag instead of expressing her feelings naturally, she all but impaled the general on it in a frightful manner. Miss Millward and Mr Terriss and the rest of the company must bear with my irreverent way of describing the performance. I quite appreciate their skill, which is perhaps more indispensable for nonsense of this kind than for plays good enough to be comparatively "actor-proof"; but the better the skill, the more annoying it is to see it nine-tenths wasted.

All the same, the evening was not a dull one. The play is not good drama, nor good melodrama; but it is tolerable pastime. I have spun out my criticism of it in order to leave as little room as possible for another play which was not tolerable even as pastime. When Mr Comyns Carr came before the curtain at the end of Sardou's Delia Harding at the Comedy Theatre on Wednesday, I found myself instinctively repeating the words of Sam Weller, "You rayther want somebody to look arter you, sir, ven your judgment goes out a wisitin'." Delia Harding is the worst play I ever saw. Taking it as a work bearing the same relation to the tastes of the upper middle class as the Adelphi drama to those of the lower middle class, I declare enthusiastically in favor of the Adelphi. Sardou's plan of playwriting is first to invent the action of his piece, and then to carefully keep it off the stage and have it announced merely by letters and telegrams. The people open the letters and read them, whether they are addressed to them or not; and then they talk either about what the letters announce as having occurred already or about what they intend to do tomorrow in consequence of receiving them. When the news is not brought by post, the characters are pressed into the service. Delia Harding, for instance, consists largely of the fashionable intelligence in Bellagio. As thus: "Stanley French arrived in Bellagio this morning," "Mr Harding will arrive in Bellagio tomorrow afternoon," "Miss Harding lives in that villa on the lake," "Sir Christopher

Carstairs will remain here for another month at least," "This is my brother, Sir Arthur Studley," "Janet: we shall pack up and leave tomorrow morning," etc. etc., the person addressed invariably echoing with subdued horror, "This morning!" "Tomorrow afternoon!" "In *that* villa!" and so on. The whole business was so stale, so obviously factitious, so barrenly inept, that at last the gallery broke out into open derision, almost as if they were listening to a particularly touching and delicate passage in a really good play. As for me, I felt ashamed and remorseful. The time has now come for pity rather than vengeance on the poor old "well made play." Fifteen years ago I was almost alone in my contempt for these clumsy booby traps. Nowadays an actor cannot open a letter or toss off somebody else's glass of poison without having to face a brutal outburst of jeering. At the Comedy on Thursday, some low fellow shouted out "Rats!" in the middle of the second act. Why was he not removed by the police? Such a step would be highly popular in the gallery: ninety-nine out of every hundred people in it are incommoded by rowdyism, and are only too glad to be protected from neighbors who cannot express their disapproval or approval decently. At political meetings the public is not only allowed but expected to exercise a freedom of comment and interruption which no sane person would propose to tolerate in a theatre; but of late first nights have been disturbed by interruptions which would expose the interrupter to serious risk of a remarkably summary expulsion from a political meeting. Besides, public speakers are helped by interruptions: they deliberately provoke them for the sake of an effective retort. But the actor is helpless: he must not say a word that is not set down for him; and the nature of his work makes it terribly easy for any half drunk fool to cruelly disconcert and annoy him. Even the applause on first nights, the receptions and exit demonstrations, are silly enough: the rule ought to be silence whilst the curtain is up and as much noise as you please when it is down. But that is a matter of taste and custom rather than of police. Where the police ought to come in without mercy is in the case of offensive and disorderly remarks or exclamations shouted at the stage during the performance. One or two well chosen examples pursued to the police court would settle the matter for the next ten years.

The acting of Delia Harding calls for no special notice. Mr Mackintosh, who appeared as Stanley French, was warmly received. His acting was not lacking in force; but his gesture and facial expression were grotesque and caricatured, though there was nothing in the part to give occasion for such extravagant handling.

SPANISH TRAGEDY AND ENGLISH FARCE

MARIANA and THE SON OF DON JUAN. By José Echegaray. Translated from the Spanish by James Graham. Two volumes of the Cameo Series. London: Fisher Unwin. 1895.

THE LADIES' IDOL. A new and original farcical comedy in three acts. By Arthur Law. Vaudeville Theatre, 18 April 1895.

[27 *April* 1895]

THERE is somewhere in Froissart a record of a hardy knight who discovered, as most men do in their middle age, that "to rob and pill is a good life." When Mr Fisher Unwin sent me The Son of Don Juan I began at the end, as my custom is (otherwise I seldom reach the end at all), and found the following:

> "LAZARUS (*Speaking like a child, and with the face of an idiot*): 'Mother—the sun—the sun; give me the sun. For God's sake—for God's sake—for God's sake, mother, give me the sun.' "

To a person familiar with Ibsen's Ghosts, this was sufficient to establish a warm interest in an author who, like Froissart's knight, takes his goods so boldly where he finds them. I had never heard of José Echegaray before; but I soon learnt, from Mr Graham's sketch of his life, that he is a celebrated Spanish dramatist, and that it will be decorous for me in future to pretend to know all about him. To tell the truth, I wish I had some other authority than Mr Graham to consult; for though I have no excuse for questioning the entire trustworthiness of the little memoir he has

99

prefixed to The Son of Don Juan, I can hardly bring myself to believe more than half of it. No doubt Echegaray is a greater physicist than Newton, and a greater mathematician than De Morgan and Professor Karl Pearson rolled into one. Perhaps he really did walk out of a drawing room ignorant of a word of German, and presently return a master of that intractable tongue, and intimate with the secrets of Hegel and all the other philosophers of the Fatherland. And why should there be any difficulty in believing in that discussion on fencing, which again made him leave the room, only to come back so consummate a swordsman that no professional in Madrid could as much as keep hold of his foil when confronted with him? And yet, somehow, I dont believe it. It is all the fault of that unfortunate musical criticism which I practised so long and assiduously. A musical critic gets supplied gratuitously with biographies of distinguished artists, compiled by musical agents or other experts in fiction, and circulated to the press and to persons with whom the artist desires to do business. These biographies seldom appear among the books of reference in first-rate libraries. They all contain at least two anecdotes, one to illustrate the miraculous powers of their hero's brain, and another to exhibit his courage and dexterity in personal combat. Mind, I do not say these anecdotes are untrue; I simply confess apologetically that I never find myself able to believe them. When I receive from an agent or from a bookseller a life of Sarasate, or Mr Edison, or any other celebrated person, I try to believe as much of it as I can; and the breakdown of my faith must not be taken as a breakdown of the celebrated person's credit. Besides, after all, Mr Graham's memoir of Echegaray may not mean anything so very staggering. There is something momentous at first sight in the statement that "the first three years of the dramatist's life were passed in the capital of Spain"; but now I come to think of it, the first three years of my life (and more) were passed in the capital of Ireland, which was a much harder trial. Again, the attention he gave to "the infinitesimal calculus, theoretical and applied mechanics, hydrostatics, curve tracing, descriptive geometry and its applications, solid geometry, and so on into the dimmest heights of the science," might have happened to many a university don. I remember once buying a book entitled How to Live on Sixpence a Day, a point on which at that time circumstances compelled me to be pressingly curious. I carried out its instructions faithfully for a whole afternoon; and if ever I have an official biography issued, I shall certainly have it stated therein, in illustration of my fortitude and self-denial, that I lived for some time on sixpence a day. On the whole, I am willing to take Mr Graham's word for it that Echegaray is, apart from his capacity as a dramatic poet, an exceptionally able man, who, after a distinguished university career, turned from the academic to the political life; attained Cabinet rank, with its Spanish inconveniences of proscription and flight at the next revolution; and in 1874, being then forty-two years of age, and in exile in Paris, took to writing plays, and found himself famous in that line by the time his political difficulties had settled themselves.

As a dramatist, I find Echegaray extremely readable. Mr Graham has translated two of the most famous of his plays into a language of his own, consisting of words taken from the English dictionary, and placed, for the most part, in an intelligible grammatical relation to one another. I say for the most part; for here and there a sentence baffles me. For example: "The hall is approached by two or three saloons, whether in front of it, whether in converging lines, but in such fashion that they are partly visible." This is a hard saying, which I humbly pass on to the stage manager in the hope that he may be able to make more out of it than I can. Happily, the dialogue is pellucid as to its meaning, even where it is least vernacular. If Mrs Patrick Campbell, for instance, plays Mariana (and she might do worse: it would be a far wiser choice than Juliet), I shall, if she uses Mr Graham's translation, listen eagerly to the effect on the audience of such a speech as "The sickness of the journey has not left me. I suspect that I am going to have a very violent megrim." I fear it is useless to pretend to accept Mr Graham's work as a translation after this: it is clearly only a crib, though in some of the burning passages it rises to considerable force and eloquence. In such passages the full meaning can be gathered from the words alone; for most nations express themselves alike when they are red-hot; but in passages of comedy the word is often nothing, and the manner and idiom everything, in proof whereof I will undertake to recast any scene from, say, The School for Scandal, in such a manner that without the least alteration of its meaning it will become duller than an average sample of the evidence in a Blue-book. Therefore, as I do not know a word of Spanish, I can only guess at the qualities which have eluded Mr Graham's crib.

Echegaray is apparently of the school of Schiller, Victor Hugo, and Verdi—picturesque, tragic to the death, shewing us the beautiful and the heroic struggling either with blind destiny or with an implacable idealism which makes vengeance and jealousy points of honor. Mariana is a lineal descendant of Ruy Blas or Don Carlos. In The Son of Don Juan, the modern scientific culture comes in, and replaces the "villain" of the older school, the Sallustio or Ruy Gomez, by destiny in the shape of hereditary disease. In spite of the line "Give me the sun, mother," for which Echegaray acknowledges his indebtedness to Ibsen, his treatment of the Ghosts theme is perfectly original: there is not in it a shadow of the peculiar moral attitude of Ibsen. Echegaray remorselessly fixes all the responsibility on Don Juan (Alving), who is as resolutely vicious as Shelley's Count Cenci. Ibsen, on the contrary, after representing Mrs Alving as having for years imputed her late husband's vices to his own wilful dissoluteness, brings home to her the conviction that it was really she herself and her fellow Puritans who, by stamping men and women of Alving's temperament into the gutter, and imposing shame and disease on them as their natural heritage, had made the ruin into which Alving fell. Accordingly, we have those terrible scenes in which she desperately tries to reverse towards the son the conduct that was fatal to the father, plying Oswald with champagne and conniving at his intrigue with his own half-sister. There is not the slightest trace of this inculpation of respectability and virtue in The Son of Don Juan. Indeed, had Echegaray adapted Ibsen's moral to the conditions of domestic life and public opinion in Spain, the process

would have destroyed all that superficial resemblance to Ghosts
which has led some critics hastily to describe Echegaray's play as
a wholesale plagiarism. The fact that the doctor who is only mentioned in Ghosts actually appears on the stage in The Son of Don
Juan is a point, not of resemblance, but of difference; whilst the
fact that Mrs Alving and Manders have no counterparts in the
Spanish play, and that the dissipated father, who does not appear
in Ghosts at all, is practically Echegaray's hero, will make it plain
to anyone who has really comprehended Ghosts that the story
has been taken on to new ground nationally, and back to old
ground morally. Echegaray has also created a new set of characters.
Paca, the woman of Tarifa; the poor little consumptive Carmen,
betrothed to Lazarus (Oswald); Timoteo and Nemesio, the shattered old boon companions of Don Juan; Dolores, the wife of
Don Juan, who is not even twentieth cousin to Mrs Alving: all
these are original creations. Echegaray makes his puppets dance
ruthlessly. He writes like a strong man to whom these people are
all "poor devils" whom he pities and even pets, but does not
respect. This again contrasts strongly with the Norwegian feeling.
Ibsen never presents his play to you as a romance for your entertainment: he says, in effect, "Here is yourself and myself, our
society, our civilization. The evil and good, the horror and the
hope of it, are woven out of your life and mine." There is no
more of that sort of conscience about Echegaray's plays than there
is about Hernani, or, for the matter of that, The Babes in the
Wood. The woman who looks at Hedda Gabler or Mrs Alving
may be looking at herself in a mirror; but the woman who looks
at Mariana is looking at another woman, a perfectly distinct and
somewhat stagy personality. Consequently the howl of rage and
dread that follows each stroke of Ibsen's scalpel will not rise when
one of our actresses pounces on Mariana: we shall only whimper
a little because our childish curiosity is not indulged in the last
scene to the extent of letting us see whether Daniel kills Pablo and
then himself, or whether Pablo kills Daniel. This last scene, or
epilogue, as it is called, is magnificently dramatic; so much so that
if some adapter will change the name of the piece from Mariana to

Daniel, and transfer all the lady's best speeches to the gentleman, some of our actor-managers will probably produce it as soon as they realize its existence—say in twenty years or so. Unless, indeed, the actress-manageress arrives in the meantime and snaps it up.

I can best convey a notion of the style and dramatic method of Echegaray by a couple of quotations. In both of the plays just translated, a narrative by the principal character makes an indelible impression on the imagination, and comes into action with great effect at the climax of the tragedy. Both narratives are characteristically modern in their tragi-comedy. Here is Mariana's:

"Listen. I was eight years old. It must have been two or three o'clock in the morning. I was sleeping in my crib; and I dreamt that I was giving a great many kisses to my doll, because it had called me 'mamma.' The doll soon began to kiss me in return, but so fiercely that it caused me pain; and the doll became very large; and it was my mother. She was holding me in her arms; and I—I was not sleeping now: it was no dream: I was awake. Behind my mother there was a man standing. It was Alvarado, who was saying, 'Come.' My mother said, 'No: not without her.' And he said, 'Devil take it, then, *with* her.' The rest was like another dream—a nightmare—anything that whirls you away and will not let you breathe. My mother dressed me as people dress lunatics or dolls, pulling me about, shaking me, nearly beating me. And Alvarado was all the time hurrying her with whispers of 'Quick, quick, make haste.' I have never gone through anything like it: trivial—ludicrous as it was, it was horrible. She could not get the little socks rightly on me; she could not manage to button my boots; my drawers were put on the wrong way, the petticoats left with the opening at the side, my dress half loose, though I kept saying, 'It wants to be fastened: it should be fastened.' And all the time Alvarado was saying, 'Quick, quick, make haste, make haste.' I was wound up in a cloak of my mother's; and a hat ribbon was tied round my head so that it nearly choked me. Then my mother snatched me up in her arms; and we got into a carriage and went very fast. Then I heard a kiss; and I thought, 'My God, who was that for, who was that for: nobody has kissed me.' Ah, my own mother, my own mother!"

At the end of the play, Daniel, Mariana's lover, in persuading her to elope, picks up her cloak, and by trying to wrap her in it and carry her out to the carriage, reminds her of this passage in her childhood, and of Alvarado, whose son Daniel is. She calls in her husband, who kills her; and the two men disappear to fight it out to the death in the garden as the curtain falls.

Don Juan's narrative is an instance of the same dramatic device.

"It was a grand night—a grand supper. There were eight of us —each with a partner. Everybody was drunk—even the Guadalquiver. Aniceta went out on the balcony and began to cry out, 'Stupid, insipid, waterish river: drink wine for once,' and threw a bottle of Manzanilla into it. Well, I was lying asleep along the floor, upon the carpet, close to a divan. And on the divan there had fallen, by one of the usual accidents, the Tarifena—Paca the Tarifena. She was asleep; and in her tossings to and fro her hair had become loose—a huge mass; and it fell over me in silky waves —a great quantity, enfolding me as in a splendid black mantle of perfumed lace. The dawn arrived—a delightful morning, the balcony open, the East with splendid curtains of mist and with little red clouds; the sky blue and stainless; a light more vivid kindling into flame the distant horizon. Slowly the crimson globe ascended. I opened my eyes wide; and I saw the sun, I saw it from between the interlaced tresses of the Tarifena. It inundated me with light; and I stretched forth my hand instinctively to grasp it. Something of a new kind of love—a new desire—agitated me; great brightness, much azure, very broad spheres, vague yet burning aspirations for something very beautiful. For a minute I understood that there is something higher than the pleasures of the senses: for a minute I felt myself another being. I wafted a kiss to the sun, and angrily pulled aside the girl's hair. One lock clung about my lips: it touched my palate and gave me nausea. I flung away the tress; I awoke the Tarifena; and vice dawned through the remains of the orgie, like the sun through the vapors of the night, its mists, and its fire-colored clouds."

I need only add that Don Juan is on the stage at the end of the play when the heir to his debauchery says, "Give me the sun, mother." On the whole, though I am afraid some of our critics will be as nauseated as Don Juan was by that stray lock of the Tarifena's hair, I suspect the Spaniards will compel us to admit that they have produced a genius of a stamp that crosses frontiers, and that we shall yet see some of his work on our own stage.

Mr Arthur Law, the author of The Ladies' Idol, the latest Vaudeville piece, did not remind me of Echegaray in any way; but his piece is not bad fun for all that. Only, when I come upon as clever an actor as Mr Weedon Grossmith, I like to see his powers well drawn out; and this social duty Mr Arthur Law has not, I regret to say, performed. The audience, convinced that Mr Grossmith is one of the funniest of men, laughs whenever he opens his mouth. He accordingly opens his mouth very often, and shuts it again, with hilarious results; but he has really very little more to do. Mr Beauchamp's Purley is a capital piece of acting; Mr Volpé, as Wix, is a credible and natural Brixton paterfamilias, and does not "character-act"; and Mr Little, though still rather too much the funny man and too little the artist, is amusing. Miss Beringer, Miss Palfry, and Miss Homfrey acquit themselves competently in the women's parts. It is true that The Ladies' Idol is not a very difficult piece to play; but after the exasperatingly bad acting one constantly sees at the theatres where high comedy and "drama" prevail, it is a relief to see even simple work creditably done.

AT THE THEATRES

Vanity Fair. A Caricature. By G. W. Godfrey. Court Theatre, 27 April 1895.

The Passport. By B. C. Stephenson and W. Yardley. Terry's Theatre, 25 April 1895.

A Human Sport. A Drama in one act. By Austin Fryers. Globe Theatre, 1 May 1895.   [4 *May* 1895]

On the whole, I am inclined to congratulate Mr Godfrey on Mrs John Wood, rather than Mrs John Wood on Mr Godfrey, in the matter of Vanity Fair. Mrs John Wood is herself a character; and by providing her with some new dialogue Mr Godfrey has given himself an air of creation; but I doubt if the other parts can be said to bear him out on this point. When I saw the piece, on the third night, Mr Arthur Cecil was still so unequal to the mere taskwork of remembering long strings of sentences which were about as characteristic and human as the instructions on the back of a telegram form, that he had to be spoon-fed by the prompter all the evening. Mr Anson as Bill Feltoe, the blackmailer, had a part which was certainly memorable in the sense that he could preserve the continuity of his ideas; but it did not go beyond that. The play, as a drama, is nothing. As an entertainment "written round" Mrs John Wood, it is a success. But it also pretends to be Vanity Fair, a picture of society. Mr Godfrey guards himself by calling it a caricature; but he none the less presents it as a morality, a satire, a sermon. And here he appeals to the love of the public for edification. Dickens's group of cronies at the Maypole inn, with their cry of "Go on improvin' of us, Johnny," exactly typifies the playgoing public in England. When an English playgoer is not by temperament, if not by actual practice, nine-tenths a chapel-goer, he is generally ten-tenths a blackguard; and so, if you cannot produce a genuine drama, and conquer him legitimately in that way, you must either be licentious at the cost of your respectability, or else moral and idealistic. Mr Godfrey, running short for the moment of character and drama, of course chose the respectable alternative, and resorted to idealism. He moralizes on fine lady spectators at murder trials, on matrimonial scandals in high life, on Christianity conquering Africa with the Maxim gun, and on the prevarications of the Treasury Bench. As further evidence of the corruption of society, he instances the interest taken by it in eminent explorers, in Buffalo Bill, and in foreign violinists, the inference being, as I understand it, that to invite Mr Stanley to dine, or Herr Joachim to play a partita by Bach, is a proceeding as fraught with degenerate heartlessness as to shew your "horror" of a crime by rushing down to the court to gloat over the trial, or to give a gentleman who pays your wife's bills the right to call you to account for being seen in her company. Mr Godfrey's explanation of all this depravity is simple. It is the work of the New Woman and of the Problem Play.

You are now in a position to appreciate the scene at the beginning of the third act, where Mr Arthur Cecil, as the gently cynical Thackerayan observer of Vanity Fair, receives, with the assistance of the prompter, the wondering questions of Miss Nancy Noel as to whether the relations between young men and young women ever really were as they are represented in the novels of Sir Walter Scott. To which I regret to say Mr Cecil does not hesitate to reply in the affirmative, without mentioning that no change that has taken place in this century has been more obviously a change for the better than the change in the relations between men and women. "Goodnight, little girl," he adds with unction, after a brief reference to his guide, philosopher, and friend in the prompter's box. "Trust to the teachings of your own pure heart. God bless you!"

Mr Godfrey must excuse me; but that sort of social philosophy is not good enough for me. It does not matter, perhaps, because I am far from attributing to the claptrap play the devastating social influence he apparently attaches to the problem play (which I am getting rather anxious to see, by the way). But I must at least declare my belief that Mr Godfrey will never succeed as a critic of society by merely jumbling together all the splenetic commonplaces that sound effective to him, and tacking on an Adelphi moral. In order to make a stage drawing room a microcosm of Vanity Fair, you may, I grant, mix your sets to any extent you please; but you need not therefore produce an impression that the sort of man who never reads a serious book or ventures above burlesque and farcical comedy at the theatre, has been led into his habit of not paying his bills, and of winking at his wife's relations with useful acquaintances, by The Heavenly Twins and Ibsen's plays. I do not say that Mr Godfrey has produced such impressions intentionally: my quarrel with him is that he has begun to criticize life without first arranging his ideas. The result is, that it is impossible for the most credulous person to believe in Mrs Brabazon Tegg's Grosvenor Square reception even to the extent of recognizing it as a caricature. It is not that the real thing is more respectable, or that the most extravagant bits (the scene with the sham millionaire, for instance) are the least lifelike: quite the contrary. But a drawing room is not like Margate sands for all that: however loose the selection of guests, there is enough logic in it to keep the music, bad though it may be, in one predominant key. It requires a very nice knowledge of what is reasonable to be safely outrageous in society of any grade; and this knowledge is as essential to the dramatist depicting society on the stage as to the diner-out who wishes to be allowed the privilege of unconventionality. In putting the drawing room on the stage, Mr Godfrey's master is obviously Mr Oscar Wilde. Now Mr Wilde has written scenes in which there is hardly a speech which could conceivably be uttered by one real person at a real at-home; but the deflection from common-sense is so subtle that it is evidently produced as a tuner tunes a piano: that is, he first tunes a fifth perfectly, and then flattens it a shade. If he could not tune the perfect fifth he could not produce the practicable one. This condition is imposed on the sociological humorist also. For instance, Don Quixote's irresistibly laughable address to the galley slaves, like the rest of his nonsense, is so close to the verge of good sense that thick-witted people, and even some clever ones, take the Don for a man of exceptionally sound understanding. None the less he is a hopeless lunatic, the sound understanding which he skirts so funnily being that of Cervantes. Mr Godfrey fails to produce the same effect because he tries to say the absurd thing without precisely knowing the sensible thing, with the result that, though he makes epigrams most industriously, he never tickles the audience except by strokes of pure fun, such as Mrs Brabazon-Tegg's "Dont disturb my maid: she's upstairs doing my hair." There are passages which are effective because they give voice to grievances or allude to abuses upon which the audience feels, or feels obliged to pretend to feel, highly indignant; but this is not art or drama: the effect would be the same if the point were made on a political platform: indeed, it would be better there. For example, in Mrs Brabazon-Tegg's dream of her trial for bigamy, she is made to complain of the practice of eminent counsel accepting retainers in more cases than they can possibly attend to. The complaint would be more effective at an ordinary public meeting, because the trial represented on the stage is precisely the sort of one from which no counsel would dream of absenting himself. Such effect, then, as Mrs Brabazon-Tegg's speech from the dock actually does produce is due, not to the author's knowledge of his subject, but to the extraordinary spontaneity and conviction with which Mrs John Wood delivers herself.

There is one point on which I am unable to say whether Mr Godfrey was satirical or sincere. When Mrs Brabazon-Tegg's conscience is awakened, she does what most rich people do under similar circumstances: that is to say, the most mischievous thing possible. She begins to scatter hundred pound cheques in conscience-money to various charities. Whether Mr Godfrey approves of this proceeding I do not know; but he at any rate conquered my respect by remorselessly making his woman of fashion presently reduce all the cheques to five pounds and replunge into fashionable life not a whit the better for her hard experience. This seems to indicate that Mr Godfrey has that courage of his profession in which most of our dramatists are shamelessly wanting. For its sake he may very well be forgiven his random satire, and even—on condition that he undertakes not to do it again— the insufferable conversations of Mr Arthur Cecil and Miss Granville.

The Passport, at Terry's, is an amusing piece, with thirteen parts, of which no less than eight are very well acted. I was not surprised at this except in the case of Miss Gertrude Kingston, who, when I last saw her, was a clever lady with a certain virtuosity in the art of dress, and made of metal hard enough to take a fine edge, but still not then a skilled actress, though the critics had instinctively recognized her as a person to whom it was best to be civil, perhaps because she so suggested that terrible person, the lady who has walked straight from her drawing room on to the stage. Most of that is gone now, except what was worth keeping in it. Miss Kingston's utterance and movements are acquiring a definite artistic character; and the circulation of feeling, which is more important to the stage artist than the circulation of the blood, seems to be establishing itself in spite of the refractory nature of the conducting medium; whilst her cleverness is still conspicuous, and her dresses make me feel more keenly than ever that I have left one corner of critical journalism unconquered: to wit, the fashion article. In short, Miss Kingston confronted me in The Passport as a rising actress, holding my interest from her entrance to her final exit, and indeed determining the success of the play, which, without her, might have broken down badly in the second and third acts, hampered as they are with the stuff about Bob, Algy, and Violet which is neither sensible, amusing, nor credible. The main thread of the story is presented by a very powerful combination of artists: Mr Yorke Stephens, Mr Maltby, Mr Giddens, Mr Mackay, Miss Gertrude Kingston, Miss Cicely Richards, and Miss Fanny Coleman. Their parts are all funny; and some of them are individual and interesting, notably the exasperating but fascinating young widow with the impossible memory, and the perfectly normal respectable maid, an excellent character, played admirably by Miss Cicely Richards. Mr Yorke Stephens is a little underparted: after the first act, which he carries off with all the debonair grace and smartness of style which distinguish him, he takes the part a little too easily. Even a widower could not be so completely unembarrassed on his wedding-day; and however obvious it may be that the misunderstandings created by the widow can be explained away, still, whilst they last, they need the assistance of a little alarm on the part of the bridegroom. As to the play, it is not a mere farcical imbroglio in which neither the figures who work the puzzle nor the places in which they work it have any real individuality: the scenes and circumstances, both in the frontier railway station and in the London house, are fully imagined and realized. The value and, alas! the rarity of this is shewn by the comparative freshness and interest of the action, and the genial indulgence with which the audience accepts the complications of the last two acts, which are, it must be confessed, anything but ingenious, not to mention the silly episode of Algy, Violet, and Bob as aforesaid.

The one act piece, A Human Sport (in the evolutionary sense), by Mr Austin Fryers, produced at the Globe Theatre at a matinée in aid of the Actors' Benevolent Fund on Wednesday last, is hardly a drama at all: it is rather the exhibition of an incident which does not develop in any way. An ironmaster (I think it was an ironmaster) has some operation spoiled by a workman getting drunk at the critical moment. In order to prevent this occurring again, he resolves to take a step which, simple and obvious as it is, has not, as far as I am aware, ever been thought of before: namely, to take the man into partnership so as to increase his self-respect. With this view he invites him to tea. The drunkard recognizes in his master's wife and mother-in-law his own deserted daughter and wife. Finding that respectability will involve a reunion with his family, he pretends to get drunk again, and is promptly kicked out as incorrigible. This unconventional and rather amusing notion has been ruined by Mr Austin Fryers' inveterate sentimentality. The "human sport," instead of behaving sportively, plunges into the stalest maudlin pathos over his longlost daughter. If Mr Austin Fryers will cut out the daughter, and make the sport get really drunk in order to escape from respectability and his wife, the play will do very well. Or if he will write a temptation scene round the decanter of brandy, and make the wife rush in and struggle with her husband for the glass until the contest is decided in her favor by the sound of their daughter's voice singing a hymn in the next room, the whole ending with the partnership and domestic bliss, that will be equally satisfactory. But I implore Mr Austin Fryers not to mix his *genres*. Let us have the new ideas in the new style, or the old tricks in the old style; but the new ideas combined with the old tricks in no style at all cannot be borne. Mr James Welch, as the sport, pulled the play through by a piece of acting impressive enough to keep the audience believing, up to the last moment, that something really interesting was imminent. If only for Mr

Welch's sake, Mr Austin Fryers, who is by no means deficient in ability, should extirpate that daughter, and build up the part into something worthy of the actor's rare talent.

MR IRVING TAKES PAREGORIC

BYGONES. By A. W. Pinero. A STORY OF WATERLOO. By A. Conan Doyle. A CHAPTER FROM DON QUIXOTE. By the late W. G. Wills. Lyceum Theatre, 4 May 1895. [11 *May* 1895]

IT was Mr Grant Allen, I think, who familiarized us with the fact that all attempts to sustain our conduct at a higher level than is natural to us produce violent reactions. Was there not a certain African divine, the Reverend Mr Creedy, who tamed the barbarian within him and lived the higher life of the Caledonian Road for a while, only to end by "going Fantee" with a vengeance? This liability to reaction is a serious matter for the actor —not, perhaps, for the actor of villains, who becomes by reaction the most amiable of men in private life, but certainly for the actor of heroes, who is occasionally to be found off the stage in a state of very violent reaction indeed. But there are some actors —not many, but some—who have solid private characters which stand like rocks in the midst of the ebb and tide of their stage emotions; and in their case the reaction must take place in their art itself. Such men, when they have to be unnaturally dignified on the stage, cannot relieve themselves by being ridiculous in private life, since the good sense of their private characters makes that impossible to them. When they can bear it no longer, they must make themselves ridiculous on the stage or burst. No actor suffers from the tyranny of this grotesque necessity more than Mr Irving. His career, ever since he became a heroic actor, has been studded by relapses into the most impish buffoonery. I remember years ago going into the Lyceum Theatre under the impression that I was about to witness a performance of Richard III. After one act of that tragedy, however, Mr Irving relapsed into an impersonation of Alfred Jingle. He concealed piles of sandwiches in his hat; so that when he afterwards raised it to introduce himself as "Alfred Jingle, Esq., of No Hall, Nowhere," a rain of ham and bread descended on him. He knelt on the stage on one knee and seated Miss Pauncefort (the spinster aunt) on the other, and then upset himself and her, head over heels. He beat a refractory horse with a bandbox; inked the glimpses of shirt that appeared through the holes in his coat; and insulted all the other characters by turning their coats back with the idiotic remark, "From the country, sir?" He was not acting: nothing less like the scenes created by Dickens could possibly have been put on the stage. He was simply taking his revenge on Shakespear and himself for months of sustained dignity. Later on we had the same phenomenon repeated in his Robert Macaire. There was, and, I suppose, still is in the market a version of that little melodrama by Mr Henley and the late Louis Stevenson which was full of literary distinction; but Mr Irving stuck to the old third-class version, which gave him unlimited scope for absurdity. He made one or two memorable effects in it: a more horribly evil-looking beast of prey than his Macaire never crossed the stage; and I can recall a point or two where the feeling produced was terrible. But what Mr Irving enjoyed, and obviously what attracted him in the business, was rushing Mr Weedon Grossmith upstairs by the back of the neck, breaking plates on his stomach, standing on a barrel boyishly pretending to play the fiddle, singing a chanson to an accompaniment improvised by himself on an old harpsichord, and, above all—for here his glee attained its climax—inadvertently pulling a large assortment of stolen handkerchiefs out of his pocket whilst explaining matters to the police officer, and clinching his account by throwing one into his hat, which, having no crown, allowed it to fall through to the floor. This alternation of the grotesque, the impish, the farcical, with the serious and exalted, is characteristic of the nineteenth century. Goethe anticipated it in his Faust and Mephistopheles, obviously two sides of the same character; and it was in the foolish travesty of Faust perpetrated by Wills that Mr Irving found a part in which he could be melodramatic actor, mocker, and buffoon all in one evening. Since then he has had a trying time of it. Becket on top of Wolsey was enough to provoke a graver man to go Fantee; and Lear followed Becket. But when King Arthur capped Lear, all of us who knew Mr Irving's constitution felt that a terrific reaction must be imminent. It has come in the shape of Don Quixote, in which he makes his own dignity ridiculous to his heart's content. He rides a slim white horse, made up as Rozinante with painted hollows just as a face is made up; he has a set of imitation geese waggling on springs to mistake for swans; he tumbles about the stage with his legs in the air; and he has a single combat, on refreshingly indecorous provocation, with a pump. And he is perfectly happy. I am the last person in the world to object; for I, too, have something of that aboriginal need for an occasional carnival in me. When he came before the curtain at the end, he informed us, with transparent good faith, that the little play practically covered the whole of Cervantes' novel, a statement which we listened to with respectful stupefaction. I get into trouble often enough by my ignorance of authors whom every literate person is expected to have at his fingers' ends; but I believe Mr Irving can beat me hollow in that respect. If I have not read Don Quixote all through, I have at least looked at the pictures; and I am prepared to swear that Mr Irving never got beyond the second chapter.

Anyone who consults recent visitors to the Lyceum, or who seeks for information in the Press as to the merits of Mr Conan Doyle's Story of Waterloo, will in nineteen cases out of twenty learn that the piece is a trifle raised into importance by the marvellous acting of Mr Irving as Corporal Gregory Brewster. As a matter of fact, the entire effect is contrived by the author, and is due to him alone. There is absolutely no acting in it—none whatever. There is a make-up in it, and a little cheap and simple mimicry which Mr Irving does indifferently because he is neither apt nor observant as a mimic of doddering old men, and because his finely cultivated voice and diction again and again rebel against the indignity of the Corporal's squeakings and mumblings and vulgarities of pronunciation. But all the rest is an illusion produced by the machinery of "a good acting play," by which is

always meant a play that requires from the performers no qualifications beyond a plausible appearance and a little experience
and address in stage business. I had better make this clear by explaining the process of doing without acting as exemplified by
A Story of Waterloo, in which Mr Conan Doyle has carried the
art of constructing an "acting" play to such an extreme that I
almost suspect him of satirically revenging himself, as a literary
man, on a profession which has such a dread of "literary plays."
(A "literary play," I should explain, is a play that the actors have
to act, in opposition to the "acting play," which acts them.)

Before the curtain rises, you read the playbill; and the process
commences at once with the suggestive effect on your imagination of "Corporal Gregory Brewster, age eighty-six, a Waterloo
veteran," of "Nora Brewster, the corporal's grandniece," and of
"Scene—Brewster's lodgings." By the time you have read that,
your own imagination, with the author pulling the strings, has
done half the work you afterwards give Mr Irving credit for.
Up goes the curtain; and the lodgings are before you, with the
humble breakfast table, the cheery fire, the old man's spectacles
and bible, and a medal hung up in a frame over the chimney-
piece. Lest you should be unobservant enough to miss the significance of all this, Miss Annie Hughes comes in with a basket of
butter and bacon, ostensibly to impersonate the grandniece, really
to carefully point out all these things to you, and to lead up to
the entry of the hero by preparing breakfast for him. When the
background is sufficiently laid in by this artifice, the drawing of
the figure commences. Mr Fuller Mellish enters in the uniform
of a modern artillery sergeant, with a breech-loading carbine.
You are touched: here is the young soldier come to see the old
—two figures from the Seven Ages of Man. Miss Hughes tells
Mr Mellish all about Corporal Gregory. She takes down the
medal, and makes him read aloud to her the press-cutting pasted
beside it which describes the feat for which the medal was given.
In short, the pair work at the picture of the old warrior until the
very dullest dog in the audience knows what he is to see, or to
imagine he sees, when the great moment comes. Thus is Brew-

ster already created, though Mr Irving has not yet left his
dressing room. At last, everything being ready, Mr Fuller Mellish
is packed off so as not to divide the interest. A squeak is heard
behind the scenes: it is the childish treble that once rang like a
trumpet on the powder-waggon at Waterloo. Enter Mr Irving,
in a dirty white wig, toothless, blear-eyed, palsied, shaky at the
knees, stooping at the shoulders, incredibly aged and very poor,
but respectable. He makes his way to his chair, and can only sit
down, so stiff are his aged limbs, very slowly and creakily. This
sitting down business is not acting: the callboy could do it; but
we are so thoroughly primed by the playbill, the scene-painter,
the stage-manager, Miss Hughes and Mr Mellish, that we go off
in enthusiastic whispers, "What superb acting! How wonderfully
he does it!" The corporal cannot recognize his grandniece at
first. When he does, he asks her questions about children—children who have long gone to their graves at ripe ages. She pre-
pares his tea: he sups it noisily and ineptly, like an infant. More
whispers: "How masterly a touch of second childhood!" He
gets a bronchial attack and gasps for paregoric, which Miss
Hughes administers with a spoon, whilst our faces glisten with
tearful smiles. "Is there another living actor who could take
paregoric like that?" The sun shines through the window: the
old man would fain sit there and peacefully enjoy the fragrant
air and life-giving warmth of the world's summer, contrasting
so pathetically with his own winter. He rises, more creakily than
before, but with his faithful grandniece's arm fondly supporting
him. He dodders across the stage, expressing a hope that the flies
will not be too "owdacious," and sits down on another chair
with his joints crying more loudly than ever for some of the oil
of youth. We feel that we could watch him sitting down for ever.
Hark! a band in the street without. Soldiers pass: the old war-
horse snorts feebly, but complains that bands dont play so loud
as they used to. The band being duly exploited for all it is worth,
the bible comes into play. What he likes in it are the campaigns
of Joshua and the battle of Armageddon, which the poor dear
old thing can hardly pronounce, though he had it from "our

clergyman." How sweet of the clergyman to humor him! Blessings on his kindly face and on his silver hair! Mr Fuller Mellish comes back with the breechloading carbine. The old man handles it; calls it a firelock; and goes crazily through his manual with it. Finally, he unlocks the breech, and as the barrel drops, believes that he has broken the weapon in two. Matters being explained, he expresses his unalterable conviction that England will have to fall back on Brown Bess when the moment for action arrives again. He takes out his pipe. It falls and is broken. He whimpers, and is petted and consoled by a present of the sergeant's beautiful pipe with "a hamber mouthpiece." Mr Fuller Mellish, becoming again superfluous, is again got rid of. Enter a haughty gentleman. It is the Colonel of the Royal Scots Guards, the corporal's old regiment. According to the well-known custom of colonels, he has called on the old pensioner to give him a five-pound note. The old man, as if electrically shocked, staggers up and desperately tries to stand for a moment at "attention" and salute his officer. He collapses, almost slain by the effort, into his chair, mumbling pathetically that he "were a'most gone that time, Colonel." "A masterstroke! who but a great actor could have executed this heart-searching movement?" The veteran returns to the fireside: once more he depicts with convincing art the state of an old man's joints. The Colonel goes; Mr Fuller Mellish comes; the old man dozes. Suddenly he springs up. "The Guards want powder; and, by God, the Guards shall have it." With these words he falls back in his chair. Mr Fuller Mellish, lest there should be any mistake about it (it is never safe to trust the intelligence of the British public), delicately informs Miss Hughes that her granduncle is dead. The curtain falls amid thunders of applause.

Every old actor into whose hands this article falls will understand perfectly from my description how the whole thing is done, and will wish that he could get such Press notices for a little hobbling and piping, and a few bits of mechanical business with a pipe, a carbine, and two chairs. The whole performance does not involve one gesture, one line, one thought outside the commonest routine of automatic stage illusion. What, I wonder, must Mr Irving, who of course knows this better than anyone else, feel when he finds this pitiful little handful of hackneyed stage tricks received exactly as if it were a crowning instance of his most difficult and finest art? No doubt he expected and intended that the public, on being touched and pleased by machinery, should imagine that they were being touched and pleased by acting. But the critics! What can he think of the analytic powers of those of us who, when an organized and successful attack is made on our emotions, are unable to discriminate between the execution done by the actor's art and that done by Mr Conan Doyle's ingenious exploitation of the ready-made pathos of old age, the ignorant and maudlin sentiment attaching to the army and "the Dook," and the vulgar conception of the battle of Waterloo as a stand-up street fight between an Englishman and a Frenchman, a conception infinitely less respectable than that which led Byron to exclaim, when he heard of Napoleon's defeat, "I'm damned sorry"?

The first item in the Lyceum triple bill is Mr Pinero's Bygones, in which Mr Sydney Valentine, as Professor Mazzoni, acts with notable skill and judgment. Mr Pinero used to play the part himself; but he was bitten then, like everyone else at that time, with the notion that "character acting," especially in parts that admitted of a foreign accent, was the perfection of stage art; and his Mazzoni was accordingly worse than anyone could believe without having seen it. Matters were made worse by the detestable and irredeemable scene in which the old man proposes marriage to the girl. Mazzoni might excusably offer her, as a means of escape from her humiliating predicament, the position of his wife, and his friendly affection and fatherly care until he left her a widow; and he might make this offer being secretly in love with her, and so preserve the pathos of his subsequent disappointment. But to propose a serious love match to her as he does seems to me abominable: the scene makes my flesh creep: it always did. Mr Valentine could not reconcile me to it; nor should I have thanked him if he had; but he softened it as far as it could be softened; and his final leavetaking, with its effect of sparing us the exhibition of a grief which he nevertheless made us feel keenly behind that last sincere and kindly smile, was a fine stroke of art. He here, as elsewhere in the play, shewed himself able to do with a few light and sure touches what most of our actors vainly struggle with by publicly wallowing in self-pity for minutes at a stretch.

I hope I have not conveyed an impression that the triple bill makes a bad evening's entertainment. Though it is my steady purpose to do what I can to drive such sketches as A Story of Waterloo, with their ready-made feeling and prearranged effects, away to the music-hall, which is their proper place now that we no longer have a "Gallery of Illustration," I enjoy them, and am entirely in favor of their multiplication so long as it is understood that they are not the business of fine actors and first-class theatres. And, abortive as Don Quixote is, there are moments in it when Wills vanishes, and we have Cervántes as the author and Mr Irving as the actor—no cheap combination. Apart from the merits of the three plays, I suggest that it is a mistake—easily avoidable by a manager with Mr Irving's resources at his disposal—to cast Miss Annie Hughes and Mr Webster for parts in two different pieces. I half expected to see Miss Hughes again in the third play; but Mr Irving drew the line there, and entrusted the leading young lady's part in Don Quixote to Miss de Silva. In Bygones, Miss Ailsa Craig succeeds in giving a touch of interest to the part of the ill-conditioned servant who works the plot. Miss Hughes grows younger and prettier, and acts better, continually; only her voice still slyly contradicts her efforts to be pathetic, which are in all other respects credible and graceful enough.

THE TWO LATEST COMEDIES

THE HOME SECRETARY. An original modern play. By R. C.
Carton. Criterion Theatre, 7 May 1895.

THE TRIUMPH OF THE PHILISTINES, AND HOW MR JORGAN PRE-
SERVED THE MORALS OF MARKET PEWBURY UNDER VERY TRY-
ING CIRCUMSTANCES. An original comedy in three acts. By
Henry Arthur Jones. St James's Theatre, 11 May 1895.

[18 *May* 1895]

I MUST not stop to make an exordium before dealing with Mr
Carton's play, for, to tell the truth, I am forgetting it so rapidly
that in another half-hour it may all have escaped me. I must in
fairness add that I did not see it very well, because, though there
are only two pillars in the Criterion Theatre that you cannot see
round, and consequently only two stalls from which the stage
is not visible, I was placed in one of those two stalls. That is the
worst of having a reputation as a critic of acting. They place you
behind an obstacle which prevents you from seeing more than
one person at a time, calculating that since you will always keep
your eye on the actor-manager, your attention will be concen-
trated on him by the impossibility of your seeing anyone else.
This time, however, Mr Wyndham had nothing particular to
shew me. There was no character for him to create, and consequently nothing for him to do that was more than the merest
routine for an actor of his accomplishment. Though supposed
to be a Home Secretary, he presented us with exactly the sort
of Cabinet Minister who never goes to the Home Office. I fancy
he has formed his political style on the Foreign Office, or the
Colonial Office, perhaps even on the Duchy of Lancaster, and is
under the erroneous impression that the same sort of thing would
do for the comparatively popular Home Office. But at all events,
Mr Wyndham knows more about Home Secretaries than Mr
Carton: in fact, he could not possibly know less. Mr Carton has
a secondhand imagination and a staggering indifference to verisimilitude. Inspired by Miss Neilson's appearance in the play of

An Ideal Husband as the beautiful wife who is too truthful to approve of all the official utterances of the Cabinet Minister whom she has rashly married, he shoots Miss Neilson on to the stage in that relation to Mr Wyndham, with nothing better to account for her domestic unhappiness than the articles in the Opposition papers. Imagine Mrs Asquith's domestic peace being shattered by an article in the St James's Gazette! The rest of the play is of less recent origin; but one need go no further back than The House in the Marsh, or Captain Swift, in tracing the descent of Dangerfield the Anarchist. Anything more wantonly nonsensical than the way in which Mr Carton rearranges the facts of English society and politics so as to represent Dangerfield as being engaged in a deadly duel of the Pompey and Caesar kind with the Home Secretary, would be hard to cite. As to all the stuff about mighty secret brotherhoods, and abysses of revolution opening at the feet of society, I invite Mr Carton to manufacture his plays in future out of some less mischievous kind of absurdity.

Apart from this serious bearing of the play on life, it is amusing enough to hear Mr Lewis Waller at a west-end theatre spouting the stalest commonplaces of the Socialist platforms with the full approval of the audience. No fashionable dramatist's library will henceforth be complete without a copy of Mr Hyndman's England for All. Mr Brookfield contributes one of those little imitations of social types of which he is fond. They are amusing; and they fulfil two indispensable conditions: to wit, they impress the public as being all different from one another, thereby creating a high estimate of Mr Brookfield's skill and versatility; and they are all exactly alike, so that the public has only one taste to acquire for them. Miss Julia Neilson plays very much better than in An Ideal Husband. In that comedy she made the worst of a good part: in this, she made the best of an indifferent one, though it was hard on her to have to sit down and examine her mind and conscience very slowly just when the audience had finally made up their minds that Mr Carton had fashioned her perfectly hollow. In fact, the less interesting both the Home Secretary and his wife became, the more slowly Mr Wyndham and Miss Neilson had to play, in order to make the final scene at least mechanically impressive. The effect was a little trying. The comedy scenes, which are laughable enough, were child's play to Miss Mary Moore, Miss Maud Millet, Mr de Lange, and Mr Alfred Bishop; and Mr Lewis Waller would hardly thank me for compliments on a performance so easily within his powers as the impersonation of Captain Swift Dangerfield. Mr Sidney Brough's part enabled him to shew that rare quality of his of being at the same time a very "useful" actor and a very attractive one. On the whole, The Home Secretary is a well-acted, well-staged, occasionally entertaining, and hopelessly slovenly play.

Mr Henry Arthur Jones's comedy, with the nineteen-word title, affords material for the social essayist rather than the dramatic critic, being avowedly an object-lesson in British lower middle-class hypocrisy. And the attack is not the usual sham attack of the stage moralist: it is courageous, uncompromising, made with sharp weapons, and left without the slightest attempt to run away at the end. When Mr Jones appeared before the curtain several persons howled piteously, like dogs who had been purposely run over. Every play which is a criticism of contemporary life, must, if it is an honest play, involve a certain struggle with the public. Accordingly, Mr Jones was not so unanimously applauded when the curtain fell on poor Mr Jorgan's very mixed "triumph" as Mr Pinero was after Mrs Ebbsmith pulled the Bible out of the fire. But his courage was respected; and there, I think, he had the advantage of Mr Pinero.

There is a sense in which Mr Jones's plays are far more faulty than those of most of his competitors, exactly as a row of men is more faulty than a row of lampposts turned out by a first-rate firm. His qualities are creative imagination, curious observation, inventive humor, originality, sympathy, and sincerity; and the risks of trusting to these are, like the rewards, very great. It is safer and cheaper to depend on the taste, judgment, instinct for fashion and knowledge of the stage and the public, by which plays can be constructed out of ready-made materials, and guaranteed to pass an evening safely and smoothly, instead of, like the real live work of Mr Jones, rousing all sorts of protests and jarring all sorts of prejudices, besides disgusting the professorial critics and amateurs by its impenitent informality. And then, Mr Jones, following in the footsteps of Dickens, plays every sort of extravagant and fanciful trick with his characters, inventing insane names for them, making them express themselves in the most impossible way, and sometimes exasperating dull and literal people beyond all bounds. Thus, in The Triumph of the Philistines, we have such a freak as Thomas Blagg, the butcher's boy, clearly of the family of Trabb's boy, of immortal memory; and with him are a Pumblechookian band of local tradesmen, who are not humanity simple and direct, but humanity made fun of. Still, if the details are outrageous, the general effect is mostly right; for Mr Jones knows his Market Pewbury well enough to joke with it. On the subject of Art I find him less convincing. His identification of it with the sort of Epicurean philosophy which is always at daggers drawn with Puritanism is roughly true to life—sufficiently so, at all events, for dramatic purposes. But his identification of Puritanism with Philistinism seems to me to be a fundamental confusion. A Philistine is a prosaic person whose artistic consciousness is unawakened, and who has no ideals. A Puritan is no doubt often at the same disadvantage as the Philistine in respect of his insensibility to Art; but he is a fanatical idealist, to whom all stimulations of the sense of beauty are abhorrent; because he is only conscious of them in so far as they appeal to his sex instinct, which he regards as his great enemy. However, it is not this point that Mr Jones has missed; for his Mr Jorgan, though called a Philistine, corresponds exactly to a Puritan. Even when Sir Valentine Fellowes, a thorough Philistine, is put in opposition to the Philistines, and in sympathy with Willie Hesslewood the painter, he remains nevertheless as life-like a Philistine as Mr Jorgan is a Puritan; so that one is tempted to ask whether it matters what the twain are called, since the author's method of working upon life instead of upon theories of society and canons of art seems sure to save him from anything worse than a confusion of names. But thought has its empire after all; and when Mr Jones claims the sympathy of the audience for the Philistine as against the Puritan, the Puritan snatches the sympathy from him; for the idealist, being the higher if more dangerous animal, always does beat the Philistine. A picture of a Bacchante is exhibited on the stage, with its back to the audience, an arrangement which gives it away from the beginning as not fit to be seen. Mr Jorgan, the Puritan, having no artistic sense, denounces the artist as a mere pandar, and the picture as an artifice to make men more sensual. Sir Valentine's defence is in effect "Why not? Life would not be worth living unless people are allowed to sow a few wild oats, as I do occasionally; and if you interfere with my pleasures I'll spend my income on the Continent instead of in your shops." Mr Jones's instinct for character led him rightly to make Sir Valentine take that line. But what chance is there of the audience taking his side? They must feel, as I feel, that the Puritan's attitude is more respectable than the Philistine's. If Art were really a matter of Bacchante pictures painted by amorous young artists from rapscallionly little models, to be defended only by easygoing men of pleasure and cynical old society ladies who regard men as incurable voluptuaries, then surely we should all say Amen to Mr Skewett's "Burn it, I say. Burn it; and have done with the iniquity." The fact is, Mr Jones, revelling in his characters and scenes and dialogues, and keen on the scent of the narrowness and hypocrisy of Market Pewbury, has not got up his case thoroughly; and the result is that the plan of action which he has invented, with its studio machinery and its substitution of a picture for a question of conduct, does not strike one as being quite the right plan; whilst Market Pewbury is left, after all, with the best of the argument.

The acting is hardly as good as the play. Mr Alexander's comedy is too smart: Sir Valentine is never really distressed or at a loss, as he certainly ought to be at the end of the second act. Mr Waring, as Jorgan, is admirable in action; but before he gets to work, it is plain that the part does not naturally fit him. Mr

Esmond's Willie Hesslewood is perhaps the most entirely successful of all the impersonations involved, except Miss Juliette Nes-
ville's immense, irresistible Sally Lebrune. Mr Jones has carried
out the idea of this character to a hair's breadth; and the disadvantage at which the young woman's entire and perfect worthlessness puts all the more respectable characters is of the essence
of comedy. Lady Monckton's work is less interesting to the
audience than technically important to the play; and only the
expert can be expected to appreciate how very well she does it.
Miss Elliott Page was quite ladylike and natural as Alma Suleny;
but I am afraid the only thanks she got for not overdressing herself and forcing the significance of every sentence was a sense that
she was underacting. She certainly added nothing to her part, an
omission which would be rather serious in some plays, since
nothing plus nothing equals nothing; but it did not matter with
Mr Jones as the author. The half-dozen little sallies of character-
acting which filled up the stage with the Puritans of Market Pewbury were, of course, easily and amusingly done; but they were
too funny and too intentional to be convincing, and the total
effect was only made credible by the acting of Mr Waring.

A NEW LADY MACBETH AND A NEW
MRS EBBSMITH

[25 *May* 1895]

LAST Saturday evening found me lurking, an uninvited guest,
in an obscure corner of the Garrick Theatre, giving Mrs Ebbsmith another trial in the person of Miss Olga Nethersole. This
time I carefully regulated the dose, coming late for the preliminary explanations, and hurrying home at the end of the second
act, when Mrs Ebbsmith had put her fine dress on, and was
beginning to work up towards the stove. I cannot say I enjoyed
myself very much; for the play bored me more than ever; but
I perceived better than I did before that the fault was not altogether Mr Pinero's. The interest of the first act depends on Mrs
Thorpe really affecting and interesting her audience in her scene

with Agnes. Miss Ellice Jeffries fails to do this. I do not blame her, just as I should not blame Mr Charles Hawtrey if he were cast for the ghost in Hamlet and played it somewhat disappointingly. On the contrary, I congratulate her on her hopeless incapacity to persuade us that she is the victim of an unhappy marriage, or that she lives in a dreary country rectory where she walks like a ghost about her dead child's room in the intervals of housekeeping for her parson brother. She has obviously not a scrap of anything of the kind in her whole disposition; and that Mr Pinero should have cast her for such business in a part on which his whole first act and a good deal of the rest of the play depends, suggests that his experience of the impossibility of getting all his characters fitted in a metropolis which has more theatres than companies is making him reckless. The impression left is that the scene between Agnes and Mrs Thorpe is tedious and colorless, and that between Agnes and the Duke biting and full of character. But really one scene is as good as the other; only Mr Hare's Duke of St Olpherts is a consummate piece of acting, whilst Miss Jeffries' Mrs Thorpe is at best a graceful evasion of an impossible task. This was less noticeable before, because Mrs Patrick Campbell counted for so much in both scenes that the second factor in them mattered less. With Miss Nethersole, who failed to touch the character of Agnes at any point as far as I witnessed her performance, it mattered a great deal. I have no doubt that Miss Nethersole pulled the bible out of the stove, and played all the "emotional" scenes as well as Mrs Campbell or any one else could play them; but certainly in the first two acts, where Mrs Ebbsmith, not yet reduced to a mere phase of hysteria, is a self-possessed individual character, Miss Nethersole gave us nothing but the stage fashion of the day in a very accentuated and conscious manner. Mrs Campbell's extraordinary power of doing anything surely and swiftly with her hands whilst she is acting, preoccupation seeming an embarrassment unknown to her, is a personal peculiarity which cannot reasonably be demanded from her competitors. But Miss Nethersole seems to set a positive value on such preoccupation. When she pretends to darn a stocking she brings it down to the footlights, and poses in profile with the stockinged hand raised above the level of her head. She touches nothing without first poising her hand above it like a bird about to alight, or a pianist's fingers descending on a chord. She cannot even take up the box containing the rich dress to bundle it off into the next room, without disposing her hands round it with an unmistakeable reference to the conventional laws of grace. The effect in these first two acts, throughout which Mrs Ebbsmith is supposed to be setting Lucas Cleeve's teeth on edge at every turn by her businesslike ways, plain dress, and impatience of the effects that charm the voluptuary, may be imagined. The change of dress, with which Mrs Campbell achieved such a very startling effect, produced hardly any with Miss Nethersole, and would have produced none but for the dialogue; for Mrs Ebbsmith had been so obviously concerned all through with the effect of her attitudes, that one quite expected that she would not neglect herself when it came to dressing for dinner. The "Trafalgar Squaring" of the Duke, a complete success on Mr Hare's part, was a complete failure on Miss Nethersole's. Mrs Campbell caught the right platform tone of political invective and contemptuous social criticism to perfection: Miss Nethersole made the speech an emotional outburst, flying out at the Duke exactly as, in a melodrama, she would have flown out at the villain who had betrayed her. My inference is that Miss Nethersole has force and emotion without sense of character. With force and emotion, and an interesting and plastic person, one can play "the heroine" under a hundred different names with entire success. But the individualized heroine is another matter; and that is where Mrs Patrick Campbell comes in.

It is usual to describe Mr Hare as an actor who does not do himself justice on first nights because he is nervous. His Duke of St Olpherts is certainly not an instance of this. It is still capital; but compared to his superb performance on the first night, it is minced in diction and almost off-hand in deportment. I have come to the conclusion that Mr Forbes Robertson is only less out of place as Lucas Cleeve than Miss Jeffries as Mrs Thorpe.

In contrast to the cool intensity of Mrs Campbell, his strong, resolute manner, slackened as much as he could slacken it, barely passed muster on the first night as the manner of the weak neurotic creature described by the Duke. But with Miss Nethersole, whose Mrs Ebbsmith is really not Mrs Ebbsmith at all, but a female Lucas Cleeve, even that faint scrap of illusion vanishes, and is replaced by a contrast of personal style in flat contradiction to the character relationship which is the subject of the drama. I still do not think The Notorious Mrs Ebbsmith could be made a good play by anything short of treating Agnes's sudden resolution to make Lucas fall in love with her as a comedy motive (as it essentially is), and getting rid of the claptrap about the bible, finishing the play with Lucas's discovery that his wife is quite as good a woman as he could stand life with, and possibly— though on this I do not insist—with Agnes's return to the political platform as the Radical Duchess of St Olpherts. But I am at least quite convinced now that the play as it stands would be much more interesting if the other characters were only half as appropriately impersonated as the Duke of St Olpherts is by Mr Hare, or as Mrs Ebbsmith was by Mrs Campbell.

By the way, I have received a sixpenny pamphlet, by Mr H. Schütz Wilson, entitled The Notorious Mrs Ebbsmith, published by Messrs Bickers. My opinion being thus challenged, I cheerfully acknowledge the pre-eminence of the pamphlet, from my point of view, as the worst pamphlet I ever read on any subject whatsoever. That, however, is only a way of saying that I cannot agree with Mr Schütz Wilson. The difference may be my fault as well as my misfortune. He accepts the play as a great "spiritual tragedy," and considers that the casting of it at the Garrick Theatre was perfect in every part. And so, as he says, "Farewell, Agnes! and may all good go with you in the future. After all, you did not burn THE BOOK."

Readers who have noticed the heading of this article may possibly want to know what Lady Macbeth has to do with it. Well, I have discovered a new Lady Macbeth. It is one of my eccentricities to be old-fashioned in my artistic tastes. For instance, I am fond—unaffectedly fond—of Shakespear's plays. I do not mean actor-managers' editions and revivals; I mean the plays as Shakespear wrote them, played straight through line by line and scene by scene as nearly as possible under the conditions of representation for which they were designed. I have seen the suburban amateurs of the Shakespear Reading Society, seated like Christy minstrels on the platform of the lecture hall at the London Institution, produce, at a moderate computation, about sixty-six times as much effect by reading straight through Much Ado About Nothing as Mr Irving with his expensively mounted and superlatively dull Lyceum version. When these same amateurs invited me to a regular stage performance of Macbeth in aid of the Siddons Memorial Fund, I went, not for the sake of Sarah the Respectable, whose great memory can take care of itself (how much fresher it is, by the way, than those of many writers and painters of her day, though no actor ever makes a speech without complaining that he is cheated out of the immortality every other sort of artist enjoys!), but simply because I wanted to see Macbeth. Mind, I am no admirer of the Elizabethan school. When Mr Henry Arthur Jones, whose collected essays on the English drama I am now engaged in reading, says: "Surely the crowning glory of our nation is our Shakespear; and remember he was one of a great school," I almost burst with the intensity of my repudiation of the second clause in that utterance. What Shakespear got from his "school" was the insane and hideous rhetoric which is all that he has in common with Jonson, Webster, and the whole crew of insufferable bunglers and dullards whose work stands out as vile even at the beginning of the seventeenth century, when every art was corrupted to the marrow by the orgie called the Renaissance, which was nothing but the vulgar exploitation in the artistic professions of the territory won by the Protestant movement. The leaders of that great self-assertion of the growing spirit of man were dead long before the Elizabethan literary rabble became conscious that "ideas" were in fashion, and that any author who could gather a cheap stock of them from murder, lust, and obscenity, and formulate them in rhetorical blank verse, might make the stage pestiferous with plays that have no ray of noble feeling, no touch of faith, beauty, or even common kindness in them from beginning to end. I really cannot keep my temper over the Elizabethan dramatists and the Renaissance; nor would I if I could. The generation which admired them equally admired the pictures of Guido, Giulio Romano, Domenichino, and the Carracci; and I trust it is not nowadays necessary to offer any further samples of its folly. A masterpiece by Carracci—say the smirking Susanna in the National Gallery—would not fetch seven pounds ten at Christie's to-day; but our literary men, always fifty years behind their time because they never look at anything nor listen to anything, but go on working up what they learnt in their boyhood when they read books instead of writing them, still serve up Charles Lamb's hobby, and please themselves by observing that Cyril Tourneur could turn out pretty pairs of lines and string them monotonously together, or that Greene had a genuine groatsworth of popular wit, or that Marlowe, who was perhaps good enough to make it possible to believe that if he had been born thirty years ago he might now have been a tolerable imitator of Mr Rudyard Kipling, dealt in a single special quality of "mighty line." On the strength of these discoveries, they keep up the tradition that these men were slightly inferior Shakespears. Beaumont and Fletcher are, indeed, sometimes cited as hardly inferior; but I will not go into that. I could not do justice to it in moderate language.

As to this performance of Macbeth at St George's Hall, of course it was, from the ordinary professional standpoint, a very bad one. I say this because I well know what happens to a critic when he incautiously praises an amateur. He gets by the next post a letter in the following terms: "Dear Sir,—I am perhaps transgressing the bounds of etiquette in writing privately to you; but I thought you might like to know that your kind notice of my performance as Guildenstern has encouraged me to take a step which I have long been meditating. I have resigned my position as Governor of the Bank of England with a view to adopting the stage as a profession, and trust that the result may justify your too favorable opinion of my humble powers." Therefore I desire it to be distinctly understood that I do not recommend any members of the Macbeth cast to go on the stage. The three witches, Miss Florence Bourne, Miss Longvil, and Miss Munro, were as good as any three witches I ever saw; but the impersonation of witches, as a profession, is almost as precarious as the provision of smoked glasses for looking at eclipses through. Macduff was bad: I am not sure that with his natural advantages he could very easily have been worse; but still, if he feels himself driven to some artistic career by a radical aversion to earning an honest livelihood, and is prepared for a hard apprenticeship of twenty years in mastering the art of the stage—for that period still holds as good as when Talma prescribed it—he can become an actor if he likes. As to Lady Macbeth, she, too, was bad; but it is clear to me that unless she at once resolutely marries some rich gentleman who disapproves of the theatre on principle, she will not be able to keep herself off the stage. She is as handsome as Miss Neilson; and she can hold an audience whilst she is doing everything wrongly. The murder scene was not very good, because Macbeth belonged to the school of the Irish fiddler who, when Ole Bull asked him whether he played by ear or from notes, replied that he played "by main strength"; and you cannot get the brooding horror of the dagger scene by that method. Besides, Miss Lillah McCarthy—that is the lady's name as given in my program—is happily too young to conceive ambition and murder, or the temptation of a husband with a sickly conscience, as realities: they are to her delicious excitements of the imagination, with a beautiful, splendid terror about them, to be conveyed by strenuous pose, and flashing eye, and indomitable bearing. She went at them bravely in this spirit; and they came off more or less happily as her instinct and courage helped her, or her skill failed her. The banquet scene and the sleep-walking scene, which are the easiest passages in the part technically to a lady with the requisite pluck and personal fascination, were quite successful;

and if the earlier scenes were immature, unskilful, and entirely artificial and rhetorical in their conception, still, they were very nearly thrilling. In short, I should like to see Miss Lillah McCarthy play again. I venture on the responsibility of saying that her Lady Macbeth was a highly promising performance, and that some years of hard work would make her a valuable recruit to the London stage. And with that very rash remark I will leave Macbeth, with a fervent wish that Mr Pinero, Mr Grundy, and Monsieur Sardou could be persuaded to learn from it how to write a play without wasting the first hour of the performance in tediously explaining its "construction." They really are mistaken in supposing that Scribe was cleverer than Shakespear.

SARDOODLEDOM

FEDORA (Herman Merivale's English version). By Victorien
 Sardou. Haymarket Theatre, 25 May 1895.
GISMONDA. By Victorien Sardou. Daly's Theatre, 27 May 1895.
THE PRUDE'S PROGRESS. A Comedy in three acts. By Jerome
 K. Jerome and Eden Phillpotts. Comedy Theatre, 22 May 1895.

[1 *June* 1895]

UP to this day week I had preserved my innocence as a playgoer sufficiently never to have seen Fedora. Of course I was not altogether new to it, since I had seen Diplomacy Dora, and Theodora, and La Toscadora, and other machine dolls from the same firm. And yet the thing took me aback. To see that curtain go up again and again only to disclose a bewildering profusion of everything that has no business in a play, was an experience for which nothing could quite prepare me. The postal arrangements, the telegraphic arrangements, the police arrangements, the names and addresses, the hours and seasons, the tables of consanguinity, the railway and shipping time-tables, the arrivals and departures, the whole welter of Bradshaw and Baedeker, Court Guide and Post Office Directory, whirling round one incredible little stage murder and finally vanishing in a gulp of impossible stage poison, made up an entertainment too Bedlamite for any man with settled wits to preconceive. Even the murder was arranged, in pure wantonness, flatly contrary to common sense. The hero is suspected by the heroine of having been a Nihilist at a period when matters were so bad in Russia that refugees who made no secret of their sympathy with the Terrorists were sympathetically welcomed by the strictest Constitutionalists in every other country in Europe. He completely regains her sympathy by proving to her that he is no Nihilist at all, but a common assassin who has deliberately murdered a man out of jealousy. Surely, if dramatists are bent on the fundamentally impossible task of inventing pardonable assassinations, they should recognize that the man who, for no reward or satisfaction to his direct personal instincts, but at the risk of his own life, kills for the sake of an idea, believing that he is striking in the cause of the general weal, is at any rate more respectable than the dehumanized creature who stabs or shoots to slake a passion which he has in common with a stag. I strongly object to heroic criminals, whether political or personal; but if the stage cannot yet get on without its illustrated police news, let us at least shun the most repulsive motives for the stage crimes we are expected to condone. This Loris Ipanoff is a vulgar scoundrel as far as he is credibly human at all; and Fedora, who has at first the excuse of being the avenger of blood, sinks to his level when, on learning that her husband preferred another woman to her, she gloats over his murder, and is disappointed because Loris did not kill his wife on the spot too. Why need plays be so brutally, callously, barbarously immoral as this? I wish Sir Henry Irving would give us at least a matinée of The Lady from the Sea to shew the playgoing public how a humane gentleman acts when he finds he has had the misfortune to lose the affection of his wife. Miss Terry as Ellida would be quite as worthy of the Lyceum Theatre as Nance Oldfield as Miss Terry.

It is greatly to Mrs Patrick Campbell's credit that, bad as the play was, her acting was worse. It was a masterpiece of failure. Not, pray observe, that Mrs Campbell herself did not succeed. The moment she was seen, our reason collapsed and our judgment fled. Every time the curtain fell there was a delirious roar. If the play was not tragic, our infatuation was. I solemnly warn all and sundry that no common man's opinion of the artistic merits of that performance was worth a farthing after the first flash of the heroine's eyes. It was not Fedora; but it was Circe; and I, as sworn critic, must make the best attempt I can to be Ulysses.

It cannot, I think, be disputed now that Mrs Campbell's force, which is intense enough, has only one mode, and that one the vituperative. This was proved at one stroke in the first act, when Fedora goes to her husband's bedside and discovers him dead. Mrs Campbell uttered a shriek, as any actress would; but it was a shriek that suggested nothing of grief, or mortally wounded tenderness, or even horror. What it did suggest very strongly was that Fedora had surprised the secret which Loris reveals to her in the third act. In short, it was a scream of rage. Again in the second act, when Loris admitted the killing of Vladimir, her cry of "Murderer, assassin," might have been any abusive term hurled at a man, appropriately or not, under an impulse of violent anger. Last week I politely attributed to Mrs Campbell's sense of character her catching, as Mrs Ebbsmith, what Miss Nethersole misses: namely, the tone of invective in "Trafalgar Squaring" the Duke of St Olpherts. But it now appears that, her emotion declines to take any other form than that of invective. When she is not abusing somebody, she sits visibly concentrating her forces to restrain the vituperative pressure which is struggling to expand in reckless aggression, the general effect being that of a magnificent woman with a magnificent temper, which she holds in or lets loose with exciting uncertainty. This of course means that Mrs Campbell is not yet mistress of her art, though she has a rare equipment for it. Even her diction is technically defective. In order to secure refinement of tone, she articulates with the tip of her tongue against her front teeth as much as possible. This enters for what it is worth and no more into the method of every fine speaker; but it should not suggest the snobbish Irishman who uses it as a cheap recipe for speaking

genteel English; and once or twice Mrs Campbell came danger-
ously near to producing this mincing effect. For instance, "One
absorbing thought which meeks a sleeve of me," is clearly not
the excess of a genuine refinement of diction, like Sir Henry
Irving's pure vowel method, which would lead him to say "One
ap-sorbing thot which měks a slěv of me" (the p in absorbing
being a German b, and the italic letters pronounced as in the
French *fidèle*). I am only moderately pedantic in this matter, and
do not object at all to Mrs Campbell's saying "Forgimme" for
"Forgive me," or the traditional and ugly "Be't so" for the
correct and pretty "Be it so"; but I protest against "hatrid" and
"disseived," which are pure inaccuracies produced by that Irish
recipe. I make no apology for going into these details; for stage
usage is one of our few standards of diction; and it is rather
alarming to hear the extent to which our younger actresses are
left to pick up the stage trick of speech without in the least
understanding the phonetic part of it.

The death scene begins like a feeble drawing room plagiarism
of the murder of Nancy by Bill Sykes, and ends with the Gilbertian absurdity of the woman, as she realizes with disgust that
her husband actually proposes to commit the vulgarity of strang-
ling her, rising with a dignity which paralyzes him, and saying,
"Oh, if you are determined to behave in that way, I will poison
myself like a lady; and you, I hope, will look on quietly like
a gentleman," or words to that effect. Here Mrs Campbell did
for a moment produce the effect which Sardou has so tediously
and laboriously lath-and-plastered up, and produce it in a way
which shewed unmistakeably that she is quite capable of the
modern equivalents of the whole Bernhardtian range of sensational
effects—effects so enormously popular and lucrative that, though
their production is hardly more of a fine art than lion-taming,
few women who are able for them can resist the temptation to
devote their lives to them. At every other point, Mrs Campbell
threw Sardou out of the window and substituted her own personal magnetism for the stale mechanical tragedy of Fedora. It
was irrelevant; but it was effective.

Sardou's latest edition of the Kiralfian entertainment which Madame Bernhardt has for years past dragged from sea to sea in her Armada of transports, is called Gismonda, and is surpassingly dreary, although it is happily relieved four times by very long waits between the acts. The scene being laid in the Middle Ages, there are no newspapers, letters, or telegrams; but this is far from being an advantage, as the characters tell each other the news all through except when a child is dropped into a tiger's cage as a cue for Madame Bernhardt's popular scream; or when the inevitable stale, puerile love scene is turned on to shew off that "voix céleste" stop which Madame Bernhardt, like a sentimental New England villager with an American organ, keeps always pulled out; or when, in a paroxysm of the basest sensationalism, we are treated to the spectacle of Gismonda chopping a man to death with a hatchet as a preliminary to appearing as a mediæval saint with a palm in her hand at the head of a religious procession. What does it matter whether such an entertainment is called Gismonda, or Theodora, or Venice, or Constantinople, or The Orient, or Captain Boyton's water show? Personally, I prefer the water show, because the sixty-foot header interested me, which Madame Bernhardt has long ceased to do; and the sensation of shooting the chute thrilled me, which Gismonda does not. As a pageant the affair may pass very well with people who, never having been touched by the peculiar spiritual beauty of the art of the Middle Ages, compare the scene-painter's titivated imitations with the Lord Mayor's Show and the architecture of Regent Street instead of with the originals; but it is no more to be compared to the pageantry of King Arthur at the Lyceum than the clever but thoroughly shoppy stage business of Madame Bernhardt is to be compared to the acting of Miss Ellen Terry. I confess I regard with a certain jealousy the extent to which this ex-artist, having deliberately exercised her unquestioned right to step down from the national theatre in which she became famous to posture in a travelling show, is still permitted the privileges and courtesies proper to her former rank. It is open to all actresses to say either, "Give me a dignified living wage and let me work at my art," or, "Give me as much money and applause as can possibly be got out of me, and let my art go hang." Only, when the choice is made, it is the business of the critic to see that the chooser of the lower level does not take precedence of the devoted artist who takes the higher one. Madame Bernhardt has elected to go round the world pretending to kill people with hatchets and hairpins, and making, I presume, heaps of money. I wish her every success; but I shall certainly not treat her as a dramatic artist of the first rank unless she pays me well for it. As a self-respecting critic I decline to be bought for nothing.

It seems a strange thing to me that we should still be so little awake to the fact that in these plays which depend wholly on poignant intensity of expression for the simple emotions the sceptre has passed to the operatic artist. What surprises me is not that this exhibition of Madame Bernhardt's should be flagrantly vulgar and commercial, or that it should be hackneyed and old-fashioned, but that we should dream of going to see it now that we have seen Calvé as Carmen and La Navarraise. In the front ranks of art there is a place for the methods of Duse, and for the drama in which emotion exists only to make thought live and move us, but none for Sarah Bernhardt and the claptraps which Sardou contrives for her. To me, at least, the whole affair seems anti-quated and ridiculous, except when I regard it as a high modern development of the circus and the waxworks. I have seen it, just as I have seen, in my time, Madame Celeste in Green Bushes and The Red Woman. Though I always preferred Buckstone to Sardou as a tragic dramatist, and still do, I used to think Madame Bernhardt a greater actress than Celeste. But I almost believe now that this must have been a delusion of the departed days when Madame Bernhardt was so slim that when she went for a trip in a captive balloon, it was said that her stepping into the car had the same effect as throwing out ballast. At all events, I am quite sure that if I had to choose between seeing Miami and Gismonda again, I should vote eagerly for Miami, who was at least amusing.

To revert for a moment to Fedora, I hope Mrs Campbell will

note that Sarah Bernhardt's career cannot be repeated now—that her art is out of date and her dramas dead. The proof is that Mrs Campbell cannot act Fedora, although to any actress over forty-five Fedora is more natural than Mrs Tanqueray. By the way, I have forgotten to say that Mrs Bancroft is in the cast, and is as amusing and skilful as ever. Mr Tree, confronted with the impossible Loris Ipanoff, was forced to take the part seriously, and, with the help of a Polish make-up, try to pull it through by a creditably awkward attempt at conventional melodramatic acting. Besides, Mrs Campbell ruined his clothes. Wherever her beautiful white arms touched him they left their mark. She knelt at his feet and made a perfect zebra of his left leg with bars across it. Then she flung her arms convulsively right round him; and the next time he turned his back to the footlights there was little to choose between his coatback and his shirtfront. Before the act was over a gallon of benzine would hardly have set him right again. Mr Tree had his revenge at the end of the play, when, in falling on Fedora's body, he managed to transfer a large black patch to her cheek, which was strikingly in evidence when she bowed her acknowledgment of the frantic applause with which the evening ended; but he was still so unhinged by the futility of Loris and the ill-treatment of his garments, that when the audience called for Mr Bancroft he informed them that Mr Bancroft was prevented from coming forward by modesty, but that Mrs Bancroft —and here Mrs Bancroft came forward smiling; and the audience naturally chuckled hugely.

May I suggest that soap and water is an excellent cosmetic for the arms, and that it does not mark coats? Also that this white-washing malpractice has become an intolerable absurdity, and that there is at least one critic who means to try whether ridicule can kill it.

It is an unspeakable relief to get away from Sardou to Mr Jerome K. Jerome, whose Prude's Progress is much better than its name. Happy is the nation that has no history, and happy the play that has no criticism in this column. The Prude's Progress is a shrewd, goodnatured, clever cockney play (Mr Jerome will not think me foolish enough to use cockney as a term of disparagement), interesting and amusing all through, with pleasantly credible characters and pleasantly incredible incidents, ending happily but not fatuously; so that there is no sense of facts shirked on the one hand nor of problems stage-solved on the other. The play, from which, thanks to its unattractive name, not much was expected, won its way and was very favorably received. It is capitally acted, Miss Lena Ashwell being much better fitted than she was in King Arthur as Elaine, and Mr Cyril Maude having at last got a real part to act, instead of being condemned to paint wrinkles on his face, take snuff, and say "damn." Miss Brough and Mr Righton, who does a clever piece of acting by himself in the third act, keep the piece going with their accustomed comic vigor and geniality.

TWO PLAYS

MACAIRE. A melodramatic farce in three acts, by William Ernest Henley and Robert Louis Stevenson. In the New Review, June 1895.

LA FEMME DE CLAUDE. By Alexandre Dumas *fils*. Drury Lane Theatre, 5 June 1895. [8 *June* 1895]

I SEE that Mr William Henley has just published in the New Review the version of Robert Macaire which he made in collaboration with the late R. L. Stevenson. I read the work myself for the first time before the revival of the old version at the Lyceum Theatre; and it has always struck me as a part illustration of the divorce of the stage from literature that we should have had, on the one hand, a famous writer of fiction collaborating with a born master of verse to rescue a famous old harlequinade from obsolescence, and, on the other, a revival of this harlequinade by our leading actor managing our leading theatre; yet that there was no thought of combining the two opportunities, the revival at the theatre proceeding contentedly with the old cheap and common dialogue, written originally with the idea that the play was a serious blood-and-thunder melodrama, whilst the new version circulated quietly in private as a booklet, and finally appears as a magazine contribution. It is a pity that Mr Henley could not very well print the old version in his Review side by side with the new, in order to shew, not only that the old is quite unreadable, and the new so wittily and whimsically turned that every phrase tickles, but that even the stage technique of the new is hugely superior to that of the old. Instead of two elaborate scenes, causing a long interval which a harlequinade will not bear, and entailing extra labor and expense, there is one scene all through, enabling the curtain to be dropped for a moment to point the situations and express conventionally the change from morning to bedtime, and from bedtime to murder-time, without perceptibly breaking the continuity of the extravaganza. The incongruous relics of the original folly of the author are swept away, and the whole brought into the vein of the fantastic variation by which Lemaître rescued the theme from obscurity. The effective situations are preserved and improved; Macaire retains all his old business except the creaking snuff-box, in exchange for which he acquires an epigrammatic philosophy expressed in lines which a distinguished actor need not be ashamed to speak; the ridiculous long-lost wife disappears; the gendarme and the innkeeper become amusing; the murder has the true touch of nightmare: in short, the two "literary men" have beaten the bungling stage "author" at his own craft in every point; outwritten him, outwitted him, outstaged him, and erased him from all future possibility in the eyes of every person of ordinary culture and intelligence who makes the comparison. And yet I have a grim conviction that actors will feel a mysterious "suitability to the stage" in the old version which is missing in the new. This divination of mine is not due to my unaided insight and sympathy, but to the fact that my education as a critic has not been confined to West End theatres. I remember finding myself one evening in the Whitechapel Road with a company of active-minded people, including two well-known ladies of distinguished attainments in oratory and poetry, and a few gentlemen addicted, like myself, to art, literature, and politics. Presently we came upon a specimen of the humblest sort of theatre—a "penny gaff"; and as none of us had ever been in one, and we were all intelligent enough to desire to see the drama of today with its adventitious trappings stripped off, we went in, raising the receipts at the box-office (so to speak) to such an extent that the performance, which had been "just going to begin" for half an hour or so, actually did begin. First, however, the leading lady, who divided her attention between the stage and her baby, which was tucked into the box-seat of the orchestra (an old-fashioned street organ placed close to the door), responded to a certain kindly interest on the part of our poetess in the baby by asking her to warn "her gentleman" to cover up his watch chain, as many of the other gentlemen were "very forgetful." The drama proved intolerable, except so far as it was complicated by an optical illusion of the Pepper's Ghost order, turned on and off at random or at the caprice of a prompter who was no doubt drunk; so, as insect life abounded in the auditorium, we did not wait for the end. But in the fifteen minutes we spent in that gaff, I saw the origin of all the associations which the old actor still misses in the literary man. The conception of theatrical art as the exploitation of popular superstition and ignorance, as the thrilling of poor bumpkins with ghosts and blood, exciting them with blows and stabs, duping them with tawdry affectations of rank and rhetoric, thriving parasitically on their moral diseases instead of purging their souls and refining their senses: this is the tradition that the theatre finds it so hard to get away from. This is why you have one version of Macaire in the New Review and the other at the Lyceum—why an artist of the rank of Coquelin informs his interviewers that there is no author who understands the stage like the author of La Tosca—why an actor so highly respected as Mr Hare produced that genteel edition of the Whitechapel Road drama at the Garrick Theatre without the least scruple—why, too, so many fairly intelligent and reasonable people regard a visit to the theatre as an offence against morality, and others, who go to the theatre themselves, do not consider that a clergyman can fitly be seen there.

Macaire, then, looked at in this light, immediately betrays innumerable deficiencies. The authors have brought a policeman

on the stage without any sense of the audience's fear of a policeman and dreadful joy in seeing someone else arrested; they have
introduced a nobleman without allowing his rank to strike at our
servility or his gold at our envy; they have, with the insensibility
of men who have never been hungry, brought wine and choice
dishes on the stage without knowing their value when flourished
properly in the faces of needy men; they have passed unconsciously
over the "love" interest, forgetting that half the popular use of
the boards is as a pedestal on which to set a well-painted, well-
dressed woman in a strong light, to please the man who is tired
of the mother of sorrows and drudgery at home; and they have
put murder on the stage without calculating on the fact that
murder is only a forbidden joy to people who know no other
reasons than the gallows and the sixth commandment for not
killing those whom they hate or whose property they covet.
When the manager says of a play, "It is not suited to the stage,"
and the critic who has been long enough at his profession to pick
up the managerial point of view follows with his "*Ce n'est pas
du théâtre*": that is fundamentally what they both mean, though
superficially the matter may have a very different air. And it is because Stevenson and Mr Henley substituted for the low cunning
and the cynical experience which makes effective melodramas
out of such calculations, the higher qualities of wit, imagination,
romance, and humor, applied with a literary workmanship which
is at once curiously skilful and carelessly happy, that even the
Lyceum Theatre dared not rise to their level.

Now that the collaboration of the authors of Macaire is broken
up by the death of Stevenson, who must, I think, be admitted to
have got on without the managers rather better than the managers
have got on without him, one wonders whether Mr Henley will
carry on the business alone. The charm of the pair was their combination of artistic faculty with a pleasant boyishness of imagination. Stevenson, always the older of the twain, shewed signs of
growing up, and could even, when kept to the point by the collaboration of his stepson, produce stories that were not obviously
the penny numbers of our boyhood rewritten by a fine hand. But

Mr Henley defies the ravages of time. That amusing mixture of pedantry and hero-worship which marks the schoolboy's cult of athletics survives unabated and unenlightened in Mr Henley's cult of literature. He delights in puerile novels about prize-fighters like Cashel Byron's Profession; he has imagination without sense; he not only adores his literary and artistic heroes, but is violently jealous for their sakes of the reputations of all the others; his attitudes are reverently traditional; experience means to him the works of fiction he has read; at every turn of his pen he shews that cardinal quality of youth, its incapacity for apprehending life at first hand as distinguished from appreciating its presentations and formulations in art and social or scientific theory. And yet he has the romantic imagination and the fine gift of poetic speech which only need some concrete subject-matter—for really plays cannot, like poems or even articles, be made out of purely abstract indignation, scorn, defiance, and so on — to provide Macaire, Admiral Guinea, and the rest with more than worthy successors.

The appearance of Duse at Drury Lane on Wednesday in La Femme de Claude, is too recent for my judgment to have recovered from the emotional disturbance produced by such an appeal as she made to my passion for very fine acting. The furthest extremes of Duse's range as an artist must always, even in this greatest art centre in the world, remain a secret between herself and a few fine observers. I should say without qualification that it is the best modern acting I have ever seen, were it not that the phrase suggests a larger experience of first-rate acting in this department than I possess. I have only seen Salvini and Ristori in their historic-heroic parts, or in Shakespear; and my experience of Coquelin is limited to Molière and such plays of our own day as Les Surprises de Divorce. The work of these three great artists seemed to me (humanly speaking) quite thorough and perfect in its application to their conception of the parts they played; and their conception was, for the most part, adequate, and more than adequate, to the culture of their generation. But their incubatory period was the period before the theatre had advanced to the point at which Wagner and Ibsen became its master spirits. Duse is the first actress whom we have seen applying the method of the great school to characteristically modern parts or to characteristically modern conceptions of old parts. Her style is not, to the attentive observer of the stage, entirely new: nothing arrives at such perfection without many tentative approaches to it. I remember years ago, when The Lady of Lyons was first produced at the Lyceum, being struck with two things about it: first, the fact that Henry Irving, after much striving and, if I may be allowed the expression, not a little floundering, had at last discovered the method of heroic acting; and, second, that in the scene where Claude brings Pauline home after their wedding, Miss Ellen Terry, by a number of delicate touches, slipped into the scene a play of subtle emotion quite foreign to its traditions, with such effect that I can conjure up those moments perfectly to this day, though my utmost effort of memory cannot bring back the very faintest adumbration of any other scene in Pauline's part, which was as useless as material for Miss Terry's peculiar genius as most of those twenty-three Lyceum heroines—Catherine Duval in A Dead Heart, and so forth—of which Mr Clement Scott has made a list for my benefit, evidently to make me cry afresh over the wicked waste of so rare a talent. Of course the twenty-three parts are not all bad parts as parts are reckoned conventionally; and equally of course Miss Terry has not exactly played any of them badly. But neither is Shakespear's Cleopatra a bad part; and neither did Duse exactly play it badly. Yet who on earth would know that Duse was a great actress if he had never seen her play anything but Cleopatra? And who on earth will ever know what Miss Terry can do if we are never to see her except in plays that date, in feeling if not in actual composition, from the dark ages before the Married Women's Property Act? I can only guess at her powers myself from my recollections of the old Court Theatre, and the little interpolations in the Lyceum parts by which her genius so often instinctively thrusts through the old play to the new style, only, of course, to be beaten back by the giving out of the material. Still, just in these thrustings you could see Duse's style coming.

Long after the Lady of Lyons came Miss Janet Achurch, whose playing as Alexandra, in Voss's play, came nearer to Duse's work in subtlety, continuity and variety of detail, and in beauty of execution, than anything I have seen on the English stage. But Duse has been helped to her supremacy by the fortunate sternness of Nature in giving her nothing but her genius. Miss Ellen Terry is a woman of quite peculiar and irresistible personal charm. Miss Achurch has been kept in constant danger of missing the highest distinction in her art by having, as an extra and cheaper string to her bow, an endowment of conventional good looks, and a large share of that power of expressing all the common emotions with extraordinary intensity which makes the vulgar great actress of the Bernhardt school. Consequently you have two Miss Achurches: the Miss Achurch of Nora and Alexandra, and the Miss Achurch of Adrienne and Forget-me-not; and there are moments when the two get mixed. But in Duse you necessarily get the great school in its perfect integrity, because Duse without her genius would be a plain little woman of no use to any manager, whereas Miss Terry or Miss Achurch, if they had no more skill than can be acquired by any person of ordinary capacity in the course of a few years' experience, would always find a certain degree of favor as pretty leading ladies. Duse, *with* her genius, is so fascinating that it is positively difficult to attend to the play instead of attending wholly to her. The extraordinary richness of her art can only be understood by those who have studied the process by which an actress is built up. You offer a part to a young lady who is an enthusiastic beginner. She reads it devoutly, and forms, say, half a dozen great ideas as to points which she will make. The difficulty then is to induce her to do nothing between these points; so that the play may be allowed at such moments to play itself. Probably when it comes to the point, these intervals will prove the only effective periods during her performance, the points being ill chosen or awkwardly executed. The majority of actresses never get beyond learning not to invent new points for themselves, but rather to pick out in their parts the passages which admit of certain well worn and tried old points being reapplied. When they have learnt to make these points smoothly and to keep quiet between whiles with a graceful air of having good reasons for doing nothing, they are finished actresses. The great actress has a harder struggle. She goes on inventing her points and her business determinedly, constantly increasing the original half-dozen, and constantly executing them with greater force and smoothness. A time comes when she is always making points, and making them well; and this is the finishing point with some actresses. But with the greatest artists there soon commences an integration of the points into a continuous whole, at which stage the actress appears to make no points at all, and to proceed in the most unstudied and "natural" way. This rare consummation Duse has reached. An attentive study of her Marguerite Gauthier, for instance, by a highly trained observer of such things, will bring to light how its apparently simple strokes are combinations of a whole series of strokes, separately conceived originally, and added one by one to the part, until finally, after many years of evolution, they have integrated into one single highly complex stroke. Take, as a very simple illustration, the business of Camille's tying up the flowers in the third act. It seems the most natural thing in the world; but it is really the final development of a highly evolved dance with the arms—even, when you watch it consciously, a rather prolonged and elaborate one. The strokes of character have grown up in just the same way. And this is the secret of the extraordinary interest of such acting. There are years of work, bodily and mental, behind every instant of it—work, mind, not mere practice and habit, which is quite a different thing. It is the rarity of the gigantic energy needed to sustain this work which makes Duse so exceptional; for the work is in her case highly intellectual work, and so requires energy of a quality altogether superior to the mere head of steam needed to produce Bernhardtian explosions with the requisite regularity. With such high energy, mere personal fascination becomes a thing which the actress can put off and on like a garment. Sarah Bernhardt has nothing but her own charm, for the exhibition of which Sardou contrives love scenes—save the mark. Duse's own

private charm has not yet been given to the public. She gives you
Césarine's charm, Marguerite Gauthier's charm, the charm of La
Locandiera, the charm, in short, belonging to the character she
impersonates; and you are enthralled by its reality and delighted
by the magical skill of the artist without for a moment feeling any
complicity either on your own part or hers in the passion represented. And with that clue to the consistency of supreme admiration for the artist with perfect respect for the woman—a combination so rare that some people doubt its possibility—I must
leave discussion of the plays she has appeared in this week to my
next article.

DUSE AND BERNHARDT

[15 *June* 1895]

Mr William Archer's defence of the dramatic critics against
Mr Street's indictment of them for their indifference to acting appears to be falling through. Mr Archer pleads that whereas Hazlitt and Leigh Hunt had frequent opportunities of comparing
ambitious actors in famous parts, the modern dramatic critic
spends his life in contemplating "good acting plays" without any
real people in them, and performers who do not create or inter-
pret characters, but simply lend their pretty or popular persons,
for a consideration, to fill up the parts. Mr Archer might have
added another reason which applies to nearly all modern works:
to wit, the operation of our copyright laws, whereby actors and
actresses acquire the right not only to perform new plays but to
prevent anyone else from performing them. Nevertheless we
critics can now at last outdo Hazlitt and Leigh Hunt if we have a
mind to; for we have just had two Mrs Ebbsmiths to compare,
besides a fourth Fedora, and Duse and Sarah Bernhardt playing
La Dame aux Camélias and Sudermann's Heimat against one
another at Daly's Theatre and at Drury Lane. Clearly now or
never is the time for a triumphant refutation of the grievance of the
English actor against the English Press: namely, that hardly any
critic knows enough about acting to be able to distinguish between an effective part and a well played one, or between the bag

of tricks which every old hand carries and the stock of ideas and sense of character which distinguish the master-actor from the mere handy man.

This week began with the relapse of Sarah Bernhardt into her old profession of serious actress. She played Magda in Suder-mann's Heimat, and was promptly challenged by Duse in the same part at Drury Lane on Wednesday. The contrast between the two Magdas is as extreme as any contrast could possibly be between artists who have finished their twenty years apprentice-ship to the same profession under closely similar conditions. Madame Bernhardt has the charm of a jolly maturity, rather spoilt and petulant, perhaps, but always ready with a sunshine-through-the-clouds smile if only she is made much of. Her dresses and diamonds, if not exactly splendid, are at least splendacious; her figure, far too scantily upholstered in the old days, is at its best; and her complexion shews that she has not studied modern art in vain. Those charming roseate effects which French painters produce by giving flesh the pretty color of strawberries and cream, and painting the shadows pink and crimson, are cunningly reproduced by Madame Bernhardt in the living picture. She paints her ears crimson and allows them to peep enchantingly through a few loose braids of her auburn hair. Every dimple has its dab of pink; and her finger-tips are so delicately incarnadined that you fancy they are transparent like her ears, and that the light is shining through their delicate blood-vessels. Her lips are like a newly painted pillar box; her cheeks, right up to the languid lashes, have the bloom and surface of a peach; she is beautiful with the beauty of her school, and entirely inhuman and incred-ible. But the incredibility is pardonable, because, though it is all the greatest nonsense, nobody believing in it, the actress herself least of all, it is so artful, so clever, so well recognized a part of the business, and carried off with such a genial air, that it is impossible not to accept it with good-humor. One feels, when the heroine bursts on the scene, a dazzling vision of beauty, that instead of imposing on you, she adds to her own piquancy by looking you straight in the face, and saying, in effect: "Now who would ever suppose that I am a grandmother?" That, of course, is irresistible; and one is not sorry to have been coaxed to relax one's notions of the dignity of art when she gets to serious business and shews how ably she does her work. The coaxing suits well with the childishly egotistical character of her acting, which is not the art of making you think more highly or feel more deeply, but the art of making you admire her, pity her, champion her, weep with her, laugh at her jokes, follow her fortunes breathlessly, and applaud her wildly when the curtain falls. It is the art of finding out all your weaknesses and practising on them—cajoling you, harrowing you, exciting you—on the whole, fooling you. And it is always Sarah Bernhardt in her own capacity who does this to you. The dress, the title of the play, the order of the words may vary; but the woman is always the same. She does not enter into the leading character: she substitutes herself for it.

All this is precisely what does not happen in the case of Duse, whose every part is a separate creation. When she comes on the stage, you are quite welcome to take your opera-glass and count whatever lines time and care have so far traced on her. They are the credentials of her humanity; and she knows better than to obliterate that significant handwriting beneath a layer of peach-bloom from the chemist's. The shadows on her face are grey, not crimson; her lips are sometimes nearly grey also; there are neither dabs nor dimples; her charm could never be imitated by a bar-maid with unlimited pin money and a row of footlights before her instead of the handles of a beer-engine. The result is not so discouraging as the patrons of the bar might suppose. Wilkes, who squinted atrociously, boasted that he was only quarter of an hour behind the handsomest man in Europe: Duse is not in action five minutes before she is quarter of a century ahead of the hand-somest woman in the world. I grant that Sarah's elaborate Monna Lisa smile, with the conscious droop of the eyelashes and the long carmined lips coyly disclosing the brilliant row of teeth, is effec-tive of its kind—that it not only appeals to your susceptibilities, but positively jogs them. And it lasts quite a minute, sometimes longer. But Duse, with a tremor of the lip which you feel rather than see, and which lasts half an instant, touches you straight on the very heart; and there is not a line in the face, or a cold tone in the grey shadow that does not give poignancy to that tremor. As to youth and age, who can associate purity and delicacy of emotion, and simplicity of expression, with the sordid craft that repels us in age; or voluptuous appeal and egotistical self-insistence with the candor and generosity that attract us in youth? Who ever thinks of Potiphar's wife as a young woman, or St Elizabeth of Hungary as an old one? These associations are horribly unjust to age, and undeserved by youth: they belong of right to differences of character, not of years; but they rule our imaginations; and the great artist profits by them to appear eternally young. However, it would be a critical blunder as well as a personal folly on my part to suggest that Duse, any more than Sarah Bernhardt, neglects any art that could heighten the effect of her acting when she is impersonating young and pretty women. The truth is that in the art of being beautiful, Madame Bernhardt is a child beside her. The French artist's stock of attitudes and facial effects could be catalogued as easily as her stock of dramatic ideas: the counting would hardly go beyond the fingers of both hands. Duse produces the illusion of being infinite in variety of beautiful pose and motion. Every idea, every shade of thought and mood, expresses itself delicately but vividly to the eye; and yet, in an apparent million of changes and inflexions, it is impossible to catch any line at an awkward angle, or any strain interfering with the perfect abandonment of all the limbs to what appears to be their natural gravitation towards the finest grace. She is ambidextrous and supple, like a gymnast or a panther; only the multitude of ideas which find physical expression in her movements are all of that high quality which marks off humanity from the animals, and, I fear I must add, from a good many gymnasts. When it is remembered that the majority of tragic actors excel only in explosions of those passions which are common to man and brute, there will be no difficulty in understanding the indescribable distinction which Duse's acting acquires from the fact that behind every stroke of it is a distinctively human idea. In nothing is this more apparent than in the vigilance in her of that high human instinct which seeks to awaken the deepest responsive feeling without giving pain. In La Dame aux Camélias, for instance, it is easy for an intense actress to harrow us with her sorrows and paroxysms of phthisis, leaving us with a liberal pennyworth of sensation, not fundamentally distinguishable from that offered by a public execution, or any other evil in which we still take a hideous delight. As different from this as light from darkness is the method of the actress who shews us how human sorrow can express itself only in its appeal for the sympathy it needs, whilst striving by strong endurance to shield others from the infection of its torment. That is the charm of Duse's interpretation of the stage poem of Marguerite Gauthier. It is unspeakably touching because it is exquisitely considerate: that is, exquisitely sympathetic. No physical charm is noble as well as beautiful unless it is the expression of a moral charm; and it is because Duse's range includes these moral high notes, if I may so express myself, that her compass, extending from the depths of a mere predatory creature like Claude's wife up to Marguerite Gauthier at her kindest or Magda at her bravest, so immeasurably dwarfs the poor little octave and a half on which Sarah Bernhardt plays such pretty canzonets and stirring marches.

Obvious as the disparity of the two famous artists has been to many of us since we first saw Duse, I doubt whether any of us realized, after Madame Bernhardt's very clever performance as Magda on Monday night, that there was room in the nature of things for its annihilation within forty-eight hours by so comparatively quiet a talent as Duse's. And yet annihilation is the only word for it. Sarah was very charming, very jolly when the sun shone, very petulant when the clouds covered it, and positively angry when they wanted to take her child away from her. And she did not trouble us with any fuss about the main theme of Sudermann's play, the revolt of the modern woman against that ideal of home which exacts the sacrifice of her whole life to its care, not by her grace, and as its own sole help and refuge, but as a right which it has to the services of all females as abject slaves.

In fact, there is not the slightest reason to suspect Madame Bernhardt of having discovered any such theme in the play; though
Duse, with one look at Schwartze, the father, nailed it to the stage
as the subject of the impending dramatic struggle before she had
been five minutes on the scene. Before long, there came a stroke
of acting which will probably never be forgotten by those who
saw it, and which explained at once why those artifices of the
dressing-table which help Madame Bernhardt would hinder
Duse almost as much as a screen placed in front of her. I should
explain, first, that the real name of the play is not Magda but
Home. Magda is a daughter who has been turned out of doors for
defying her father, one of those outrageous persons who mistake
their desire to have everything their own way in the house for a
sacred principle of home life. She has a hard time of it, but at last
makes a success as an opera singer, though not until her lonely
struggles have thrown her for sympathy on a fellow student, who
in due time goes his way, and leaves her to face motherhood as
best she can. In the fullness of her fame she returns to her native
town, and in an attack of homesickness makes advances to her
father, who consents to receive her again. No sooner is she in-
stalled in the house than she finds that one of the most intimate
friends of the family is the father of her child. In the third act of
the play she is on the stage when he is announced as a visitor. It
must be admitted that Sarah Bernhardt played this scene very
lightly and pleasantly: there was genuine good fellowship in the
way in which she reassured the embarrassed gallant and made
him understand that she was not going to play off the sorrows of
Gretchen on him after all those years, and that she felt that she
owed him the priceless experience of maternity, even if she did
not particularly respect him for it. Her self-possession at this point
was immense: the peach-bloom never altered by a shade. Not so
with Duse. The moment she read the card handed her by the
servant, you realized what it was to have to face a meeting with
the man. It was interesting to watch how she got through it when
he came in, and how, on the whole, she got through it pretty
well. He paid his compliments and offered his flowers; they sat

down; and she evidently felt that she had got it safely over and might allow herself to think at her ease, and to look at him to see how much he had altered. Then a terrible thing happened to her. She began to blush; and in another moment she was conscious of it, and the blush was slowly spreading and deepening until, after a few vain efforts to avert her face or to obstruct his view of it without seeming to do so, she gave up and hid the blush in her hands. After that feat of acting I did not need to be told why Duse does not paint an inch thick. I could detect no trick in it: it seemed to me a perfectly genuine effect of the dramatic imagination. In the third act of La Dame aux Camélias, where she produces a touching effect by throwing herself down, and presently rises with her face changed and flushed with weeping, the flush is secured by the preliminary plunge to a stooping attitude, imagination or no imagination; but Magda's blush did not admit of that explanation; and I must confess to an intense professional curiosity as to whether it always comes spontaneously.

I shall make no attempt to describe the rest of that unforgettable act. To say that it left the house not only frantically applauding, but actually roaring, is to say nothing; for had we not applauded Sarah as Gismonda and roared at Mrs Patrick Campbell as Fedora? But there really was something to roar at this time. There was a real play, and an actress who understood the author and was a greater artist than he. And for me, at least, there was a confirmation of my sometimes flagging faith that a dramatic critic is really the servant of a high art, and not a mere advertiser of entertainments of questionable respectability of motive.

LA PRINCESSE LOINTAINE

LA PRINCESSE LOINTAINE. By Edmond Rostand. Daly's Theatre, 17 June 1895. [22 *June* 1895]

THE romance of chivalry has its good points; but it always dies of the Unwomanly Woman. And M. Rostand's Princess Far Away will die of Melissinde. A first act in which the men do nothing but describe their hysterical visions of a wonderful goddess-princess whom they have never seen is bad enough; but it is pardonable, because men do make fools of themselves about women, sometimes in an interesting and poetic fashion. But when the woman appears and plays up to the height of their folly, intoning her speeches to an accompaniment of harps and horns, distributing lilies and languors to pilgrims, and roses and raptures to troubadours, always in the character which their ravings have ascribed to her, what can one feel except that an excellent opportunity for a good comedy is being thrown away? If Melissinde would only eat something, or speak in prose, or only swear in it, or do anything human—were it even smoking a cigaret— to bring these silly Argonauts to their senses for a moment, one could forgive her. But she remains an unredeemed humbug from one end of the play to the other; and when, at the climax of one of her most deliberately piled-up theatrical entrances, a poor green mariner exclaims, with open-mouthed awe, "The Blessed Virgin!" it sends a twinge of frightful blasphemous irony down one's spine. Having felt that, I now understand better than before why the Dulcinea episodes in Don Quixote are so coarse in comparison to the rest of the book. Cervantes had been driven into reactionary savagery by too much Melissinde.

It is a pity that the part of M. Rostand's play which deals with the shipful of enthusiasts did not get over the footlights better; for it is touched here and there with a certain modern freedom of spirit, and has some grace, youth, and imagination in it. But it lacks the force which comes from wisdom and originality. The prettiest descriptions of Melissinde are spoiled by the reflection —inevitable in an audience saturated with the Bernhardt tradition—that they are only leading up to the entrance of the star. Besides, they are in the verse of a rhythmless language. I know that many English people declare that they appreciate this verse; and I know also that they sometimes follow up their declaration by asking you whether you pronounce Fédora as Fay'dera or Fido'ra, a question which no Frenchman could even understand. But to me French verse is simply not verse at all. I know it as a blind man knows color: that is, by the current explanations of it. When I read alexandrines, I cook them, in spite of myself, so as to make them scan like the last line of a stanza in Childe Harold: for instance, if I may illustrate by combining Rostand and Byron:

> Te voyant accoutré d'une manière telle,
> He rushed into the field, and, foremost fighting, fell,
> Pour porter monseigneur vers sa Dame Lointaine
> And fertilize the field that each pretends to gain.

This, I know, is deplorable; but it would be useless for me to attempt to conceal my hopeless deficiencies as a linguist. I am very sorry; but I cannot learn languages. I have tried hard, only to find that men of ordinary capacity can learn Sanscrit in less time than it takes me to buy a German dictionary. The worst of it is that this disability of mine seems to be most humiliatingly exceptional. My colleagues sit at French plays, German plays, and Italian plays, laughing at all the jokes, thrilling with all the fine sentiments, and obviously seizing the finest shades of the language; whilst I, unless I have read the play beforehand, or asked someone during the interval what it is about, must either struggle with a sixpenny "synopsis" which invariably misses the real point of the drama, or else sit with a guilty conscience and a blank countenance, drawing the most extravagantly wrong inferences from the dumb show of the piece. The torture of this can only be adequately apprehended when it is considered that in ordinary novels, or plays, or conversations, the majority of sentences have no definite meaning at all; and that an energetic intellectual effort to grapple with them, such as one makes in trying to understand a foreign language, would at once discover their inconclusiveness, inaccuracy, and emptiness. When I listen to an English play I am not troubled by not understanding when there is nothing to understand, because I understand at once that there is nothing to understand. But at a foreign play I do not understand this; and every sentence that means nothing in particular—say five out of six in the slacker moments of the action—seems to me to be a sentence of which I have missed the meaning through my unhappy and disgraceful ignorance of the language. Hence torments of shame and inefficiency, the betrayal of which would destroy my reputation as a critic at one blow. Of course I have a phrase or two ready at the end of my tongue to conceal my ignorance. My command of operatic Italian is almost copious, as might be expected from my experience as a musical critic. I can make love in Italian; I could challenge a foe to a duel in Italian if I were not afraid of him; and if I swallowed some agonizing mineral poison, I could describe my sensations very eloquently. And I could manage a prayer pretty well. But these accomplishments are too special for modern comedy and ordinary conversation. As to French, I can neither speak it nor understand it when spoken without an impracticably long interval for reflection; and I am, besides, subject to a curious propensity, when addressed by Italian or French people, to reply in fluent German, though on all other occasions that language utterly baffles me. On the whole, I come off best at the theatre in such a case as that of Magda, where I began by reading the synopsis, then picked up a little of the play in French at Daly's Theatre, then a little more in Italian at Drury Lane, then a little more in German from the book, and finally looked at Duse and was illuminated beyond all the powers of all the books and languages on earth.

I may now return to M. Rostand's play with an easy conscience, since I have made it plain that my sense that its versification is a drawback to it may be the effect of pure ignorance on my part. Certainly it made it verbose, and destroyed the illusion of the seafaring scenes by setting all the sailors monotonously bawling their phrases like street cries, in the manner of M. Mounet Sully and the Comédie Française, though of course they stopped short of the worst declamatory horrors of that institution. And in some subtle way, it led on the two troubadours, Joffroy Rudel and Bertrand d'Allamanon, to make themselves ridiculous. About Joffroy (M. de Max) there was no mistake from the very beginning. As he lay moribund on his litter, his large dark eyes were fixed in profound pity for himself; and his lips were wreathed in a smile of ineffable complacency at the thought of how well his eyes looked. He smiled all poor M. Rostand's poetry overboard within a minute of his entrance; and it then became a question whether Bertrand (M. Guitry) could raise it from the depths in the second and third acts, in which Joffroy does not appear. But though M. Guitry did not smile at all, being, in fact, as serious a man as any poet could desire, the audience laughed outright at Bertrand. In vain did Madame Bernhardt work up his entrance by tearing off her white sleeves and throwing them out of the window to him, enjoining him to redden them in the gore of the gigantic green knight. In vain did he dash in spinning with the impetus of his charge, whirling his falchion in the air, and bearing on his brow a gash which suggested that the green knight, before succumbing, had sliced the top off his head like the lid of a saucepan. The audience only laughed. They laughed again when he fainted; they shrieked when Sorismonde (the inevitable confidante) said "He is better"; and they might have ended by laughing the piece off the stage had he not reminded Melissinde that she had no sleeves on, whereupon she became conscious of herself, and a blushing silence fell on the house. It was really not M. Guitry's fault: for the life of me I cannot see what he could have done other than what he did; but I cannot pretend that I take a very severe view of the bad manners of the audience in laughing. However, his entrance, like several of the exciting events on the ship in the first act, might have been better stage-managed. The great modern master of such effects is Richard Wagner, with regard to whom the French nation is still in a comparatively benighted condition. The stage manager who wishes to work up the arrival of a champion or the sighting of land from a ship had better go to Bayreuth and watch the first acts of Lohengrin and Tristan, unless he is content to run the risk of making modern audiences laugh. But I do not think very much could be done with M. Rostand's scene leading up to Bertrand's arrival in any case. Melissinde and Sorismonde describing the attack from the window—"Oh, quel superbe élan!" and so on —is not to be compared either to Rebecca describing the onslaught of the black knight to Ivanhoe, or Klingsor's running commentary to Kundry on the havoc made by Parsifal among the knights of the flower maidens.

As to Madame Bernhardt's own performance, it is not humanly possible for an actress to do very much with a play in which, when the other characters are not describing what a peerlessly beautiful and wonderful creature she is, she is herself on the stage accepting that ridiculous position. But the moment Madame Bernhardt entered one very welcome reform was evident. The elaborate make-up which I took the liberty of describing in some detail in my last article, and which made Gismonda and Magda so impossibly like goddesses in a Tiepolesque ceiling, had all but disappeared. Melissinde had a face, not a stucco mask: she was a real woman, not a hairdresser's shop-window image. And what an improvement it was! How Madame Bernhardt can ever have supposed that her face is less interesting or attractive than the complexion which she carries in her dressing-bag, or that she has anything to gain by trying to make herself look like the silliest sort of lady of fashion, would be a mystery to me if it were not only too evident that she no longer brings to her art the immense pressure of thought and labor which earns for the greatest artists that rarest of all faiths, faith in their real selves. She looked much better; but there was very little thought, very little work, and consequently very little interest in her performance. Fortunately for her, she still has exceptional nervous power; and she has not altogether forgotten those situations in her old parts which repeat themselves with more or less inessential modification in her new ones. This, to so clever a woman, with such a reputation, is enough to enable her to play the great actress still. But it should not satisfy London criticism. Take, for example, the end of the third act of this Princesse Lointaine, which she selects as her opportunity for one of those displays of vehemence which are expected from her as part of the conventional Bernhardt exhibition. It is pure rant and nothing else. When once she begins to tear through her lines at the utmost pitch and power of her voice, she shews no further sense of what she is saying, and is unable to recover herself when, in the final speech, the feeling changes. As her physical endurance threatens to fail she tears along the faster, and finally rushes off the stage in a forced frenzy. I do not deny that there is something very exciting in a blind whirlwind of roaring energy. I have seen a working-class audience spring to their feet and cheer madly for three minutes at it. But then the artist was Mr John Burns, who can give Madame Bernhardt a start of several miles at that particular sort of effect, and beat her easily. And I am bound to say, in justice to Mr Burns, that I have never seen him bring down the curtain in this fashion until the play was really over, or substitute the peroration for the business part of the speech, whereas Madame Bernhardt does deliberately substitute rant for the business of the play. Again, Mr Burns does it to amuse an election meeting of working men who are tired of sitting still: he does not offer it as serious political oratory in the House of Commons. I need hardly say that it is not the sort of effect that improves as the artist grows older, since it can only be produced by sustained physical violence. It is quite different from those effects which great players produce at a dramatic climax by working up the scene, through sheer force of acting, to the pitch at which, when the crucial moment comes, the effect makes itself, the artist's work being then over, though the audience is persuaded that some stupendous magnetic explosion has taken place. No doubt some of my readers have witnessed that scene in which Queen Elizabeth and her court seemed to vanish miraculously from the stage, apparently swept into nothingness when Ristori let loose her wrath as Marie Stuart; or they may have seen the same effect produced by Salvini when the king flies in disorder from the play scene in Hamlet. But it is only the critic, watching and listening with the same intensity with which the performer acts, who, when asked what extraordinary thing Ristori or Salvini did at that supreme moment to work such a miracle, is able to reply that they did nothing. Elizabeth and Claudius ran off the stage with their courts after them: that was all. Ristori and Salvini simply looked on, having already wrought the scene to the point at which the flight of the rest produced the necessary effect on the imagination of the audience. I need hardly refer again to the effect made last week by the third act of Sudermann's Home, as Duse played it. I only ask anyone who saw that performance to try to imagine —if he has the heart to do it—such an artistic scandal as that great actress suddenly throwing her part to the winds and substituting for it a good two minutes rant, like the finish to the third act of La Princesse Lointaine. The public should learn to distinguish in these matters consciously as well as unconsciously. Ranting is not, as it is generally assumed to be, bad acting. It is not acting at all, but the introduction of an exhibition of force for the sake of force. And let us not affect to deny that when the performer has strength enough to raise the pressure to hurricane pitch, a successful rant is attractive and exciting, provided only the performer is clearly doing it on purpose, and is not an epileptic or a lunatic. But it takes not only purpose but reason to humanize force and raise it to the rank of a factor in fine art. It is the strength that is completely controlled and utilized that takes the crown: it is your Ristori, your Salvini, your Duse, with their unfailing hold and yet exquisitely delicate touch upon their parts, their sleeplessly vigilant sense of beauty of thought, feeling, and action, and their prodigious industry, that are recognized as the real athletes of the stage, compared with whom the ranters are weaklings and sluggards. That, at least, must be the judgment of London. Artists of international fame do not come to this capital of the world for money, but for reputation; and the London critic should be jealous above all things of letting that reputation go cheaply. When Duse gives us her best work, we cannot be too emphatic in declaring that it is best of the best and magnificent; so that our hall-mark may be carried through the nations on a piece of sterling gold. But when Madame Bernhardt gives us pinchbeck plays and acting that is poor in thought and eked out with odds and ends stripped from her old parts; when she rants at us and brings down the house in a London theatre just as she brings it down in a provincial American one, we must tell her that she can do better than that, and that we will have nothing less than her best. When she offers us her reputation instead of first-rate acting, we must reply that we give reputations instead of taking them, and that we accept nothing in exchange except first-rate acting down on the counter, without a moment's credit. Already there are signs that she is waking up to the situation. The failure of Gismonda to elicit any expression of the deep respect which really fine work imposes, even on those who prefer something cheaper; the sudden and complete obliteration of her Magda by Duse's first five minutes in the part; the fatal compliments by which her most enthusiastic champions have exposed the commonness and obviousness of the intellectual material of her acting: something of all this may have penetrated to her through the barrier of language and the incense-clouds of flattery; for it looked as if on Monday the disappearance of the Gismonda make-up were only a symptom of a more serious attitude towards London. I suggest, now, that the rant should be discarded as well, and replaced by a genuine study and interpretation of the passages which are sacrificed to it. I further suggest, as a musical critic, that the shallow trick of intoning which sets so many of my musically neglected colleagues babbling about the "golden voice" should be discarded too. Miss Rehan, who is coming next week, will expose the musical emptiness of Madame Bernhardt's habit of monotonously chanting sentences on one note, as effectually as Duse has exposed the intellectual emptiness of her Magda. Of course, intoning is easy—as easy as holding down one key of an accordion and keeping up a mellifluous smile all the time; but it dehumanizes speech, and after some minutes becomes maddening, so that a flash of fun or a burst of rage is doubly welcome because it for a moment alters that eternal pitch and timbre. Some critics speak of "the melody" of it, as to which I can only say that the man who finds melody in one sustained note would find exquisite curves in a packing case. I therefore respectfully urge Madame Bernhardt to add a complete set of strings to her lyre before Miss Rehan comes. Otherwise there will be fresh comparisons of the most disparaging kind.

My apologies for postponing notice of the Ducal Court Company of Saxe-Coburg and Gotha and their orchestra until next week.

MR DALY FOSSILIZES

The Railroad of Love. Comedy in four acts adapted by Augustin Daly from the German of Frau von Schonthan. Daly's Theatre, 25 June 1895.

The Strange Adventures of Miss Brown. A new and original farcical play by Robert Buchanan and Charles Marlowe. Vaudeville Theatre, 26 June 1895.   [29 *June* 1895]

Yet another foreign language—that of Amurrica! And Mr Augustin Daly again! What is to be done with Mr Daly? How shall we open his mind to the fact that he stands on the brink of the twentieth century in London and not with Mr Vincent Crummles at Portsmouth in the early Dickens days? I have in my hand the program of last Tuesday's performance. One character is described as "a polished relic of wasted energies," another as "not half a bad sort of parent, and an excellent judge of— Latour '70." A lady is catalogued as "a goldfish of much experience—not to be caught on the fly." This program measures twenty-one inches by seven and a quarter, and the decorative printing is in blue ink. Why is it not printed on tissue paper; why does not the blue come off on my fingers; why did I not buy it from an orange seller outside the theatre? Not, I am sure, from any desire on Mr Daly's part to break with the tradition of my boyhood, but doubtless because the manufacture of the old playbill is a lost art here. I picture Mr Daly, vainly searching London for that particular sort of tissue paper and that crayon-like blue ink, trembling lest the public should think him outlandish and unprofessional without them. Bless your innocence, dear Mr Daly, such things have not been known in London for so long that I am regarded as an old fogey because they were once familiar to me. As for the facetious comments on the characters, they linger, perhaps, in pantomime season, when the clock goes back fifty years by general consent; but at a West End theatre at the

163

end of June we stare at them in polite amazement as we did at the Strand Theatre years ago, when you first came over and bereaved us of breath by ending up each act of your comedies by a harlequinade rally in which negro servants entered and upset each other over the furniture.

Things have changed in many respects since those old days at the Strand. Mr Daly, the lessee of one of the handsomest of our London theatres, is in quite a different position to Mr Daly the manager of an American company making a holiday experiment in a house not associated with dramatic work of the finest class. Furthermore, our standard of fineness in dramatic work has gone up since then. The German sentimental farce in several acts, Americanized by Mr Daly, was natural, frank, amusing, and positively lifelike in comparison with the plays which were regarded as dramatic masterpieces in the eighties. Diplomacy and Peril, Clancarty and Still Waters Run Deep, Our Boys, New Men and Old Acres, and, by way of advanced psychological drama dealing with the question of the sexes, Forget-me-Not went not an inch deeper into life than Mr Daly's adaptations, and were, on the whole, less genial and worse acted. Mrs Gilbert and Miss Rehan, Mr Lewis and Mr Drew, were individually quite equal to their most formidable competitors in the days when Mrs and Mr Kendal were at the height of their popularity; and the combination of the four in one company was irresistible.

I wonder how far Mr Daly realizes how completely that state of things has gone by. When Mr Charrington produced Ibsen's Doll's House at the Royalty in 1889, he smashed up the British drama of the eighties. Not that the public liked Ibsen: he was infinitely too good for that. But the practical business point is not how people like Ibsen, but how they liked Byron, Sardou, and Tom Taylor after Ibsen. And that is the point that our managers miss. It seems easy to count the money that the public paid to see A Doll's House, and the money it paid to see Diplomacy, and to conclude from the huge excess of the latter sum that there is more money in Sardou than in Ibsen. But when Mr Comyns Carr proceeds to apply this conclusion by producing

Sardou's Delia Harding, after nine plays of Ibsen's had been seen in London, he finds it received with open derision, and with such slender pecuniary results that it would have paid him better to produce even Emperor or Galilean, the most impossible, commercially speaking, of all Ibsen's works. That does not prove, however, that the substitution of Ibsen for Sardou is the worldly wise course for the manager, since Ibsen's work is much further above the public capacity than Sardou's is below it. What the manager has to do is to measure as exactly as possible the effect on public taste produced by the series of artistic experiments, by the Independent Theatre Society and others, included between Mr Charrington's production of A Doll's House and that of Arms and the Man at the Avenue Theatre last year. Never mind whether these experiments were pecuniary successes or not: the question is how far they altered the fashion in pecuniarily successful pieces. A glance at the contemporary stage shews the difference. Compare Lady Windermere's Fan, The Second Mrs Tanqueray, and The Case of Rebellious Susan with the repertory whose gems, from the box-office point of view, were The Ironmaster and A Scrap of Paper, not to repeat my former instances! The change is evident at once. In short, a modern manager need not produce The Wild Duck; but he must be very careful not to produce a play which will seem insipid and old-fashioned to playgoers who have seen The Wild Duck, even though they may have hissed it.

This is the lesson that Mr Daly has not learnt. When he first came, there was nothing more old-fashioned about his productions than the archaic playbills, the horseplay at the ends of the acts, and the doggerel tags before the final curtain. But nowadays the plays themselves are old-fashioned with the most dangerous sort of old-fashionedness: that is, they are ten years out of date, whereas the playbill smartnesses and the doggerel, being fifty years out of date, have a certain rococo quaintness about them which appeals to our indulgence. All that can be said for The Railroad of Love now is that it is not an absolute outrage on the public and on Miss Rehan's genius, as Dollars and Cents was, and that in the third act the part of Valentine Osprey can still be raised, by a rapture of over-acting on Miss Rehan's part, to the point of rescuing the play from utter impossibility. But that terrible milliterry lewt'nent, with his company manners, his badinage and repartee, and his dashing manner of chucking the parlor-maid under the chin, is hard to bear, especially now that Mr Drew has left the company, and no successor can be found with his grace of style and apologetic humor. And then the fathers, with their interminable "preeliminerries" and explanations! Except when Miss Rehan or Mr Lewis or Mrs Gilbert is on the stage the play is hardly tolerable—the less so because Mr Daly's stage management is of the most fatal kind, being founded throughout on a boyish sense of fun instead of on a sense of comedy and character. What he calls acting I should call larking. For example, the part of Benny Demaresq, described in the bill as "condemned by the judge and waiting sentence from the judge's daughter," is taken by an actor who, though young and not as yet very proficient, could quite easily do himself credit in the part under artistic guidance. But he has been apparently encouraged to set about it in the broadly burlesqued, rough-and-ready, physically violent style of the circus. We do not accept that sort of thing in first-rate theatres in London; and when Mr Otis Skinner made the part agreeable years ago he did it by making the least, and not the most, of the tomfoolery (the expression is really unavoidable) laid out for him. The same criticism, in a greater or less degree, applies to all those members of the company who do not know their business better than Mr Daly does. The comic negro servant and the parlormaid who flirts with the visitors discharge their duty of destroying the illusion without adding to the entertainment, with the fullest efficiency, and, I doubt not, with the warmest approval of the manager. The whole atmosphere of the play is one of stale pleasantry of a kind for which we are not just now in the humor.

As to Miss Rehan, without whom the performance would be a hopeless failure, I would prefer to speak more fully of her when we have seen the play which Mr Daly has founded on Shakes-

pear's Two Gentlemen of Verona (for Mr Daly shews himself
a thorough disciple of the old school in his conviction that
Shakespear was a wretchedly unskilful dramatic author). The
scene of Valentine Osprey's entrance and introduction to the
milliterry hero is vulgar beyond redemption; and the vulgarity
seems less excusable now than it did at the last performance seven
years ago, when Miss Rehan's personal charm was more cap-
ricious and youthful, and less earnest and womanly than it has
since become. But the misgiving caused by this is only momentary. She soon shews that she is going to repeat her old feat in
this play of seizing the author's silly idea, sillily expressed, of a
superlatively fascinating woman, and substituting for it her own
sympathetic idea, beautifully expressed. It is true that as Miss
Rehan's style grows nobler, and takes her further away from
the skittish hoyden of Mr Daly's dramatic imagination, it becomes more and more obvious that the part she acts is not in
the play; but the moment you hear her deliver such lines as
"Did you squander it?"—referring to the milliterry gentleman's
heart—you see that she will extract enough feeling from Frau
Schonthan's German sentiment and her adapter's Irish blarney
to maintain enough congruity between her Valentine Osprey
and the author's.

The latest successor to Mr Drew is Mr Frank Worthing,
who has good looks and a pleasant address without much grip
or individual style. Perhaps, however, it is unfair to speak of
want of grip when there is so little to get hold of. Mr Drew
always played these parts with a cold reserve of insincerity
under a pretty varnish of drollery. This was not only amusing
in itself, but saved your respect for him by suggesting that
he thoroughly despised the heroes he represented. Mr Worthing
takes Lieutenant Everett seriously; and the part rather breaks
down under the treatment.

It is not just now enlightened critical policy to pay Mr Daly
compliments. In spite of the effort he made some time ago to get
abreast of the modern movement by giving Mr Burnand a commission to write a comedy with puns in it, he remains behind the

times; and the humane course is to make him aware that unless he realizes that the public at present wishes to forget everything he has ever learnt, and will be only too glad if he forgets it too, he will risk being classed with those managers who are fit for nothing but to be stuffed and mounted under glass to adorn the staircase of the Garrick Club. For various reasons, this would be a pity. His company, his enterprise, his theatre are all exceptionally interesting; so that he could pursue a forward policy with the utmost advantage. Miss Rehan is a treasure too costly to be wasted on stale farce and old-world rhetorical drama. And Mr Daly is virtually the only manager left us who is not an actor-manager, except Mr Comyns Carr, since Messrs Gatti and Sir Augustus Harris deal only in popular melodrama and in opera. It remains to be seen whether he can get sufficiently into touch with the present decade to take advantage of all these opportunities. For the last few years he has been playing the part of Rip van Winkle; and I submit to him that he had better leave that to Mr Jefferson.

Now that the brief revival of The Second Mrs Tanqueray is nearly over, I may without malice say that it was too heavy a joke for the hot weather. Miss Evelyn Millard, with her convincingly respectable and well-conducted air, is as admirable an eighteenth-century *ingénue* in Sowing the Wind as she is a wildly impossible *fin-de-siècle* demirep in Mr Pinero's play. She made a very elaborate study of Paula, and failed with a completeness that left nothing to be desired. Her method was simple. She divided the part into sympathetic passages and bursts of temper. The sympathetic passages she played in her most ladylike and virginal style: the bursts of temper she laboriously manufactured into that conscious, amateurish comedy that would make her, if she were only quarter of a century older, such a very conventional spinster aunt in a stage version of Pickwick. The lightning changes from the Pamela Amanda to the spinster aunt style produced a strongly comic effect, and made the play oddly unlike itself. The house was highly complimentary—in more senses than one, I am afraid—and Mr Alexander, as Aubrey, kept up appearances with grim suavity, whilst Mr Esmond had to put forth visible energy to combat a lassitudinous tendency to forget where he was and what he was doing. Jayne and Misquith, in the first scene, succumbed to the heat, and would not act. Lady Monckton rattled through Mrs Cortelyon's part as she might have rattled through anything else that she had not thought much about; and at the end of the second act I silently melted away and resolved to say nothing until the twelve nights were almost fulfilled.

The Strange Adventures of Miss Brown, at the Vaudeville, is said to resemble a piece called Charley's Aunt (which I have not seen) in point of introducing a man disguised as a woman. Such disguises are usually more or less disagreeable; but this is not so in the present case. The piece, which is by Mr Robert Buchanan and Mr Charles Marlowe, offers itself unashamedly as pure fun and pastime for a couple of hours; and it succeeds perfectly. It is not silly or tedious, like most pieces with the same aim; it cannot tax the most ordinary brain, though the interest is kept up throughout; and it is irresistibly laughable. Mr Frederick Kerr, as a huge schoolgirl in a red wig, is as pleasant and popular, and—to heighten the joke—as manly, as he usually is in the costume proper to his sex. Youth, good looks, and a pretty audacity serve Miss Palfrey's turn better than the moderate degree of art she has so far acquired; Miss Esmé Beringer acts, and acts well, as the dark parlor boarder from Demerara; Mr Robb Harwood made a hit as the German master; Mr Beauchamp is a very Irish major struggling with a very English accent; and Miss Victor, Mr Lionel Brough, and Miss Homfrey, assisted by half a dozen lesser lights, make up a cast that could hardly be improved. On the whole, I can recommend Miss Brown, even for the warmest nights.

POOR SHAKESPEAR! .

MA COUSINE. By H. Meilhac. Garrick Theatre, 1 July 1895.
THE TWO GENTLEMEN OF VERONA. Daly's Theatre, 2 July 1895.
[6 *July* 1895]

THE piece founded by Augustin Daly on Shakespear's Two
Gentlemen of Verona, to which I looked forward last week,
is not exactly a comic opera, though there is plenty of music in
it, and not exactly a serpentine dance, though it proceeds under
a play of changing colored lights. It is something more old-
fashioned than either: to wit, a vaudeville. And let me hasten to
admit that it makes a very pleasant entertainment for those who
know no better. Even I, who know a great deal better, as I shall
presently demonstrate rather severely, enjoyed myself tolerably.
I cannot feel harshly towards a gentleman who works so hard
as Mr Daly does to make Shakespear presentable: one feels that
he loves the bard, and lets him have his way as far as he thinks it
good for him. His rearrangement of the scenes of the first two
acts is just like him. Shakespear shews lucidly how Proteus lives
with his father (Antonio) in Verona, and loves a lady of that
city named Julia. Mr Daly, by taking the scene in Julia's house
between Julia and her maid, and the scene in Antonio's house
between Antonio and Proteus, and making them into one scene,
convinces the unlettered audience that Proteus and Julia live in
the same house with their father Antonio. Further, Shakespear
shews us how Valentine, the other gentleman of Verona, travels
from Verona to Milan, the journey being driven into our heads
by a comic scene in Verona, in which Valentine's servant is over-
whelmed with grief at leaving his parents, and with indignation
at the insensibility of his dog to his sorrow, followed presently
by another comic scene in Milan in which the same servant is
welcomed to the strange city by a fellow-servant. Mr Daly, however, is ready for Shakespear on this point too. He just represents
the two scenes as occurring in the same place; and immediately
the puzzle as to who is who is complicated by a puzzle as to

where is where. Thus is the immortal William adapted to the requirements of a nineteenth-century audience.

In preparing the text of his version Mr Daly has proceeded on the usual principles, altering, transposing, omitting, improving, correcting, and transferring speeches from one character to another. Many of Shakespear's lines are mere poetry, not to the point, not getting the play along, evidently stuck in because the poet liked to spread himself in verse. On all such unbusinesslike superfluities Mr Daly is down with his blue pencil. For instance, he relieves us of such stuff as the following, which merely conveys that Valentine loves Silvia, a fact already sufficiently established by the previous dialogue:

> My thoughts do harbor with my Silvia nightly;
>   And slaves they are to me, that send them flying:
> Oh, could their master come and go as lightly,
>   Himself would lodge where senseless they are lying.
> My herald thoughts in thy pure bosom rest them,
>   While I, their king, that thither them importune,
> Do curse the grace that with such grace hath blessed them,
>   Because myself do want my servant's fortune.
> I curse myself, for they are sent by me,
>   That they should harbor where their lord would be.

Slaves indeed are these lines and their like to Mr Daly, who "sends them flying" without remorse. But when he comes to passages that a stage manager can understand, his reverence for the bard knows no bounds. The following awkward lines, unnecessary as they are under modern stage conditions, are at any rate not poetic, and are in the nature of police news. Therefore they are piously retained:

> What halloing, and what stir, is this today?
> These are my mates, that make their wills their law,
> Have some unhappy passenger in chase.
> They love me well; yet I have much to do,
> To keep them from uncivil outrages.
> Withdraw thee, Valentine: whos this comes here?

The perfunctory metrical character of such lines only makes them more ridiculous than they would be in prose. I would cut them out without remorse to make room for all the lines that have nothing to justify their existence except their poetry, their humor, their touches of character—in short, the lines for whose sake the play survives, just as it was for their sake it originally came into existence. Mr Daly, who prefers the lines which only exist for the sake of the play, will doubtless think me as great a fool as Shakespear; but I submit to him, without disputing his judgment, that he is, after all, only a man with a theory of dramatic composition, going with a blue pencil over the work of a great dramatist, and striking out everything that does not fit his theory. Now, as it happens, nobody cares about Mr Daly's theory; whilst everybody who pays to see what is, after all, advertised as a performance of Shakespear's play entitled The Two Gentlemen of Verona, and not as a demonstration of Mr Daly's theory, does care more or less about the art of Shakespear. Why not give them what they ask for, instead of going to great trouble and expense to give them something else?

In those matters in which Mr Daly has given the rein to his own taste and fancy: that is to say, in scenery, costumes, and music, he is for the most part disabled by a want of real knowledge of the arts concerned. I say for the most part, because his pretty fifteenth-century dresses, though probably inspired rather by Sir Frederic Leighton than by Benozzo Gozzoli, may pass. But the scenery is insufferable. First, for "a street in Verona" we get a Bath bun colored operatic front cloth with about as much light in it as there is in a studio in Fitzjohn's Avenue in the middle of October. I respectfully invite Mr Daly to spend his next holiday looking at a real street in Verona, asking his conscience meanwhile whether a manager with eyes in his head and the electric light at his disposal could not advance a step on the Telbin (senior) style. Telbin was an admirable scene painter; but he was limited by the mechanical conditions of gas illumination; and he learnt his technique before the great advance made during the Impressionist movement in the painting of open-air effects, especially of brilliant sunlight. Of that advance Mr Daly has apparently no conception. The days of Macready and Clarkson Stanfield still exist for him; he would probably prefer a water-color drawing of a foreign street by Samuel Prout to one of Mr T. M. Rooke; and I daresay every relic of the original tallow candlelight that still clings to the art of scene-painting is as dear to him as it is to most old playgoers, including, unhappily, many of the critics.

As to the elaborate set in which Julia makes her first entrance, a glance at it shews how far Mr Daly prefers the Marble Arch to the loggia of Orcagna. All over the scene we have Renaissance work, in its genteelest stages of decay, held up as the perfection of romantic elegance and beauty. The school that produced the classicism of the First Empire, designed the terraces of Regent's Park and the façades of Fitzroy Square, and conceived the Boboli Gardens and Versailles as places for human beings to be happy in, ramps all over the scenery, and offers as much of its pet colonnades and statues as can be crammed into a single scene, by way of a compendium of everything that is lovely in the city of San Zeno and the tombs of the Scaligers. As to the natural objects depicted, I ask whether any man living has ever seen a pale green cypress in Verona or anywhere else out of a toy Noah's Ark. A man who, having once seen cypresses and felt their presence in a north Italian landscape, paints them lettuce color, must be suffering either from madness, malice, or a theory of how nature should have colored trees, cognate with Mr Daly's theory of how Shakespear should have written plays.

Of the music let me speak compassionately. After all, it is only very lately that Mr Arnold Dolmetsch, by playing fifteenth-century music on fifteenth-century instruments, has shewn us that the age of beauty was true to itself in music as in pictures and armor and costumes. But what should Mr Daly know of this, educated as he no doubt was to believe that the court of Denmark should always enter in the first act of Hamlet to the march from Judas Maccabæus? Schubert's setting of Who is Silvia? he knew, but had rashly used up in Twelfth Night as

Who's Olivia. He has therefore had to fall back on another modern setting, almost supernaturally devoid of any particular merit. Besides this, all through the drama the most horribly common music repeatedly breaks out on the slightest pretext or on no pretext at all. One dance, set to a crude old English popular tune, sundry eighteenth and nineteenth century musical banalities, and a titivated plantation melody in the first act which produces an indescribably atrocious effect by coming in behind the scenes as a sort of coda to Julia's curtain speech, all turn the play, as I have said, into a vaudeville. Needless to add, the accompaniments are not played on lutes and viols, but by the orchestra and a guitar or two. In the forest scene the outlaws begin the act by a chorus. After their encounter with Valentine they go off the stage singing the refrain exactly in the style of La Fille de Madame Angot. The wanton absurdity of introducing this comic opera convention is presently eclipsed by a thunderstorm, immediately after which Valentine enters and delivers his speech sitting down on a bank of moss, as an outlaw in tights naturally would after a terrific shower. Such is the effect of many years of theatrical management on the human brain.

Perhaps the oddest remark I have to make about the performance is that, with all its glaring defects and blunders, it is rather a handsome and elaborate one as such things go. It is many years now since Mr Ruskin first took the Academicians of his day aback by the obvious remark that Carpaccio and Giovanni Bellini were better painters than Domenichino and Salvator Rosa. Nobody dreams now of assuming that Pope was a greater poet than Chaucer, that Mozart's Twelfth Mass is superior to the masterpieces of Orlandus Lassus and Palestrina, or that our "ecclesiastical Gothic" architecture is more enlightened than Norman axe work. But the theatre is still wallowing in such follies; and until Mr Comyns Carr and Sir Edward Burne-Jones, Baronet, put King Arthur on the stage more or less in the manner natural to men who know these things, Mr Daly might have pleaded the unbroken conservatism of the playhouse against me. But after the Lyceum scenery and architecture I decline to accept a relapse without protest. There is no reason why cheap photographs of Italian architecture (sixpence apiece in infinite variety at the bookstall in the South Kensington Museum) should not rescue us from Regent's Park Renaissance colonnades on the stage just as the electric light can rescue us from Telbin's dun-colored sunlight. The opera is the last place in the world where any wise man would look for adequate stage illusion; but the fact is that Mr Daly, with all his colored lights, has not produced a single Italian scene comparable in illusion to that provided by Sir Augustus Harris at Covent Garden for Cavalleria Rusticana.

Of the acting I have not much to say. Miss Rehan provided a strong argument in favor of rational dress by looking much better in her page's costume than in that of her own sex; and in the serenade scene, and that of the wooing of Silvia for Proteus, she stirred some feeling into the part, and reminded us of what she was in Twelfth Night, where the same situations are fully worked out. For the rest, she moved and spoke with imposing rhythmic grace. That is as much notice as so cheap a part as Julia is worth from an artist who, being absolute mistress of the situation at Daly's Theatre, might and should have played Imogen for us instead. The two gentlemen were impersonated by Mr Worthing and Mr Craig. Mr Worthing charged himself with feeling without any particular reference to his lines; and Mr Craig struck a balance by attending to the meaning of his speeches without taking them at all to heart. Mr Clarke, as the Duke, was emphatic, and worked up every long speech to a climax in the useful old style; but his tone is harsh, his touch on his consonants coarse, and his accent ugly, all fatal disqualifications for the delivery of Shakespearean verse. The scenes between Launce and his dog brought out the latent silliness and childishness of the audience as Shakespear's clowning scenes always do: I laugh at them like a yokel myself. Mr Lewis hardly made the most of them. His style has been formed in modern comedies, where the locutions are so familiar that their meaning is in no danger of being lost by the rapidity of his quaint utterance; but Launce's phraseology is another matter: a few of the funniest lines missed fire because the audience did not catch them. And with all possible allowance for Mr Daly's blue pencil, I cannot help suspecting that Mr Lewis's memory was responsible for one or two of his omissions. Still, Mr Lewis has always his comic force, whether he makes the most or the least of it; so that he cannot fail in such a part as Launce. Miss Maxine Elliot's Silvia was the most considerable performance after Miss Rehan's Julia. The whole company will gain by the substitution on Tuesday next of a much better play, A Midsummer Night's Dream, as a basis for Mr Daly's operations. No doubt he is at this moment, like Mrs Todgers, "a dodgin' among the tender bits with a fork, and an eatin' of 'em"; but there is sure to be enough of the original left here and there to repay a visit.

What is to be said of Rejane, the inimitable, at the Garrick? How shall I excuse myself for having enjoyed Ma Cousine? It is a masterpiece of levity; and to say that Rejane plays it unscrupulously is to convey but a faint idea of the unconscionable allurements which she brings to the aid of her drollest and cleverest comedy. The play is improper without being offensive, because it makes no more pretension to morality than Rejane does to fastidiousness. Ma Cousine is not difficult to follow. Even I understood a full quarter of the dialogue; and some of Rejane's most effective strokes can be appreciated by Englishmen without the least knowledge of the French tongue. I would not go again merely to see the ingenious blend of skirt dance and cancan in the second act, or the—how shall I put it?—the petticoat chase in the third act, or the witcheries of the sofa in the first, though I confess to having laughed at them all with the greatest frailty; but there is much more in Rejane's acting than this: it has the quick sensibility which is the really moving quality in fine comic acting, and it is perfectly honest and self-respecting in its impudence. Integrity consists in obeying the morality which you accept; and neither Meilhac nor Rejane pretend for a moment to accept the morality which they both disregard in Ma Cousine.

Mr Alexander's revival of The Idler at the St James's Theatre promises to be a success. Mr Haddon Chambers is a rough and ready playwright with the imagination of a bushranger; but it is imagination, all the same, and it suffices. The house received the play with enthusiasm.

TOUJOURS DALY

MADAME SANS-GÊNE. Garrick Theatre, 8 July 1895.
A MIDSUMMER NIGHT'S DREAM. Daly's Theatre, 9 July 1895.

[13 *July* 1895]

BEFORE Madame Sans-Gêne I think it best to retire in good order without committing myself. I have never seen a French play of which I understood less; and that, for me, is saying a good deal. Many of the sallies of Rejane which provoke the loudest laughter are just those which escape me. Napoleon is an inscrutable person, as becomes the Man of Destiny. I do not catch a solitary word he says, no doubt because of his Corsican accent. With the rest I can pick my way along sufficiently to be almost as much bored as if the play were in English. Surely the twenty minutes or so of amusement contained in the play might be purchased a little more cheaply than by the endurance of a huge mock historic melodrama which never for a moment produces the faintest conviction, and which involves the exhibition of elaborate Empire interiors requiring half an hour between the acts to set, and not worth looking at when they are set. Of course I admire the ingenuity with which Sardou carries out his principle of combining the maximum of expenditure and idle chatter with the minimum of drama; but I have admired that so often that it is beginning to pall on me. And I think something better could be done with Rejane's talent than this business, funny as it is for once in a way, of playing the washerwoman like a real duchess and the duchess like a stage washerwoman. Rejane, to say the least, is not exacting as to the quality of her parts provided they are popular; and it rests with the dramatists to make the best or worst of her. How Sardou proceeds when he has *carte blanche* in that way may be learnt from the pages of the Sardou-Bernhardt repertory—though please observe that I do not imply that he ever makes the worst of anything; because to go to that extreme requires a good deal of conviction, which is just the sort of force that he lacks. I can no more believe in Madame Sans-Gêne than in Theodora or La Tosca. She is more amusing: that is all.

The Two Gentlemen of Verona has been succeeded at Daly's Theatre by A Midsummer Night's Dream. Mr Daly is in great form. In my last article I was rash enough to hint that he had not quite realized what could be done with electric lighting on the stage. He triumphantly answers me by fitting up all his fairies with portable batteries and incandescent lights, which they switch on and off from time to time, like children with a new toy. He has trained Miss Lillian Swain in the part of Puck until it is safe to say that she does not take one step, strike one attitude, or modify her voice by a single inflexion that is not violently, wantonly, and ridiculously wrong and absurd. Instead of being mercurial, she poses academically, like a cheap Italian statuette; instead of being impish and childish, she is elegant and affected; she laughs a solemn, measured laugh, like a heavy German Zamiel; she announces her ability to girdle the earth in forty minutes in the attitude of a professional skater, and then begins the journey awkwardly in a swing, which takes her in the opposite direction to that in which she indicated her intention of going: in short, she illustrates every folly and superstition that still clings round what Mr Daly no doubt calls "the legitimate." Another stroke of his is to make Oberon a woman. It must not be supposed that he does this solely because it is wrong, though there is no other reason apparent. He does it partly because he was brought up to do such things, and partly because they seem to him to be a tribute to Shakespear's greatness, which, being uncommon, ought not to be interpreted according to the dictates of common sense. A female Oberon and a Puck who behaves like a page-boy earnestly training himself for the post of footman recommend themselves to him because they totally destroy the naturalness of the representation, and so accord with his conception of the Shakespearean drama as the most artificial of all forms of stage entertainment. That is how you find out the man who is not

an artist. Verse, music, the beauties of dress, gesture, and movement are to him interesting aberrations instead of being the
natural expression which human feeling seeks at a certain degree
of delicacy and intensity. He regards art as a quaint and costly
ring in the nose of Nature. I am loth to say that Mr Daly is
such a man; but after studying all his Shakespearean revivals with
the thirstiest desire to find as much art as possible in them, I
must mournfully confess that the only idea I can see in them is
the idea of titivation. As to his slaughterings of the text, how can
one help feeling them acutely in a play like A Midsummer Night's
Dream, in which Shakespear, having to bring Nature in its most
enchanting aspect before an audience without the help of theatrical
scenery, used all his power of description and expression in verse
with such effect that the utmost any scene-painter can hope for
is to produce a picture that shall not bitterly disappoint the
spectator who has read the play beforehand? Mr Daly is, I should
say, one of those people who are unable to conceive that there
could have been any illusion at all about the play before scenery
was introduced. He certainly has no suspicion of the fact that
every accessory he employs is brought in at the deadliest risk
of destroying the magic spell woven by the poet. He swings Puck
away on a clumsy trapeze with a ridiculous clash of the cymbals
in the orchestra, in the fullest belief that he is thereby completing
instead of destroying the effect of Puck's lines. His "panoramic
illusion of the passage of Theseus's barge to Athens" is more
absurd than anything that occurs in the tragedy of Pyramus and
Thisbe in the last act. The stage management blunders again and
again through feeble imaginative realization of the circumstances
of the drama. In the first act it should be clear to any stage
manager that Lysander's speech, beginning, "I am, my lord, as
well derived as he," should be spoken privately and not publicly
to Theseus. In the rehearsal scene in the wood, Titania should
not be conspicuously exhibited under a limelight in the very
centre of the stage, where the clowns have, in defiance of all
common sanity, to pretend not to see her. We are expected, no
doubt, to assume that she is invisible because she is a fairy,

though Bottom's conversation with her when she wakes and addresses him flatly contradicts that hypothesis. In the fourth act, Theseus has to enter from his barge down a bank, picking his way through the sleeping Lysander and Hermia, Demetrius and Helena. The four lions in Trafalgar Square are not more conspicuous and unoverlookable than these four figures are. Yet Theseus has to make all his hunting speeches in an impossible unconsciousness of them, and then to look at them amazedly and exclaim, "But soft, what nymphs are these?" as if he could in any extremity of absence of mind have missed seeing them all along. Most of these absurdities are part of a systematic policy of sacrificing the credibility of the play to the chance of exhibiting an effective "living picture."

I very soon gave up the attempt to keep a record of the outrages practized by Mr Daly on the text. Everyone knows the lines:

> I swear to thee by Cupid's strongest bow,
> By his best arrow with the golden head,
> By the simplicity of Venus' doves,
> By that which knitteth souls and prospers loves, etc.

Mr Daly's powerful mind perceived at a glance that the second and third lines are superfluous, as their omission does not destroy the sense of the passage. He accordingly omitted them. In the same scene, Shakespear makes the two star-crossed lovers speak in alternate lines with an effect which sets the whole scene throbbing with their absorption in one another:

LYSANDER. The course of true love never did run smooth.
    But either it was different in blood—
HERMIA. O cross! too high to be enthralled to low!
LYSANDER. Or else misgraffed in respect of years,
HERMIA. O spite! too old to be engaged to young!
LYSANDER. Or else it stood upon the choice of friends,
HERMIA. O hell! to choose love by another's eye!
LYSANDER. Or if there were a sympathy in choice,
    War, death, or sickness did lay siege to it, etc.

With a Hermia who knew how to breathe out these parentheses, the duet would be an exquisite one; but Mr Daly, shocked, as an American and an Irishman, at a young lady using such an expression as "Oh hell!" cuts out the whole antiphony, and leaves Lysander to deliver a long lecture without interruption from the lady. At such moments, the episode of the ass's head rises to the dignity of allegory. From any other manager I should accept the excuse that the effects of verse for which I am pleading require a virtuosity of delivery on the part of the actor which is practically not to be had at present. But Mr Daly has Miss Rehan, who is specially famous for just this virtuosity of speech; and yet her lines are treated just as the others are. The fact is, beautiful elocution is rare because the managers have no ears.

The play, though of course very poorly spoken in comparison with how it ought to be spoken, is tolerably acted. Mr George Clarke, clad in the armor of Alcibiades and the red silk gown of Charley's Aunt, articulates most industriously, and waves his arms and flexes his wrists in strict accordance, not for a moment with the poetry, but with those laws of dramatic elocution and gesture which veteran actors are always willing to impart to novices at a reasonable price per dozen lessons. Mr Lewis as Bottom is not as funny as his part, whereas in modern plays he is always funnier than his part. He seemed to me to miss the stolid, obstinate, self-sufficient temperament of Bottom altogether. There is a definite conception of some particular sort of man at the back of all Shakespear's characters. The quantity of fun to be got out of Bottom and Autolycus, for instance, is about the same; but underneath the fun there are two widely different persons, of types still extant and familiar. Mr Lewis would be as funny in Autolycus as he is in Bottom; but he would be exactly the same man in both parts.

As to Miss Rehan, her scenes in the wood with Demetrius were very fine, although, in the passage where Hermia frightens her, she condescends to arrant clowning. Her treatment of Shakespearean verse is delightful after the mechanical intoning of Sarah Bernhardt. She gives us beauty of tone, grace of measure, delicacy of articulation: in short, all the technical qualities of verse music, along with the rich feeling and fine intelligence without which those technical qualities would soon become monotonous. When she is at her best, the music melts in the caress of the emotion it expresses, and thus completes the conditions necessary for obtaining Shakespear's effects in Shakespear's way. When she is on the stage, the play asserts its full charm; and when she is gone, and the stage carpenters and the orchestra are doing their best to pull the entertainment through in Mr Daly's way, down drops the whole affair into mild tedium. But it is impossible to watch the most recent developments of Miss Rehan's style without some uneasiness. I wonder whether she is old enough to remember the late Barry Sullivan when he was still in his physical prime. Those who do will recall, not an obsolete provincial tragedian, trading on the wreck of an unaccountable reputation, but an actor who possessed in an extraordinary degree just the imposing grace, the sensitive personal dignity of style, the force and self-reliance into which Miss Rehan's style is settling. Miss Rehan's exit in the second act of A Midsummer Night's Dream, with the couplet,

> I'll follow thee, and make a heaven of hell
> To die upon the hand I love so well,

is an exact reproduction of the Barry Sullivan exit. Again, in the first act, when Miss Rehan, prone on a couch, raises herself on her left hand, and, with her right raised "to heaven," solemnly declaims the lines:

> For ere Demetrius look'd on Hermia's eyne
> He hailed down oaths, that he was only mine;
> And when this hail some heat from Hermia felt,
> So he dissolved, and showers of oaths did melt,

you are, once more, not forward with Duse, but back with Barry Sullivan, who would in just the same way, when led into it by a touch of stateliness and sonority in the lines, abandon his part, and become for the moment a sort of majestic incarnation of abstract solemnity and magnificence. His skill and intense belief in himself gave him the dangerous power of doing so without making himself ridiculous; and it was by this power, and by the fascination, the grace, and the force which are implied by it, that he gave life to old-fashioned and mutilated representations of Shakespear's plays, poorly acted and ignorantly mounted. This was all very well whilst the fascination lasted; but when his voice lost its tone, his figure its resilience and grace, and his force its spontaneity and natural dignity, there was nothing left but a mannered, elderly, truculent, and, except to his old admirers, rather absurd tragedian of the palmy school. As I was a small boy when I first saw Barry Sullivan, and as I lost sight of him before his waning charm had quite vanished, I remember him, not as he is remembered by those who saw him only in the last ten years of his life, but as an actor who was in his day much further superior in pictorial, vocal, and rhetorical qualities to his next best rival than any actor or actress can easily be nowadays. And it strikes me forcibly that unless Miss Rehan takes to playing Imogen instead of such comparatively childish stuff as Julia or even Helena, and unless she throws herself into sympathy with the contemporary movement by identifying herself with characteristically modern parts of the Magda or Nora type, she may find herself left behind in the race by competitors of much less physical genius, just as Barry Sullivan did. Miss Rehan is clearly absolute mistress of the situation at Daly's Theatre: nobody can persuade me that if she says Cymbeline, Mr Daly can say The Two Gentlemen of Verona, or that if she says Sudermann or Ibsen, Mr Daly can insist on the author of Dollars and Cents. But the self-culture which has produced her superb graces of manner and diction seems to have isolated her instead of quickening her sympathy and drawing closer her contact with the world. Every woman who sees Duse play Magda feels that Duse is acting and speaking for her and for all women as they are hardly ever able to speak and act for themselves. The same may be said of Miss Achurch as Nora. But no woman has ever had the very faintest sensation of that kind about any part that Miss Rehan has yet played. We admire, not what she is doing, but the charm with which she does it. That sort of admiration will not last. Miss Rehan's voice is not henceforth going to grow fresher, nor her dignity less conscious, nor her grace of gesture less studied and mannered, nor her movements swifter and more spontaneous. Already I find that young people who see her for the first time cannot quite agree that our raptures about her Katharine and her Rosalind are borne out by her Julia and Helena. Five years hence she will be still more rhetorical and less real: further ahead I dare not look with Barry Sullivan in my mind. There is only one way to defy Time; and that is to have young ideas, which may always be trusted to find youthful and vivid expression. I am afraid this means avoiding the company of Mr Daly; but it is useless to blink the fact that unless a modern actress can and will force her manager, in spite of his manly prejudices, to produce plays with real women's parts in them, she had better, at all hazards, make shift to manage for herself. With Grandfather Daly to choose her plays for her, there is no future for Ada Rehan.

CRITICISM ON THE HUSTINGS

TWELFTH NIGHT. Acted after the manner of the sixteenth century before the members of the Elizabethan Stage Society, Burlington Hall, 21 June 1895. [20 *July* 1895]

THE holding of a General Election at the end of the London season should be made unlawful. Involving, as it does, an outburst of the keenest political criticism, it should not be fixed for the moment when all the men who are professionally trained in criticism—that is to say, the critics of art—are exhausted by three months' continuous work. I am asked, sometimes sympathetically, sometimes sarcastically, whether the critic of art is in his place on the political platform. I reply that he is indispensable there, and that the recognition of that fact is spreading. The reason is obvious. Criticism with a foregone conclusion is a contradiction in terms; and criticism by politicians always has its conclusion foregone, because the critics are party men. Try to imagine what my criticism would be worth if I had first to ascertain the politics of Sir Henry Irving, Mr Tree, Mr Alexander, Mr Wyndham, Mr Hare, and so on, and then to enthusiastically praise all the enterprises on one side, and to denounce and disparage those on the other. For example, Manager A and Manager B are, let us suppose, on opposite sides in politics. Manager A produces a new Pinero play of the Mrs Tanqueray order. I extol it as a masterpiece of dramatic psychology. Manager B promptly orders another such play from Mr Pinero. I denounce it as an outrage on decency. Manager A abolishes fees and raises the price of admission to the pit from two shillings to half a crown. I rejoice in his spirited attack on an insufferable system of cadging and extortion, and in his self-sacrificing regard for the comfort and convenience of the public. Manager B follows suit. I expose the snobbish trick by which he has provided his aristocratic friends in the stalls with free programs at the expense of the honest, hardworking pit. That is what party criticism is like. One political party brings in a Land Purchase Bill which is immediately opposed and denounced by the opposite party. Presently that opposite party becomes the Government, and, since society does not evolve on party lines, and something must be done, has to proceed with the Land Purchase Legislation itself. Immediately the Land Purchasers of the day before are denouncing Land Purchase as an unspeakable infamy. Even articles descriptive of parliamentary debates are written on party lines. Sir William Harcourt and Mr Goschen may make bad speeches, and Mr Asquith and Mr Balfour good ones. No matter: the division made in the article between the good and bad speeches must be a party division with Sir William and Mr Asquith on one side, and Mr Balfour and Mr Goschen on the other. How superior is the position of the art critic, who can choose his side and change it as he likes when there is a side to choose at all! He is free to write like Mr Ruskin if he can; whereas the political critic hardly dares emulate even the moderate degree of detachment attained in histories by Macaulay and Mr Justin M'Carthy. Nobody wonders what he will say about anything, but only how he will say it. You would no more dream of buying the

Standard or the Chronicle to see what opinion they had of the West Birmingham election than you would go to Euston to see in which direction the locomotive attached to the Scotch express would take it into its head to travel.

One more feature of the situation remains to be taken into account. The public, whilst submitting to the party manner of criticism as it submits to any other institution under which it has been reared, brightens up significantly when anyone drops that manner for a moment. It displays a personal curiosity about the art critic which the political leader writer never excites. Nobody knows or cares who writes the political articles in the Daily Telegraph. But Mr Clement Scott's name cannot be concealed. And it is so with every paper. If the name of a contributor bursts through the veil of anonymity, it is sure to be that of a writer on literature or art, never that of a reliable party leader writer. As in the press, so on the platform, the more independent a speaker is, the more interest the public takes in him. Political party speeches, like leading articles, are essentially nothing but party advertisements; and people do not trust advertisements: the more concerned they are with the benefits held out by the advertiser, the more anxious they are to have the opinion of a disinterested expert as to whether the advertisement can be trusted. Get on your legs and talk the current party Manichæism, according to which there are two great parties representing two great principles, the one wholly malign and the other wholly beneficent, composed of two different orders of beings, the one angelic and the other diabolic; and everything silly, everything drunken, infatuated, fanatical, envious, quarrelsome, in short, foolish in the audience responds to you at once. Assume, on the other hand, that one Government is very like another, and that nothing will wreck a Government except a refusal to go where it is driven, or an attempt to go where it is not driven (especially if the recalcitrance be made a matter of party principle), and at once your audience is as happy and sensible as it is in the nature of an audience to be. But nobody at present combines the requisite political detachment with the requisite critical training except the art critic. I therefore look forward to the time when election meetings will be advertised by placards headed "No politics," and displaying a list of speakers headed, in the largest type, with the name of some noted critic of pictures, music, the drama, or literature. And the end of that will be that some bold editor will at last take the step I have vainly urged for years, and conduct the criticism of politics in his paper exactly as he now conducts the criticism of art.

At the same time, I do not urge this reform on parliamentary candidates as necessarily advantageous to them. Out of half a dozen candidates in London and the provinces, on whose behalf I spoke impartially in the heat of the election, five were defeated, and the sixth had his formerly triumphant majority reduced to a mere margin. My real aim is to widen the horizon of the critic, especially of the dramatic critic, whose habit at present is to bring a large experience of stage life to bear on a scanty experience of real life, although it is certain that all really fruitful criticism of the drama must bring a wide and practical knowledge of real life to bear on the stage. One result of this is just the reverse of what might be expected. When I devoted myself to the criticism of music, I was compelled, like all musical critics, to give close attention to the execution of the works performed, because, as these were for the most part masterpieces of established fame, their merit as compositions had been settled long ago. If you hear Beethoven's C minor symphony played ten times in a season, you cannot criticize the symphony every time: you can only criticize the manner in which it is played. The dramatic critic, constantly criticizing new plays that are (to say the least) not masterpieces, would seem to be in quite a different predicament; yet the same result might very well be anticipated, for this reason, that as the great majority of these new plays are merely reshufflings of a tattered and thumbed pack of old stage cards, and are, in fact, infinitely less novel and suggestive than a Beethoven symphony is the hundredth time you hear it, one would expect the dramatic critic to be thrown back far more than even his musical colleague upon the criticism of technical execution. That this is notoriously the reverse of what has actually happened I can only account for by concluding that our dramatic critics specialize themselves to such an extent that they lose the character of men and citizens, and become mere playgoers, in which unhappy condition, since stageland then appears a quite real place to them, and the laws of Nature are supplanted in their minds by the conventions of the stage, every fresh permutation and combination of the old stage situations and effects appeals to them as a historical, evolutional development. They tell the story of Fedora and discuss her motives and character when there is really nothing whatever to discuss except how Sarah Bernhardt, or Mrs Bernard Beere, or Mrs Patrick Campbell make this or that effect. In the same way, if you construct one of those dolls which close their eyes when you lay them on their backs, and squeak plaintively when you nip them in the epigastric region, any imaginative little girl will explain to you at great length and in minute detail how the doll got tired and sleepy, and what it means by the squeak. The most popular dramatic criticisms of today are stories of dolls, prettily invented and touchingly told. And when you give the critic a woman to criticize instead of a doll, and scenes from real life instead of turns of the stageland kaleidoscope to consider, he protests that you are confronting him with the morbid, the unmanageable, the diseased. Political activity would soon cure him of this. We shall presently have to re-elect the retiring thirds of the London vestries. Let every dramatic critic offer himself as a candidate, and woo his ward thoroughly, and we shall never hear another word about the "Norwegian parochialism" of Ibsen's Enemy of the People. And yet—horrid thought—suppose the dupes of stage illusion became the dupes of platform illusion too, and turned rabid party politicians, every man of them! To do without illusions and ideals, and to keep a fast grip on the real stuff of life, is hard enough anywhere. I am not sure, on reflection, that it is easier out of the theatre than in it. Still, even a new set of illusions would enliven dramatic criticism.

I welcome the advent of The Elizabethan Stage Society, founded "to give practical effect to the principle that Shakespear should be accorded the build of stage for which he designed his plays." Last month the Society played Twelfth Night in the Burlington Hall: next December they will give us The Comedy of Errors in Gray's Inn Hall, where it was originally acted in 1594. It is only by such performances that people can be convinced that Shakespear's plays lose more than they gain by modern staging. I do not, like the E.S.S., affirm it as a principle that Shakespear's plays should be accorded the build of stage for which he designed them. I simply affirm it as a fact, personally observed by myself, that the modern pictorial stage is not so favorable to Shakespearean acting and stage illusion as the platform stage. Years ago, comparing the effect of Much Ado as performed at the Lyceum and as read through by a number of amateurs seated in evening dress on the platform at the London Institution, I found that the amateur performance was more vivid and enjoyable, and that the illusion, though flatly contradicted by the costumes and surroundings, was actually stronger. I happened to witness, too, a performance of Browning's Luria under circumstances still more apparently ludicrous. It was acted—not merely read—in a lecture theatre at University College, against a background of plain curtains, by performers also in evening dress. The effect was so satisfactory in comparison to the ordinary pictorial stage effect that I have ever since regarded the return to the old conditions of stage representation for old plays as perfectly practical and advisable. The success of the combinations of platform action with stage scenery at the Ober Ammergau Passion Play, and of the Maeterlinckian treatment of Pelléas et Mélisande by the Théâtre de l'Œuvre, shews that the staging of the poetic drama may be modified in various directions with much greater boldness than I or anyone else could have supposed safe if our prejudices had not been broken up by these little amateur tentatives, which so many of us make the fatal mistake of passing by as not worth attention. The performance of Twelfth Night now in question brought out another point with remarkable distinctness, and that was the immense advantage of the platform stage to the actor. It places him in so intimate a relation to the spectators that the difficulty of getting delicate play "across the footlights," and of making vehement play forcible enough to overcome the remoteness of the "living picture" stage, all but vanishes. Is there not some story to the effect that Garrick, when it was proposed to alter the stage in the modern direction in his time, replied that if he were ten feet further from his audience there would be no difference between him and any of his rivals. After the Twelfth Night performance I can quite believe this. I am convinced that if Burbage were to rise from the dead and accept an invitation from Sir Henry Irving to appear at the Lyceum, he would recoil beaten the moment he realized that he was to be looked at as part of an optical illusion through a huge hole in the wall, instead of being practically in the middle of the theatre. The acting at Burlington Hall was for the most part bad acting, done by amateurs who were acutely conscious of themselves and of Shakespear, and very feebly conscious, indeed, of the reality and humanity of the characters they represented. Sir Toby Belch, Sir Andrew Aguecheek, and the rest of the comic personages, with the honorable exception of Malvolio, grinned continuously at the humor of their own parts. The clown made no pretence of understanding a single sentence he uttered: it sufficed for him that he *was* a clown. Orsino was an inhumanly well-conducted, well-spoken, well-dressed, considerate, and reasonable lover. Olivia, played by a young lady of obvious possibilities as an actress, will not realize those possibilities unless she promptly abandons the artificial rhetorical drama, and never touches it again until she is able to play a modern comedy and a modern melodrama with frankness and conviction. Viola spoke some of her lines very prettily; but she was not—well, all that is necessary for my argument is to say that she was not as good as Miss Rehan. Antonio, a very handsome young man with a sensitive style and, like Olivia, unmistakeable possibilities, had not experience enough to make the most of himself. In short, nobody can pretend that the Society had any advantage over Mr Daly or Sir Henry Irving in the histrionic talent at its disposal. But what it had went so much further under the Elizabethan conditions that everyone present took the acting to be much better than it really was; whereas at Daly's, or the Lyceum, only the most gifted players can make any considerable effect, the other parts invariably seeming colorless and unduly subordinate. With skilful and rapid declamation, which would have rendered the curtailment of the play unnecessary, the performance would have beaten its modern rivals completely, especially as Mr Dolmetsch with his viol and lute, and Miss Helen Dolmetsch with her viola da gamba, were there with their little party of viol and virginal players to give us some of the music of the days when England really could produce music. On the whole, though I will not urge Sir Henry Irving to rebuild the Lyceum on the old inn yard model, I do seriously suggest that our leading actors might occasionally come down and take a turn on the stage of the E.S.S., at Gray's Inn Hall or elsewhere, just to shew us what they could do on the sort of stage which helped Burbage to become famous.

THE SEASON'S MORAL

[27 *July* 1895]

Now that the theatrical season is over, is there any moral to be drawn? I do not mean by literary factions—Ibsenites and anti-Ibsenites and the like—but by, let us say, a manager with enough money at stake to make him anxious to get some guidance for next season. To him, as far as I can see, the season has been like Ibsen's plays: the moral is that there is no moral. The outcry against Ibsen has been deferred to carefully. Little Eyolf has been boycotted; and none of the older plays have been touched in English, whilst there has been a plentiful supply of what was described the other day, in contradistinction to Ibsen's work, as "the drama that the public likes and the public pays for." Need I add that in most cases the public has not liked it and has declined to pay for it. What is a manager to do? He responds to the demand for honest, wholesome, English murder, suicide, and adultery, by commissioning M. Sardou to supply those solid native articles; and lo! bottomless disaster, worse than the worst Ibsen ever threatened. He tries the newest English psychological drama, with an interestingly improper heroine who throws the Bible into the fire.

The press proclaims a masterpiece: where is that masterpiece now? The infallible Mrs Tanqueray is revived, and does not draw a sixpence. Mr Grundy, as an expert in "construction," with daring views on the great marriage question, is called in; but his Slaves of the Ring perishes without having enjoyed a seventieth part of the popularity of A Doll's House. Even Henry Arthur Jones, the strong and successful, has no more than a Norwegian success: the manager might have produced The League of Youth instead of The Triumph of the Philistines without being any the poorer. What a muddle it all seems! That safe old hand Sardou, playing the safe old game according to the safe old rules, fails ignominiously. Those safe old hands Pinero, Grundy, and Jones, cautiously playing the new game according to the safe old rules, fail to retrieve the situation. One must not forget, however, that performances have to be taken into account as well as plays. Sardou's contribution, Delia Harding, was adequately acted—much better than it deserved in Miss Marion Terry's case—and may be dismissed as having failed hopelessly on its merits. Mrs Ebbsmith, badly cast and badly acted except for Mrs Campbell's Agnes and Mr Hare's Duke of St Olpherts, did not begin to flag until the withdrawal of Mrs Campbell brought out all the defects in the performance. Slaves of the Ring, though better cast, was worse acted than Mrs Ebbsmith; and The Triumph of the Philistines never got fairly on to the stage, the strong and sympathetic parts being just enough underplayed to take the edge off the performance. This points to the difficulty which has been apparent for the last five or six years: namely, that the public are getting tired of the old-fashioned plays faster than the actors are learning to make the new ones effective. The unfortunate new dramatist has, therefore, to write plays so extraordinarily good that, like Mozart's operas, they succeed in spite of inadequate execution. This is all very well for geniuses like Ibsen; but it is rather hard on the ordinary purveyor of the drama. The managers do not seem to me yet to grasp this feature of the situation. If they did, they would only meddle with the strongest specimens of the new drama, instead of timidly going to the old firms and ordering

moderate plays cut in the new style. No doubt the success of The
Second Mrs Tanqueray and The Case of Rebellious Susan seemed
to support the view that the new style had better be tried cautiously by an old hand. But then Mrs Tanqueray had not really the
faintest touch of the new spirit in it; and recent events suggest
that its success was due to a happy cast of the dice by which the
play found an actress who doubled its value and had hers doubled
by it. For we have this season seen the play without the actress
and the actress without the play, with disappointing results in
both cases. As to Rebellious Susan it was, on the outside, an amusing and naughty comedy, acted by the company which has since
made a success of Mr Carton's scatterbrained and conventionally
sentimental Home Secretary. The fact that The Triumph of the
Philistines, in which the element of social criticism was pushed
well to the front of the play, and in which the element of amusing
and naughty comedy was confined to one part, only succeeded
in respect of this very part, and did not hold the stage long, completes the demonstration that the moral drawn from the success of
Mrs Tanqueray and Rebellious Susan was the wrong moral, and
that for the present it is dangerous to meddle with plays of the
new type unless they are strong enough to be "actor proof." Thus
it would appear that Mr Alexander was ill advised to produce The
Triumph of the Philistines with such a work as Sudermann's
Home (Magda) up his sleeve. Home will hold as much acting as
even Duse can put into it; but the play was handicapped in Duse's
hands by a language that the audience did not understand. The
general complaints made that the situation in the last act was
strained and weak, were due, I suspect, to the failure of the audience to catch the meaning, or at least the full force, of the speech
which brings about the catastrophe. Magda, after many years of
work and finally of great success as an independent woman,
working as a public singer, becomes reconciled to her father, a
fanatical believer in the old ideals of family honor and manly
supremacy. She has a child whose father turns up among the intimate friends of the family. Her father demands that she shall
marry this man as a point of honor. She submits to this and to the

sacrifice of her profession until the man demands also that she shall part with the child in order to save appearances. Magda then turns on him and overwhelms him with scorn. Her father insists. She defies her father, who attempts to kill her and is struck down by paralysis in the act. To anyone who is only following in a general way what is happening, this catastrophe must indeed appear inadequately motived and over-strained. So would the story of Othello under the same circumstances. But when the dialogue is fully understood, there are few strokes of drama more effective and convincing than the climax of the final scene between the father and daughter, when she at last asks him the terrible question, "How do you know that he was the only one?" After that, the catastrophe comes quite inevitably; and there is no reason to doubt that in an English version it would justify itself fully. Mr Alexander could not easily have got Magda played as Duse played her; but he could have got her played well enough to make much more effect than those parts in Mr Jones's play which missed fire through underacting. In truth, Magda is so excellent an acting part that it would be very hard for an actress of any standing to fail in it. All this, however, is wisdom after the event. At the beginning of the season Sudermann was an unknown quantity; and everything pointed to the expediency of producing The Triumph of the Philistines. Besides, Mr Alexander had already made a heroic contribution to the cause of art by venturing on Mr Henry James's Guy Domville, and producing it with great care and unstinted liberality, though the result was one for which he could hardly have been quite unprepared. The play, delicately written and admirably performed, was too fine for the audience; and the gallery first-nighters behaved very badly, as they did subsequently, more excusably, at Delia Harding, though after that they happily pulled themselves together, and conducted themselves decently during the rest of the season. The production of Guy Domville was an attempt to conquer new territory by a *coup de main*; and that sort of enterprise needs a heavier weapon than Mr Henry James forges. Then, too, Mr Henry James's intellectual fastidiousness remains untouched by the resurgent energy and wilfulness of the new spirit. It takes us back to the exhausted atmosphere of George Eliot, Huxley, and Tyndall, instead of thrusting us forward into the invigorating strife raised by Wagner, Ibsen, and Sudermann. That verdant dupe of the lunacy specialists, Dr Max Nordau, would hardly recognize in Mr Henry James "the stigmata of degeneration," which no dramatist at present can afford to be without. Mr Alexander should have struck his blow with the arm of Ibsen or Sudermann, or else kept to the old ground. And it appears that neither Mr Pinero, Mr Grundy, nor Mr Jones could have helped him any better than Mr Henry James. Moral, apparently: those who make half revolutions dig their own graves.

But it must be remembered, as a check to the folly of moralizing, that the plays which belong to no "movement," and in which the authors have gratified their fancies without reference to any views, have prospered—at least, they have not been withdrawn. In The Passport, The Prude's Progress, and The Strange Adventures of Miss Brown, you have imagination, humor, and a sense of character within the limits of good fellowship. These qualities will carry a good deal of psychology and social doctrine about the unhappiness of marriage, the emancipation of woman, and so forth, if the loading be judiciously done. But the psychology and the doctrine can be done without, whereas the imagination, the humor, the sympathetic sense of character, whether blunt and vulgar or acute and subtle, are indispensable. It was the purest snobbery of criticism which this season reverently hailed The Notorious Mrs Ebbsmith as a masterpiece, and saluted The Prude's Progress with a supercilious nod. I rather congratulate myself on having been polite to the three unpretending successes, and on having cut Mrs Ebbsmith dead at first sight.

Here again it should be noted that these three successful plays, unlike Mrs Ebbsmith and The Philistines, are very well cast and very well acted, The Passport especially being played for all it is worth by an exceptionally strong and well suited company. Another apparently successful play was Mr Carton's Home Secretary. Mr Carton, beside the pleasant gift of lightness of heart, has at least imagination and humor enough to assimilate the imaginative and humorous work of other authors, and to make up a pasticcio of the parts in which a London audience delights to see certain favorite artists: Mr Lewis Waller as Captain Swift, Miss Neilson as the austerely angelic wife of an erring mortal man, Miss Moore as a bewitching flirt, Mr Sydney Brough as a good-hearted young gentleman with a sympathetically comic love affair, and Mr Wyndham as a reformed rake. For my part, I wish Mr Wyndham had never reformed. In the old days, when he sipped every flower and changed every hour, when he sowed acres of wild oats and violated every moral obligation, one foresaw that the pace would not last, and one hoped that he would presently go deeper into life and art, and do the fullest justice to his admirable talent as an actor. Unhappily, instead of doing this, he played the insufferable John Mildmay, became serious, and gave up acting altogether to exhibit himself as a quiet gentleman, who can act in the old scandalous fashion if he likes, but prefers, as a man of heart, to refrain. The refraint is no doubt impressive; but it is getting tiresome as a pose, though I should be delighted to see it in a real part. Rosmer, for instance, would be an excellent part for Mr Wyndham in his latest vein.

I now propose to banish the theatre from my mind for a couple of months at least. Since January I have devoted to it far too much of what was meant for mankind. I could hardly have gone back to it even for the above retrospect had I not been led gently by Miss Cissie Loftus, whose imitations of popular actors I studied with much interest at the Palace Theatre the other evening. Nothing teaches a critic more than a study of how far a great artist can be imitated. As a musical critic I learnt a great deal from a comparison of Miss Nettie Carpenter with Sarasate, and Miss Szumowska with Paderewski; and I am the wiser now for seeing how much more of Sarah Bernhardt Miss Loftus can reproduce than of Miss Rehan. But it is not as a mimic that Miss Loftus fascinates the public. The imitation, clever and delicate as it is, is only an excuse for the reality, which is Miss Loftus herself; and I shall not analyse the qualities which go to make up her very attractive personality until I see her on another stage acting at first hand. Among other artists whom I saw at the Palace were Miss Clara Wieland and the illustrious Miss Lottie Collins. Miss Wieland is very interesting from the critic's point of view. Her singing, her dancing, her pantomime, her ogling, her cleverness, even her plump sort of prettiness, are as smart and artistic as they need be; and yet it is impossible to detect in her any enjoyment of what she does, or any sympathetic sense of its charm. She seems to have observed that such things are effective, and to have industriously learnt to do and to be accordingly. Miss Lottie Collins, on the other hand, has still her Tarararesque *diable au corps*; but all the music has gone from her singing, because, in her determination to deliver her lines pointedly, she forgets to keep up the swing of the tune, and allows her comic-song singing to decay into mere seventh-rate character acting. A tune treated in that way is a tune spoilt; and the words of a music-hall song are never worth spoiling the tune for. I respectfully assure Miss Collins that unless she promptly recaptures the art of keeping the musical lilt perfectly in step with every syllable of the words, she will soon find her popularity degringolading from the summit to which the Tarara craze exalted it.

ROMEO AND JULIET

Romeo and Juliet. Lyceum Theatre, 21 September 1895.

[28 *September* 1895]

How we lavish our money and our worship on Shakespear without in the least knowing why! From time to time we ripen for a new act of homage. Great preparations are made; high hopes are raised; everyone concerned, from the humblest *persona muta* on the stage to the sworn first-nighter in the gallery, is full of earnest belief that the splendor of the Swan will be revealed at last, like the Holy Grail. And yet the point of the whole thing is missed every time with ludicrous ineptitude; and often a ruined actor-manager spends the rest of his life, like the Ancient Mariner, in telling the tale of what it cost, and how So-and-So got his (or her) first chance in it, and how such and such other eminent people declared that nothing like it had ever been done before, and so on and so forth. Still, there is nothing for it but to try and try and try again. Every revival helps to exhaust the number of possible ways of altering Shakespear's plays unsuccessfully, and so hastens the day when the mere desire for novelty will lead to the experiment of leaving them unaltered. Let us see what there is to learn from Mr Forbes Robertson's revival of Romeo and Juliet, before that goes the way of all the other revivals. I hardly like to call Mr Forbes Robertson an artist, because he is notoriously a gentleman with a taste for painting, and the two things are usually incompatible. Your Englishman always conceives that to be romantic and to have a susceptible imagination is to be potentially a painter. His eye for form may be that of a carpenter, his sense of color that of a haberdasher's window-dresser in the Old Kent Road: no matter, he can still imagine historical scenes—"King James receiving the news of the landing of William of Orange" or the like—and draw them and color them, or he can dress up his wife as Zenobia or Dante's Beatrice or Dolly Varden, according to her style, and copy her. I do not level these disparaging observations at Mr Forbes Robertson: I only wish to make it clear that I approach his latest enterprise completely free from the common assumption that he is likely to stage Romeo and Juliet better than anyone else because he paints pictures and sends them to the exhibitions occasionally. To be quite frank, I am rather prejudiced against him by that fact, since I learnt in the days when I criticized pictures that his sense of color is essentially and Britannically an imaginative and moral one: that is, he associates low tones ("quiet colors" they call them in Marshall & Snellgrove's) with dignity and decency, and white linen with cleanliness and respectability. I am therefore not surprised to find the dresses at the Lyceum, though handsome and expensive, chastened by the taste of a British gentleman; so that the stalls can contemplate the fourteenth century and yet feel at home there—a remarkable result, and a very desirable one for those who like it. "Mrs Patrick Campbell's dresses," says the program, "have been carried out by Mrs Mason, of New Burlington Street." I can only

say that I wish they had been carried out and buried. They belong
to Mrs Mason, and are her triumph, instead of to Mrs Campbell.
I know how to value an actress who is an artist in dressing fashion-
ably, like Miss Gertrude Kingston; and I delight in one who is an
artist in dressing originally, like Miss Ellen Terry; but a lady who
is dressed by somebody else, according to somebody else's ideas,
like any dressmaker-made woman of fashion, is artistically quite
out of the question; and I can only excuse the Lyceum Juliet costumes on the supposition that Mrs Campbell deliberately aimed
at suggesting by them the tutelage of a girl of fourteen who is not
yet allowed to choose her own dresses.

The scenery is excellent. Mr William Harford's "public place
in Verona" has only one defect, and that a very English one. The
sky is too cold, and the cypresses too pale: better have painted
them with dabs of warm brown on an actually gold sky in the
beautiful old fashion, than have risked that Constablesque suggestion, faint as it is, of English raininess and chill. But for the
rest, it is easy to imagine that the flood of the Adige is really
hurrying along behind that embankment as Mercutio leans idly
over it. Friar Laurence's cell, too, is good: one can feel the
shadowed cloisters outside, with the sunlight and the well in the
middle of the quadrangle; and though I do not believe that a
simple friar's cell often ran to the luxury of a couple of frescoes
by Giotto, yet the touch is suggestive and pardonable. Mr Ryan's
corner of Mantua in the last act would be perfect if the light could
only be forced to Italian pitch: in fact it surpasses the real thing
in respect of its freedom from the atrocious Mantuan stenches
and huge mosquitoes from the marshes. Mr Harker has only one
scene, that of Capulet's ball, a beautiful fourteenth-century loggia; whilst Mr Harford, having to do another scene in Capulet's
house, has jumped forward to genteelly elegant Renascence work
in carved white marble, in the manner of the Miracoli at Venice.
It will be inferred, and rightly inferred, that the scenery is enormously in advance of that to which Mr Augustin Daly treated
us for The Two Gentlemen of Verona. No doubt Mr Daly paid
as much as Mr Forbes Robertson; but Mr Daly's scene-painters

copied bad work, and Mr Forbes Robertson's have copied good. That makes all the difference.

Of course, in criticizing the general effect, the play and the acting cannot be altogether left out of account, though it would be unfair to lay too much stress on them. Perhaps the most difficult character in the play as far as finesse of execution goes is Mercutio. We see Mercutio in his first scene as a wit and fantasist of the most delicate order. In his next, apparently without any shock to the Elizabethan sense of congruity, he is a detestable and intolerable cad, the exact prototype of our modern 'Arry. The change gives such another glimpse into the manners of that time as you get in Much Ado from the astonishment which Benedick creates by taking to washing his face every day. By stage tradition, Mercutio is as much a leading part as Romeo, if not more so. Therefore, when the manager chooses Romeo, he should be particularly careful to choose a good Mercutio, lest he should appear to have that part purposely underplayed. Perhaps this was why Mr Forbes Robertson went so far out of his way as to cast Mr Coghlan for the part. If so, he overreached himself; for he could not possibly have made a worse choice. I really cannot express myself politely on the subject of Mr Coghlan's performance. He lounges, he mumbles, he delivers the Queen Mab speech in a raffish patter which takes, and is apparently deliberately meant to take, all beauty of tone and grace of measure out of it. It may be that Mr Coghlan has studied the part carefully, and come to the conclusion that since the visit of the Montagues to Capulet's ball is a young bloods' escapade, Mercutio should be represented as coming half drunk and lolling on the stone seat outside to repeat a tipsy rigmarole about nothing. In that case I must express my entire disagreement with Mr Coghlan's reading. Shakespear never leaves me in any doubt as to when he means an actor to play Sir Toby Belch and when to play Mercutio, or when he means an actor to speak measured verse and when slipshod colloquial prose.

Far better than Mr Coghlan's Mercutio, and yet quite the worst impersonation I have ever seen of a not very difficult old woman's part, was Miss Dolores Drummond's Nurse. Tybalt's is such an unmercifully bad part that one can hardly demand anything from its representative except that he should brush his hair when he comes to his uncle's ball (a condition which he invariably repudiates) and that he should be so consummate a swordsman as to make it safe for Romeo to fall on him with absolute abandonment, and annihilate him as Jean de Reszke used to annihilate Montariol. This is one of the great sensations of the play: unless an actor is capable of a really terrible explosion of rage, he had better let Romeo alone. Unfortunately, the "fire-eyed fury" before which Tybalt falls lies outside the gentlemanly limits of Mr Forbes Robertson's stage instinct; and it may be that his skill as an actor is not equal to the task of working-up the audience to the point at which they will imagine an explosion which cannot, of course, be real. At all events the dual scene has none of the murderous excitement which is the whole dramatic point of it: it is tamed down to a mere formal pretext for the banishment of Romeo. Mr Forbes Robertson has evidently no sympathy with Shakespear's love of a shindy: you see his love of law and order coming out in his stage management of the fighting scenes. Nobody is allowed to enjoy the scrimmage: Capulet and Montague are silenced; and the spectators of the duel are women—I should say ladies—who look intensely shocked to see gentlemen of position so grossly forgetting themselves. Mr Forbes Robertson himself fights with unconcealed repugnance: he makes you feel that to do it in that disorderly way, without seconds, without a doctor, shewing temper about it, and actually calling his adversary names, jars unspeakably on him. Far otherwise have we seen him as Orlando wrestling with Charles. But there the contest was in the presence of a court, with measured ground and due formality—under Queensberry rules, so to speak. For the rest, Mr Forbes Robertson is very handsome, very well dressed, very perfectly behaved. His assortment of tones, of gestures, of facial expressions, of attitudes, are limited to half a dozen apiece; but they are carefully selected and all of the best. The arrangements in the last scene are exceedingly nice:

the tomb of the Capulets is beautifully kept, well lighted, and conveniently accessible by a couple of broad steps—quite like a new cathedral chapel. Indeed, when Romeo, contemplating the bier of Juliet (which reflected the utmost credit on the undertaker), said:

> I still will stay with thee,
> And never from this palace of dim night
> Depart again,

I felt that the sacrifice he was making in doing without a proper funeral was greatly softened. Romeo was a gentleman to the last. He laid out Paris after killing him as carefully as if he were folding up his best suit of clothes. One remembers Irving, a dim figure dragging a horrible burden down through the gloom "into the rotten jaws of death," and reflects on the differences of imaginative temperament that underlie the differences of acting and stage-managing.

As to Juliet, she danced like the daughter of Herodias. And she knew the measure of her lines to a hairsbreadth. Did I not say, long ago, that Mrs Tanqueray's piano-playing was worth all the rest of her? And yet I was taken in by Mrs Tanqueray—also by Mrs Ebbsmith, as we all were. Woman's great art is to lie low, and let the imagination of the male endow her with depths. How Mrs Patrick Campbell must have laughed at us whilst we were giving her all the credit—if credit it were—for our silly psychologizing over those Pinero parts! As Juliet she still fits herself into the hospitable manly heart without effort, simply because she is a wonderful person, not only in mere facial prettiness, in which respect she is perhaps not superior to the bevy of "extra ladies" in the fashionable scenes in the new Drury Lane play, not even in her light, beautifully proportioned figure, but in the extraordinary swiftness and certainty of her physical self-command. I am convinced that Mrs Patrick Campbell could thread a needle with her toes at the first attempt as rapidly, as smoothly, as prettily, and with as much attention to spare for doing anything else at the same time as she can play an arpeggio. This physical talent, which is seldom consciously recognized except when it is professedly specialized in some particular direction (as in the case, for instance, of Miss Letty Lind), will, when accompanied by nimbleness of mind, quick observation, and lively theatrical instinct, carry any actress with a rush to the front of her profession, as it has carried Mrs Patrick Campbell. Her Juliet, nevertheless, is an immature performance at all the exceptional points which, please remember, are not very numerous, much of Juliet's business being of a kind that no "leading lady" of ordinary ability could possibly fail in. All the conscious ideas gathered by her from the part and carried out in planned strokes of her own are commonplace. There is not a touch of tragedy, not a throb of love or fear, temper instead of passion: in short, a Juliet as unawakened as Richard III, one in whose death you dont believe, though you would not cry over it if you did believe. Nothing of it is memorable except the dance—the irresistible dance.

It should never be forgotten in judging an attempt to play Romeo and Juliet that the parts are made almost impossible, except to actors of positive genius, skilled to the last degree in metrical declamation, by the way in which the poetry, magnificent as it is, is interlarded by the miserable rhetoric and silly logical conceits which were the foible of the Elizabethans. When Juliet comes out on her balcony and, having propounded the question, "What's in a name?" proceeds to argue it out like an amateur attorney in Christmas-card verse of the "rose by any other name" order, no actress can make it appear natural to a century which has discovered the art of giving prolonged and intense dramatic expression to pure feeling alone, without any skeleton of argument or narrative, by means of music. Romeo has lines that tighten the heart or catch you up into the heights, alternately with heartless fustian and silly ingenuities that make you curse Shakespear's stagestruckness and his youthful inability to keep his brains quiet. It needs a great flowing tide of passion, an irresistibly impetuous march of music, to carry us over these pitfalls and stumbling-blocks, even when we are foolish enough to mistake the good for the bad, and to reverently accept Mr

Coghlan as an authority on the subject of Mercutio. It would be folly to hold out any such hopes of rescue at the Lyceum. Of the whole company there is only one member who achieves artistic respectability as a Shakespearean player, and that is Mr Warde as Capulet. For the most part, one has to listen to the music of Shakespear—in which music, I repeat again and again, the whole worth and charm of these early plays of his lies—as one might listen to a symphony of Beethoven's with all the parts played on the bones, the big drum, and the Jew's harp. But the production is an unsparing effort, and therefore as honorable to Mr Forbes Robertson's management as the highest artistic success could make it. The more efforts of that kind we have, the sooner we shall have the artistic success.

PLAYS THAT ARE NO PLAYS

CHEER, BOYS, CHEER! A new and original drama by Sir Augustus Harris, Cecil Raleigh, and Henry Hamilton. Drury Lane Theatre, 21 September 1895.

HER ADVOCATE. A new play by Walter Frith. Duke of York's (Trafalgar) Theatre, 26 September 1895. [5 *October* 1895]

Do what I will, I cannot acquire a taste for these morbid, realistic-didactic plays on which Sir Augustus Harris lavishes his huge resources. They make me long inexpressibly for a breath of honest, wholesome, simple, straightforward Ibsen. To begin with, I cannot understand them. In vain are the first acts consumed in lawyers' offices, and front scenes laid on every ten minutes to instruct me in the relations, consanguineous, amatory, legal, psychological, and geographical between the persons concerned. I have heard it all over and over again; for in the first play of this kind I ever saw, the course of events was just the same: the hero thrashed the villain; and the villain, with his accomplice, the comic Jew, was arrested by the police in a gorgeous ballroom at the end. The one best way of bringing these sensations about must long since have been ascertained and formulated; so that I feel justified in assuming that the explanations are always the same. But no frequency of repetition can improve my grasp of them. Give me Rosmersholm or The Master Builder, and I am in my depth: their comparatively simple, natural, sympathetic situations do not puzzle me at all; but in Cheer, Boys, Cheer! I not only do not understand, but I feel that I should go mad if I tried to. I can only note that there has been a great development of the realistic element in the staging of these plays—or rather of this play; for it is always essentially the same play —and that certain new features have replaced certain old ones. For instance, the displays of fashionable life, which used to be farcically unlike anything off the stage, are now millinered and tailored, horsed and broughamed, painted and decorated, furnished and upholstered, not by costumiers and property men, but by the artists and tradesmen who equip the real fashionable world; and the verisimilitude of the whole is completed by the likeness between actors and actresses modelling themselves on gentlemen and ladies, and fashionable gentlemen and ladies modelling themselves on actors and actresses. In this way so much realism is now maintained continuously throughout the play that the old-fashioned climax, which usually meant something with real water in it, would appear ridiculous to us. We therefore have a scene with horses, a polo match or a race, to begin with, and in the fourth act a battle with magazine guns. The disappearance of the real water has led to the dropping out of the saving of the heroine's life by the hero, which used to be a matter of course, and which might, I suggest, be effectively reintroduced by supplementing the horses by a trained mad bull. Public taste has so far advanced that the introduction of the detective, followed by two policemen in uniform into the final ballroom scene, has come to be considered bad form: the villain now leaves the stage, with a cynical remark, to meet his doom downstairs. The faithful comic servant in gaiters, who used to introduce the detective, and who always punched the head of some pampered menial in powder and plush in an earlier scene, has also vanished. Otherwise the persons are the same—if one may be allowed to apply such a misleading word as persons to these conventional abstractions of gentility, virtue, innocence, vice, patriotism, and manliness. The personified natural forces who carry on the second act of Wagner's Das Rheingold are as much more human and individual than the characters in Cheer, Boys, Cheer! as the symbolism of Wotan's spear is outdone in insistence by that of Mr Neville's flashing tall hat, for which Mr J. M. Glover should certainly have composed a Wagnerian *Leitmotif*. The superb way in which Mr Neville, as Lord Chepstow, sets his shoulders back and takes off that hat to every lady who ventures into the glare of its efful- gence, is a thing to be seen, not described. Of drama proper there is hardly any. There are serio-comic discussions on law, politics, business, socialism, the effect of pigeon-shooting on the English character, the danger of the Matabele wiping out the English race with quick-firing guns (rather cool, this, in view of recent his- tory), all picked up and dropped in a scrappy way, the people on the stage putting leading questions to one another in order to bring out disjointed irrelevant little claptraps, which are immedi- ately balanced by little cynicisms, neither of them very sincere, or having anything whatever to do with the play or with the characters of the speakers. Here and there the dialogue is en- livened by a clever little sketch of the commoner foibles of humanity, or a bit of fun, or even a stroke of feeling, all stuck in as inorganically as the polo match is stuck in. This is inevitable, as there is no dramatic soil for them to grow from. The whole affair is a purely traditional entertainment, with the "novel fea- tures" which are part of the tradition brought up to date, regard- less of cost. The greater part of the audience finds itself amused by the spectacle, and interested by the magazine gun-firing, the Johannesburg hotel, the polo match, and the Worth dresses; but it would be utterly ashamed of taking the thrashing of the villain, or the "Just before the battle, mother" episode, otherwise than with its tongue in its cheek. The minority who are affected by these devices are disparaged as sentimentalists and greenhorns: it is a point of honor with the seasoned playgoer to grin cynically at such things as "rot," whilst affecting much connoisseurship in the cleverness with which they are contrived. This to me is the weak point in Drury Lane melodrama. It always contains too much stuff which neither its patrons nor its authors would condescend to take seriously, and which is a mere superstition from the time when playgoers could safely be treated as a mere mob of gaping bumpkins. There is no reason why all the attractive features of the Drury Lane displays should not be retained as integral parts of a genuine drama, which, without being very subtle, should at least be a sincere story about real men, women, and events, and not a conventional string of situations filled up with villains, heroines, and heroes whose sole proofs of heroism are outbursts of violent blackguardism of the same kind as those in which American lynching mobs display their moral indignation.

Her Advocate, at the Duke of York's Theatre, as they now snobbishly call the Trafalgar, brings forward Mr Walter Frith as an industrious apprentice to the authorship of the Drury Lane school. Stage philosophy, stage fun, stage sentiment, and stage fine writing seem to come quite easily to him; and he uses them, as he uses the stock stage figures, in a simple and direct way of business, to produce a paying play. The workmanship is terribly commonplace; but the stuff is clever and lively, and disarms criticism by making no serious pretence to artistic merit. Just as another Frith frankly said, "I cannot do you an artistic picture like Botticelli's Primavera or the like, but I'll do you a railway station or a Derby Day to the life"; so the author of Her Advocate seems to have said, "I cannot write you a dramatic poem, like Twelfth Night or Pelléas et Mélisande, nor do I pretend to any of the qualities of Molière or Labiche, Goldsmith or Sheridan, Ibsen or Sudermann; but I'll do you a criminal trial that will be as delightful as the real thing." There is a sort of greatness in this frank recognition of one's limitations. In the National Gallery it is quite possible, after breathing the finest ether of the true artistic atmosphere among the early Italian pictures for an hour, to spend a few minutes looking at The Derby Day without resenting its absolutely prosaic character any more than you do that of the fire-hose. It is the same with Her Advocate. You do not think of literary charm, of delicate wit, of flashes that light up the dark places of our nature, of the tragedy and comedy of the conflicts of men with one another and with fate: you are simply interested to see where the dock is, and the witness-box, and the jury; to watch the javelin-men and hear the judge threatening to have the court cleared; and you are amused and excited by the witness who first describes how he saw the prisoner poison someone out of a blue bottle at several yards distance, and then, at comparatively close quarters, mistakes an ink-bottle for the counsel's cigaret-case, finally breaking down altogether. It is exactly like the arrest of the forger in The Railway Station. When the witness sees the ghost of the murdered man and drops down dead in the box after confessing his guilt, you are not at all reminded of Macbeth, and you are perhaps a little sceptical as to whether that is how it really happens; but then you are ready to make some allowance for being in a theatre. On the whole, you cannot deny that you have passed the evening pleasantly enough, the more so as Mr Frith's realism is quite genuine as far as it goes. In most stage trial-scenes the external imitation of a court may be exact enough; the procedure may be as accurate as the conditions of stage representation permit; and the barristers, judge, and police may be properly placed and properly dressed. But beneath this superficial conformity to real life you generally detect the traditional stage judge, stage barrister, and stage policeman, drawn by an author who has never been for a moment in touch with legal and official life and ideas. Mr Frith knows his world better than that; and as he has been fortunate enough to get his play very well stage-managed, the effect of the sketches of life in it is unusually convincing, in spite of interpolations of cheap sentiment and fine writing stuck in as a matter of business. There is just one point at which Mr Frith's social experience fails him. He represents a lady as insisting, because she comes from the country, on opening the windows of a London room for the sake of ventilation. This suggests to me that Mr Frith has not yet been out of London. If he has ever met a human being in the country with any notion of the value of fresh air—if he has ever been in a country-house which did not still contain most of the air which was bottled up in the rooms on the day when the builders locked the door and handed over the key to the first occupier, he may regard himself as an exceptionally fortunate man.

The actors in Her Advocate have an easy task: indeed, they are for the most part wasted on the play. It is positively exasperating to see an artist like Miss Gertrude Kingston condemned to play a snivelling melodramatic police court heroine, who might just as well be represented by a lay figure with a phonograph in its mouth, a crying machine in its nose, and a label round its neck inscribed "Hospital Nurse wrongfully accused of Murder." Mr Cartwright, as "her advocate," enjoys himself immensely. He gives us the Adelphi voice, the Adelphi suffusion of suppressed emotion, and the Adelphi unction in remarking, in the character of a leading counsel in the thick of a heavy murder case, that "the happy day is enamelled blue and gold like some old missal." He leans much on the orchestra, also in the Adelphi manner, turning on the band and the deeper springs of emotion simultaneously. So tender is his nature that he devotes all his earnings at the bar to paying off the creditors of his father's bank, which broke in an unhappy hour; and, though engaged to an attractive and deserving young lady impersonated by Miss Lena Ashwell, he falls violently in love with his client, whose affections fortunately turn out to be engaged elsewhere, let us hope to a gentleman with an insatiable taste for tears. Mr Cartwright enters so thoroughly into the absurdity and staginess of his part that he must be regarded as the author's accomplice rather than his victim on these points; but he sometimes brings off a commonsense stroke intelligently, and even, in a sentimental way, forcibly, though his style and execution have none of the finer artistic qualities. Mr Volpe as the judge—a nicely touched bit of comedy —and Mr Somerset as the witness have much the best of the trial scene. Mr Barnes is amusing in the second act as a broken-down Irish barrister, the butt of the junior bar. The other parts have nothing in them: one only hopes, in the case of promising young actors like Mr Oswald Yorke and Mr Holmes Gore, that they will not forget that the traditions of style represented by Mr Cartwright are not the only successful ones, and that artists like Mr Hare and Mr Wyndham are also popular.

On the whole, these entertainments, in which there is neither real drama nor opportunity for real acting, are bad for the stage. That one or two theatres and companies should be specialized for them is reasonable enough, since the companies can consist of actors who cannot do fine work. But it is not encouraging to see an enterprise like Mr Dana's, which began so well with The Passport, a tolerable comedy made highly diverting by capital acting, declining upon a mechanical sensational entertainment like Her Advocate, which could be played as effectively by a third-rate company as by a first-rate one.

THE CHILI WIDOW

THE CHILI WIDOW. Adapted by Arthur Bourchier and Alfred Sutro from Monsieur le Directeur, by MM. Bisson and Carré. Royalty Theatre.   [12 *October* 1895]

ON paying a somewhat belated visit to The Chili Widow the other evening, I was astonished to find that Mr Bourchier has not only taken the Royalty Theatre—many have done that before him, and some have repented it—but has actually founded there, with apparent success, a new school of stage art. At least it is new to the regular professional stage, though not to the country house or the university dramatic club. It is the school of the romping, gleeful amateur, not he with the contracted brow, the Elizabethan imagination, and the patent method of voice production, but the facetious undergraduate who dresses up for a lark, the awfully jolly girl who can act like anything, and the funny man with accomplishments, including the banjo. I am not intolerant of such sportiveness: the majesty of criticism can unbend on occasion and enjoy a bit of fun, served up with ridiculous home-made art, as much as the humblest member of the domestic staff admitted to the drawing room to see the daughters of the house in their stage glory. Even at the Royalty Theatre I do not object to it: only, it is my duty to be perfectly explicit with the public as to the nature of the entertainment. Let me therefore explain.

The accomplishments which distinguish the trained actor from the amateur are not the same as the qualities which distinguish great actors from ordinary ones. Take, first, the difference between the trained actor and the man in the street—the layman. When the layman walks, his only object is to get to Charing Cross; when he makes a gesture, it is to attract the attention of a cab-driver or bus-conductor; when he speaks, it is to convey or demand information, or tell a lie, or otherwise further his prosaic ends; when he moves his hands, it is to put up his umbrella or take out his handkerchief. On the stage these merely utilitarian purposes are only simulated: the real purpose is to produce an effect on the senses and imagination of the spectator. The actor's walk is addressed to the spectator's sense of grace, dignity, or strength of movement, and his voice to the listener's sense of expressive or beautiful tone. Impersonations even of ugly or deformed creatures with harsh voices have the same artistic character, and are agreeably disagreeable, just as the most extreme discords in a symphony or opera are distinctly musical, and perfectly different to the random cacophonies which arise from the tuning of the orchestra. Now, the power of complying with artistic conditions without being so preoccupied by them as to be incapable of thinking of anything else is hard to acquire, and can be perfected only by long practice. Talma estimated the apprenticeship at twenty years. The habit can never become as instinctive as keeping one's balance, for instance, because failure in that for even an instant means a fall, so that the practice in it is lifelong and constant; whereas the artistic habit lapses more or less in the absence of an audience, and even on the stage can be forgotten for long periods without any worse consequences than a loss of charm which nothing may bring to the actor's attention. The real safeguard against such lapses is a sense of beauty—the artistic sense—cultivated to such a degree of sensitiveness that a coarse or prosaic tone, or an awkward gesture, jars instantly on the artist as a note out of tune jars on the musician. The defect of the old-fashioned systems of training for the stage was that they attempted to prescribe the conclusions of this constantly evolving artistic sense instead of cultivating it and leaving the artist to its guidance. Thus they taught you an old-fashioned stage-walk, an old-fashioned stage-voice, an old-fashioned stage way of kneeling, of sitting down, of shaking hands, of picking up a handkerchief, and so on, each of them supposed to be the final and perfect way of doing it. The end of that was, of course, to discredit training altogether. But neglect of training very quickly discredits itself; and it will now perhaps be admitted that the awakening and culture of the artistic conscience is a real service which a teacher can render to an actor. When that conscience is thoroughly awakened and cultivated, when a person can maintain vigilant artistic sensitiveness throughout a performance whilst making all the movements required by the action of a drama, and speaking all its dialogue graphically without preoccupation or embarrassment, then that person is a technically competent artistic actor, able to play a part of which he hardly comprehends one line, in a play of which he knows nothing except his own words and speeches and the cues thereto, much more intelligibly and effectively, as well as agreeably, than a statesman with ten times his general ability could. He can only be beaten, in fact, by the professional rival who has equal skill in execution, but has more numerous and valuable ideas to execute. The finest actors—Jefferson, Coquelin, Salvini, Duse— carry this technical skill to such a point that though they act so beautifully that you cannot take your eyes off them even when you do not understand what they are saying, yet the beauty seems so spontaneous and inevitable that it is generally quite impossible to persuade their admirers that there is any art or study in their acting at all.

The effect on an ordinary man of making him suddenly conscious of the artistic aspect of his movements and speech is to plunge him into a condition of terror and bewilderment in which he forgets how to do anything. It gives him stage fright, in short.

Take a humble tradesman who has demolished his boiled mutton and turnips for half a century without misgiving. Invite him to meet a peer or two at dinner in Grosvenor Square, and he will refuse dish after dish because he no longer feels sure of how he ought to eat it. Take a lady who habitually talks the heads off all her acquaintances, and put her on a platform to make the simplest statement to an audience, and she will be struck dumb. The nervous agonies of the young have caused more discomfort in the world than the torments of the Inquisition. If this happens on the large stage of the world to people who have all had at least some social training, what must be the anguish of the wretch who, with his face absurdly painted, and dressed in an outlandish costume that does not fit him, is thrust on a stage for the first time in his life to speak Elizabethan stage English as Rosencrantz or Guildenstern, or even to stand as a mute courtier and look on at some fellow creature making the like horrible exhibition of himself!

All this, however, presupposes that the victim has an artistic conscience, only just born and still blind. There are plenty of people who have either no artistic conscience at all or else one which is very easily satisfied. Just as you have soldiers who are not frightened under fire because they have not imagination enough to conceive their danger, whilst your imaginative Napoleon or Nelson turns pale, and your serene Goethe sees yellow, so there are debutters, both on the social and theatrical stage, who get through their ordeal easily because they are only imperfectly conscious of it. And there are happy people whose artistic conscience has always been awake, and to whom sufficient conscious grace and beauty to begin with are second nature. There is also the person with high animal spirits, a strong sense of fun, and a turn for mimicry. He, with an utterly unawakened artistic conscience, will flourish greatly at private theatricals, and sometimes also at public ones. With a good ear for musical pitch and tune and measure, and some physical agility, he will do excellently at the music-halls; but he very often has no ear to speak of; and then, incapable of singing, dancing, fine diction or grace-

ful movement, he delights himself with tomfoolery, and is hugely
pleased with himself when the people laugh. And since the people
do laugh, there is a constant tendency to substitute tomfoolery
for artistic comedy on the stage, since artistic comedians are in
the nature of things much scarcer than buffoons. Then it is that
the skilled critic must act as the watchdog of art, and begin to
bark vigorously. Unfortunately, he can only bark: it is the
manager who must bite. The artistic manager, as distinguished
from the man who merely takes a theatre and puts up a play,
is also a critic, and, knowing the difference between finished
stage execution and mere larking, picks and drills his company
accordingly. That is how theatres come to have styles as well as
individuals.

The nature of my criticism of the Royalty performance will
now be intelligible. I do not deny that it is amusing—sometimes;
but I do most emphatically deny that the performance, as a whole,
has any artistic character. I go further: I sorrowfully profess my
conviction, based on an attentive examination of the stage business, that the performers have been not only encouraged, but
positively ordered, to clown as much as possible so as to keep
the fun going and make the play lively. The back drawing room
has never produced a company of comedians so intensely and
ostentatiously conscious of their own funniness. Squawking voices,
grinning faces, foolish antics, pervade the play to such an extent
that though, as I have admitted (very magnanimously, believe
me), the second act amused me, yet I could not face the third, having lost my old robust schoolboy appetite for large doses of that
sort of merriment. The jar on my nerves began in Harmony, a
little play by Mr Henry Arthur Jones, one of his early pieces, in
which you can plainly see the feeling, imagination, and humor
of the future author of The Crusaders and Rebellious Susan,
along with the stage asides and soliloquies of a cruder period.
The gentleman who played the youthful lover in this nearly
drove me out of my senses with his determination to be breezy
and not to let the play down. His voice rattled and his figure
bounded, until I gave up trying to imagine that I was looking

at a scene in a primitive country parish, and fell to wondering what quality over and above a cheerful effrontery can be needed to make any able-bodied young gentleman into an actor in three weeks nowadays. Mr Kinghorne hardly improved matters by doing his business as the blind organist in the safest of old stage styles, piling it on and working it up tremendously, and never touching nature at any point. And Miss Ettie Williams, pretty, self-possessed, and resolutely metropolitan, gave the final blow to the illusion. But it was not until The Chili Widow came on that I began to suspect that breeziness, and rattle, and intense comic consciousness were parts of the managerial policy. Mr Bourchier seemed determined that there should be no mistake about our being there to make a regular evening of it; and it is possible that the profound depression into which this attitude naturally threw me—as I think it would any reasonable person—may have made me somewhat captious. At all events, I soon felt that I could willingly mow down the whole of that stage Home Office staff with a Maxim gun. It was not mere extravagance of caricature that annoyed me; for Mr Blakeley and Miss Larkin, who are hardened veterans in broad caricature, managed their business smoothly and easily, and at least did not play the part of the audience as well by laughing at their own performances; whilst Miss Phillips clowned only when a silly part absolutely forced her to, and made the most of the rest. What was wrong with the performance was its persistent Philistinism. It is fortunate for Mr Bourchier and for Miss Violet and Miss Irene Vanbrugh that they are such very pleasant people and that the play is such an amusing play. Mr Bourchier is a born comedian: he has ease, humor, geniality, and plenty of natural grace of speech and manner. Happy in these endowments, he insists on sharing the fun himself, and is evidently quite persuaded that if all the others will only rattle along in the same careless way, the result will be as pleasant in their case as in his. He enjoys himself so robustly that the audience cannot help feeling good-humored. The very thoughtlessness of his performance is an element in its popularity: one feels that a thoroughly healthy person never thinks. Miss Violet Vanbrugh is very attractive; but she is much more conscious of Miss Violet Vanbrugh than of her part: in other words, she lacks conviction. The fact is, she is not a comedian: all this man-killing archness does not belong to her: one sees that it is only her fun, not her nature; and the result is, not an artist at work, but a pretty lady at play, a spectacle always agreeable, but not to the purpose of the connoisseur in dramatic art. Miss Irene Vanbrugh has more genuine comic force, and is better fitted in her part; but as far as I saw the play she only appeared in the first act, which might with great advantage be cut out. Mr Kinghorne plays the office-keeper much more naturally than the organist in the first piece, and much more entertainingly. The others funnify their parts more or less blatantly, the whole ill-concerted attempt to produce a facetious atmosphere without any reference to the finer artistic conditions being, as I have said, discordant and amateurish. Even the audience struck me as a somewhat unsophisticated, not to say chuckleheaded one; but I am glad to be able to add that it was numerous and well pleased. It had the air of having at last discovered a play which was better fun than a smoking concert.

On a point of pronunciation may I be allowed to say that Ballymacklerush, with a strong stress on the rush, is a credible Irish name, but that Bally McKillrush, with the stress on the kill, is impossible. The only safe rule about the pronunciation of an Irish name is that whatever way comes naturally to an Englishman is quite certain to be the wrong way.

The Royalty Theatre, completely redecorated, is more itself than ever, a fact which, in view of old times, is not at all depressing. The prices have been raised to the standard customary in "no fee" houses; but I need hardly add that I paid sixpence for a program with nineteen advertisements on it and an appeal for more. The new drop scene, a gigantic pastoral in the Pompadour style, painted in the gloomiest colors, is coeval in point of taste with the days when Dean Street, Soho Square, was a fashionable London address. Mr Bourchier, however, seems likely to make it a fashionable theatrical address for some time to come, on the which, in spite of his unawakened condition, I do congratulate him.

PINERO AS HE IS ACTED

THE BENEFIT OF THE DOUBT. A new and original comedy, in three acts. By Arthur W Pinero. Comedy Theatre, 16 October 1895.

POOR MR POTTON. A new and original farce, in three acts. By Clarence Hamlyn and H. M. Paull. Vaudeville Theatre, 10 October 1895.   [19 *October* 1895]

THIS time Mr Pinero has succeeded. The Benefit of the Doubt is worth The Profligate, Mrs Tanqueray, and Mrs Ebbsmith rolled into one and multiplied by ten. It is melancholy to have to add that it has broken the back of our London stage, and may even fail through the sniffing monotony and dreary ugliness of the acting; but about the merit of the play there can be no question. Mr Pinero, concentrating himself on a phase of life and sentiment which he thoroughly understands, has extracted abundant drama from it, and maintained it at an astonishingly high and even pressure for two hours, without for a moment being driven back on the woman with a past, the cynical libertine peer, the angel of purity, the Cayley Drummle confidant, or any other of the conventional figures which inevitably appear in his plays whenever he conceives himself to be dealing as a sociologist with public questions of which he has no solid knowledge, but only a purely conventional and theatrical conceit. In the Benefit of the Doubt he keeps within the territory he has actually explored; and the result is at once apparent in the higher dramatic pressure, the closer-knit action, the substitution of a homogeneous slice of life for the old theatrical sandwich of sentiment and comic relief, and the comparative originality, naturalness, and free development of the characters. Even in the machinery by which the persons of the play are got on and off the stage there is a marked improvement. It is artificial enough—Mr Pinero has not exactly been born again—but at least there are no intercepted letters, or sendings of one set of people to France and another

217

to India in order to enable a lady to arrive unexpectedly or a gentleman to walk in by night at the drawing room window. There certainly is one nocturnal visit through a window; but it is pardonable; and for the rest, the people come and go in a normal and respectable manner. The play is of a frivolous widow with three fast, slangy, pretty daughters, two of them married. An amiable young gentleman named John Allingham, tormented by a frightfully jealous wife, confides his miseries to one of the married daughters, a Mrs Fraser (Fraser being much away from home). The jealous Mrs Allingham sues for a judicial separation, and the play opens at the point where her petition is refused. Mrs Fraser, however, only escapes very narrowly, as the Judge comments strongly on her indiscretion, and suggests nothing more complimentary for her than "the benefit of the doubt." When Mr Fraser comes home, he acts on this suggestion so very grudgingly that Mrs Fraser rushes off to throw herself upon the more sympathetic Allingham. But that ill-starred example of the perils of excessive good-nature has meanwhile succumbed to his wife's appeal for a reconciliation, she being nearly as violent in her remorse as in her jealousy, and much less reasonable. There you have your drama: first, in the suspense of awaiting the verdict, ended by the return of Mrs Fraser from the divorce court to face out her disgrace before her family and be driven to desperation by the rebuff from her husband; and second, her arrival at Allingham's house just as the demon of jealousy has been reinstalled there on the domestic throne. In handling all this Mr Pinero is never at a loss. He knows what pretty daughters and frivolous mothers are like in those circles which used to be called *demi-mondaine* before that distinction was audaciously annexed by people who are not *mondaine* at all; he knows what the divorce court and the newspapers mean to them; he knows what a jealous woman is like; and he has dramatized them all with an intensity never attained by him before. Consciously or unconsciously, he has this time seen his world as it really is: that is, a world which never dreams of bothering its little head with large questions or general ideas. He no longer attempts to dress up

Mrs Ponsonby de Tomkins like Mrs Besant, and to present the ridiculous result as a portrait of a typical modern "advanced" woman: he sticks to the Bayswater-Kensington *genre*, of which he is a master. He does not even adulterate it with conventional stage sentiment: for instance, none of Mrs Emptage's fast and rather raffish daughters burst into tears at the thought of the holy purity of their sixteenth year, when they could look angels in the face unashamed, as Paula Tanqueray did. His early weaknesses have disappeared along with his late affectations; and the happy issue is the best serious play he has yet produced.

The subject of the acting is almost too painful to face. The second act, which lasts for more than an hour, is pervaded by the violently jealous wife. She only leaves the stage to give place to her wearied and desperate rival, who ends by drinking champagne cup to save herself from fainting, and, having fed on nothing all day but excitement, naturally gets tipsy and hysterical. Such scenes, however moving and interesting they may be, and however skilfully written, can only be made tolerable by sheer beauty of execution. Tact and experience—the best substitutes our unfortunate stage can offer—may do something to steer the performance clear of positive offensiveness; but tact and experience are not enough: unless the lines are spoken by voices of which the ear never tires, with gestures and action which never lose their fascination, the result can be no better than a disagreeable experience, drawing a crowd and holding it only as a street accident does. The reason why the second act made the audience uneasy was that long before the end of it we had had enough, and more than enough, not of the play, but of the performers. We all know the melodramatic style which grew up in the days when actors who played "emotional" parts habitually got themselves into the requisite maudlin condition by making themselves half drunk. This was the true origin of the detestable veiled voice and muzzy utterance which no longer produce any illusion except that of the odor of spirits. The actor of the past did not walk across the stage to open the door: he plunged headlong at the handle, and, when he had safely grasped it, rolled his eye round to give some pretence of dramatic significance to an action which really expressed nothing but his doubts as to his ability to walk straight. He hung over the furniture, leant against the staircase, wallowed, collapsed tragically when he sat down, did everything, in short, to conceal his condition and cover up the absence of that clear, sober, elegant speech and movement which mark the self-possessed and accomplished artist. The old drunken habits have nearly passed away—at least, I hope future generations of critics will not often have to write sympathetic obituary notices deploring the "breakdown in health" of actors and actresses who notoriously drank themselves first off the stage and then out of the world—but the style of acting that arose in the days when everybody drank remains with us as a senseless superstition, and is still laboriously acquired and cultivated by perfectly sober actors. Unhappily for Mr Pinero's play, Mr Leonard Boyne, who probably has no suspicion of the real origin of the traditional style of which he has made himself, next to Mr Charles Warner, the most popular exponent, played John Allingham as he would have played an Adelphi or Drury Lane hero. Miss Lily Hanbury, as the jealous Mrs Allingham, soon proved the weakness of our system of promoting young ladies to leading parts on the strength of good looks and general intelligence and address. Miss Hanbury acted as acting is understood on the London stage. That is, she expressed emotion by catching the left side of her under lip between her front teeth, and twisting the right corner as much out of its natural place as possible. She cried, and declared that she was "bad," meaning that she was mad. Her voice, which careful cultivation might by this time have made a very agreeable one, still has all its girlish, nasal character. Five minutes of Mr Boyne and Miss Hanbury, doing some light and pleasant work in an ordinary play, would leave the impression that they were charming and clever people, and encourage our fatuous satisfaction with the most incompetent profession in the world; but half an hour of them—such a half-hour as Mr Pinero has set them— may I never spend such another! They did their best; but they were hopelessly overparted. As to Miss Winifred Emery, she

received boundless applause, but as it burst out in all its enthusiasm in the first act, before she had uttered a word or made a
gesture, it may safely be discounted. All the same, Miss Emery
played astonishingly well, considering that she is virtually a
beginner at work so difficult as that cut out for her by Mr Pinero.
She was, of course, powerfully aided by her natural charm, and
by the confidence in it which experience has given her. The champagne scene and the passages of querulous lassitude were frankly
realistic; and I rather doubt whether a less pretty and popular
lady dare have treated them so without greater art to help her.
Even as it was, Miss Emery sometimes lost her style and allowed
her intonation to become decidedly disagreeable. But for the most
part, and especially in the first act, she got far beyond any point I
have seen her reach before, and, indeed, beyond any point that is
commonly reached by our London "leading ladies." She evidently
only wants plenty of that sort of work to make her, within the
limits of her temperament, a highly accomplished actress.

Miss Rose Leclercq, not this time condemned to play the
usual caricature of herself, had a real part, and played it with
real distinction. The other parts are of the usual type; that is to
say, they require a certain professional habit for their effective
presentation, but involve little knowledge of the art of acting.
The best of them are in the hands of Miss Esme Beringer, Mr
Cyril Maude, and Mr Aubrey Fitzgerald. Mr Pinero, always a
bad hand at casting a play, has not fitted Miss Beringer very
happily—more's the pity, as she is one of the few young actresses
now on the stage who have studied their profession, or even
realized that there is anything to study in it.

Poor Mr Potton, at the Vaudeville, is called a farce, even a
new and original farce; but it is hardly more than a romp. However, it is tolerably good fun of its kind, childish fun mostly as
regards the action, clever fun occasionally as regards the lines.
The scenes, especially the last act, are not at all ill-planned: there
is a certain incongruity between the jejune flimsiness of the general
notion of the play and the comparative solidity and intelligence
with which it is put together. Probably this is a natural conse-

quence of the collaboration between Mr Clarence Hamlyn and Mr Paull. From the critical point of view the play is chiefly interesting as an example of the extent to which brutality and silliness are still in demand in our theatres, just as the performance is an example of the impudent artlessness with which long scenes can be gabbled through on the London stage without provoking as much criticism as a company of children performing in a nursery would receive from their parents. The brutality is, of course, unconscious, though that is an excellent reason for a critical attempt to induce some consciousness of it. The fun of the play lies in the engagement of Mr Potton (Mr Weedon Grossmith) to an elderly and several times widowed heroine (Miss Gladys Homfrey). Miss Gladys Homfrey is a lady of very ample proportions. I shall not attempt to estimate the excess of her weight over that of Mr Weedon Grossmith with precision; let me put it roughly and safely at not less than fifty pounds. Need I add that the main joke in Poor Mr Potton is the spectacle of Miss Homfrey throwing herself ponderously on Mr Grossmith's neck, and being petted and kissed and courted by him. I am obliged to make the strange confession that I do not enjoy this sort of stage effect; though I admit that the guffaws which it invariably elicits shew that London audiences do not agree with me. Mr Gilbert quite understood his public when he furnished his operas so carefully with stout and mature ladies for the express purpose of making fun of their age and figure. Such fun has always revolted me; and I am waiting for the time when it will revolt the public too. I have by me a book called The Elizabethan Hamlet, by Mr John Corbin, published by Mr Elkin Mathews, in which the author succeeds in fully driving home the fact, not of course hitherto unknown, but certainly hitherto underestimated, that Hamlet first became popular on the stage as a madman: that is, as a comic person according to the ideas of that time. I say of that time as a matter of politeness to my contemporaries, though anyone who has ever seen a village idiot at large must have seen also a crowd of villagers teasing him, encouraging him to make uncouth sounds and cut deplorable capers, and laughing at him with gross enjoyment as at one of Nature's primest jokes. It has always been so, I am afraid. The old-fashioned king's jester was not a clever, satirical, able person like Dumas's Chicot: he was a zany, a poor idiot, a butt, not a wit. Fortunately we have at last reached a point at which the old Hamlet play is out of the question, whilst the masterpiece which Shakespear built on it is the most popular play we have. But is there any distinction, except in degree of atrocity, between the old brutal laughter at "Hamblet's" madness and murderous cunning, and our laughter today at the Lady Janes of Mr Gilbert, and at certain comedians and music-hall artists who are commercially fortunate enough to be abnormally small or grotesque in appearance? And if Shakespear, in a much coarser age, could take subjects which were reeking with the vilest stage traditions, and lift them at one stroke to the highest tragic dignity, is it too much to ask that our modern dramatists should habitually assume that "the British public" consists of humane persons with developed sympathies, and not of rowdy undergraduates and street arabs? I presume that Miss Gladys Homfrey has an honorable ambition to distinguish herself in the art of acting, as Mrs Stirling and Mrs Gilbert have distinguished themselves. Why then should she be condemned to merely exhibit herself as a fat lady? I am not pretending to ignore the fact that personality is an element in the qualification of an actor or actress as well as skill, and that our stage affords so little training that practical dramatic authorship has become the art of exploiting the personalities of popular favorites instead of setting tasks to the executive skill of accomplished artists. If a young author were to come to me and announce his intention of striving to win fame by creating an imaginary heroine who should survive millions of real women as Imogen and Gretchen have, I should, in the paternal character of a man of the world, immediately reply, "Bless your innocence, you mustnt do that. You must vamp up a serious part that will fit Mrs Patrick Campbell, and a serio-comic part that will fit Miss Fanny Brough, bearing carefully in mind that neither of these ladies ever acts anybody but herself, nor indeed dare do it, since the public goes to the theatre to see them playing themselves and not to enjoy dramatic poetry or fine acting." Still, there are limits even to the compulsory cynicism of dramatic authorship. The author may be forced to exploit a lady's temperament and appearance because she cannot act; but he need not condescend to exploit her circumference. Characters like Falstaff are not added to dramatic literature by any process so cheap as making game of the stoutest member of the profession.

Two parts in Poor Mr Potton are well played. Mr Weedon Grossmith succeeds in making Potton perfectly real, and quite a different person from the other characters of his creation. His perplexed conviction, the apparent unconsciousness with which he allows his funniest points to make themselves, the art with which he takes care that they shall make themselves, and the adroitness of his execution, leave nothing for the critic to say except that the part is as well done as it can be done. Miss Haydon, as Mrs Potton, makes a charming old lady, preserving her own dignity and that of her art, as well as the verisimilitude of the play, without losing a scrap of comic effect. I will not say that none of the rest were amusing; but they certainly were often quite as annoying as amusing, gabbling and guying as if the play were being performed for their entertainment much more than for that of the audience. Accustomed as I am becoming to see important parts given to clowning novices and to young women whose flippant personal vanity, bad manners, vulgarly titivated costumes, and slipshod carelessness of speech and action would not be tolerated from a parlormaid by the people who are expected to pay half a guinea for a seat at the theatre, it hardly now seems worth while to complain of an outrage more or less in this direction. The Vaudeville company, apart from Mr Grossmith and Miss Haydon, is neither better nor worse than I expected to find it. The exceptions were Miss Beet, who gave a capital sketch of an irritable general servant, and Mr Tom Terriss, whose father has endowed him handsomely with an admirable voice and an attractive figure and face, disinheriting him only in the matter of his chin, which is a comparatively unfamiliar feature.

If Mr Terriss's part was not a very exacting one, he at least got a thorough grip of it, and would have pleased the audience even if his name had been an unknown one.

MORE MASTERPIECES

THE RISE OF DICK HALWARD. A new play in three acts. By Jerome K. Jerome. Garrick Theatre, 19 October 1895.

[26 *October* 1895]

WITH every possible disposition to tolerate all views of life on the stage, I cannot quite keep my patience with the pessimism of Mr Jerome K. Jerome and his school. I can endure, for a strictly limited time, the splenetic, cynical pessimist, who lashes and satirizes the abundant follies and weaknesses of mankind to excuse himself for giving it up as a bad job. But your maudlin pessimist who, like Mr Jerome K. Jerome, says "We are all hopeless scoundrels; so let us be kind and gentle to one another": him I find it hard to bear. Mr Jerome's hero Dick Halward is called Dick because that is a less harsh term than Richard. A judge might say, "Richard Halward: after a patient trial, and upon evidence which must convince every reasonable person of the justice of the verdict, you have been found guilty of one of the meanest frauds that has ever come before a court of law. By selling your professional honor and robbing your friend at one stroke, you have shewn yourself void alike of character in your public capacity and of feeling in your private relations. You are a dishonest and worthless fellow; and the sentence of the court is, etc., etc." Not thus Mr Jerome K. Jerome. He grasps the culprit's hand, and, in a voice husky with emotion, says: "Dick, old chap, not another word about that money. Not a man of us but would have done just as you did, Heaven help us, if we got the chance. You were tempted, and you fell; but you sent £5 to your sisters when you were poor; you never had a hard word for the housemaid at your chambers; and in the sterling simplicity of your heart you hid your pipe and slippers in the coal-scuttle when you had lady visitors. How many of us would do as much? You have sinned; but you have suffered; and it was love that led you astray. Let the cold world say what it will, you shall have a happy ending, Dick, dear old man. God bless you, Dick, God bless you. Go and live happily ever after. It's unmanly to—dash it, I think I'll go and smoke a pipe outside, if you dont mind, Dick." Ibsen might have been a rich man today if he had only taken that view of things. Perhaps, however, it is only fair that it should bring dramatic authors money; for it will assuredly not bring them anything else.

A criminal is not necessarily a despicable person. The man who is strongly, ably, egotistically and therefore self-respectingly wicked may be crowned or hung, as the case may be, according to his failure or success; but he is not despised. The only one insufferable and unpardonable thing for a criminal to do is to confess before he is found out. When a man goes to a police station and gives himself up for an undiscovered murder, the first uncontrollable impulse of every healthy person is one of impatient exasperation with a fool who cannot bear his cross and hold his tongue, but must tear open a healed wound for the sake of having his miserable conscience soothed by the hangman. Mr Jerome K. Jerome, by way of carrying to its possible extreme his pessimistic theory that the baser a man is, the more intensely human and sympathetic he is, completes the infamy of Dick Halward by making him volunteer a quite exceptionally gratuitous and dastardly confession at the moment when he believes he is going to commit suicide by taking his father's patent headache cure. Under such circumstances a man with any decency left in him would surely make a stage will leaving his property to the person he had robbed of it, and then slip quietly overboard, so to speak. But Halward cannot deny himself a dram of sympathy at the price of leaving everybody disgusted, ashamed, and miserably uncomfortable. He pours the headache cure into a tumbler (by the way, it is quite a genuine cure, and may be relied on not only for headache, but for ailments of all kinds—nineteen drops of hydrocyanic acid), and summons to his presence his two most intimate friends, one of whom, it is hardly necessary to say, is the youth whose inheritance he has stolen. His own betrothed and that of the young man are also sent for. He then baldly confesses; and the play immediately collapses like a punctured tyre, Mr Jerome's stagecraft collapsing visibly with it. For the unhappy four witnesses of the confession are so totally unequal to the occasion that they simply drift off the stage one after another flabbergasted, only one of them having the presence of mind to explain that he must go and think about it a little before committing himself. Fortunately for Mr Jerome, the five parties to this unexampled stage effect were artists no less popular than Miss Marion Terry, Miss Annie Hughes, Mr Willard, Mr Esmond, and Mr Barnes. If Mr Jerome will try it at the Independent Theatre with five comparatively unknown performers, he will probably be made acutely conscious of his own originality. When the disabled quartet had melted from the gaze of a dumbfounded audience, Halward proceeded to bid the world farewell and raise the headache cure to his lips. We all remembered how, in The Dancing Girl, when Mr Tree was in the like extremity, Miss Norreys slid down the banisters and seized the fatal goblet at the last moment. We were therefore not surprised to see Miss Marion Terry come back. Since it was Miss Terry's objection to marrying a man with less than five thousand a year that had given Dick his excuse for his crime, the attitude of pure derision in which we should otherwise have contemplated the heroine's reappearance was suspended in view of the possibility that the play might after all end heroically by the lady insisting on sharing the poison, and the two dying together by their own condemnation, Rosmersholmwise. But Mr Jerome knew better than that. Miss Terry did her duty according to Mr Jerome's lights—the footlights. She weaned her lover from his fell purpose, and promised to go across the seas with him and begin a new life regardless of income. At which unspeakable crisis of Mr Jerome's attempt to hold the mirror up to nature, the curtain fell.

I find it very hard to believe that Mr Jerome, in writing this play, or Mr Willard in producing it, had any other object than to make money in the cheapest possible way. So hard, in fact, that I shall not try to believe it. No doubt I shall be told that

> The drama's laws the drama's patrons give;
> And those who live to please must please to live.

But you cannot get out of an argument by simply telling a lie in a heroic couplet. The drama's laws the drama's patrons do *not* give, nor ever can give: that is the prerogative of the dramatist, and of the dramatist alone. Nor need anybody "please to live": on the contrary, the person who is willing to do anything to please everybody is a universally and deservedly despised and disastrous person. The public cannot do without the theatre; and the actor and the dramatist are therefore in a position to insist on honorable terms. The managers who are at present flinging all professional honor and artistic faith to the winds by competing with one another as to who shall secure the vulgarest and foolishest play are no more under any compulsion to do so than Sir Henry Irving is to swallow swords, balance straws on his nose, or bounce up through star-traps. Suppose Sir Henry were to join the ignoble scramble after big pecuniary successes, and to abandon the comparatively high ground on which he is now securely planted, what would be the result? Only that on the low ground he would be easily beaten by the music-halls; so that he would debauch his audiences only to lose them. That is just what too many of our managers are doing at the present time. They deliberately select melodramas of the Surrey and Marylebone types, and engage first-rate performers to present them at west end houses at west end prices. In due course these pieces are sent "on tour" through the provinces. Now "the provinces" include suburban London; and at this very moment the people who like shoddy melodrama are waking up to the fact that if they do their playgoing at the suburban houses, they can see, at reasonable prices, exactly the same plays as they are now paying exorbitant prices to see worse acted at west end houses. Take this play of Mr Jerome's, The Rise of Dick Halward. The part of Dick, from its ridiculous invocation of Mephistopheles in the first act to its sham farewell to earth in the last, is arrant fustian, better than the fustian of twenty years ago, no doubt, but still, judged by the literary and artistic standards of today, very sorry fustian. Mr Willard does not play it more effectively than a strong transpontine leading man would: he plays it less effectively. As to Miss Marion Terry, I could name half a dozen young ladies, not to be compared to her for a moment in artistic power and accomplishment, who might replace her with advantage, as the heroine. The part in her hands is only a bad misfit. Miss Hughes, Mr Esmond, and the rest are equally, if less grotesquely, thrown away on their parts. The Prude's Progress was far more successfully represented, not only because it was a better play, but because it had a weaker cast. When The Rise of Dick Halward is performed by actors just fit for the class of people to whose level the play has been written down, it will go ten times better than it does at the Garrick, although the sums paid to the leading performers will be less by about five-sixths.

In Mr Oscar Wilde's Ideal Husband there was a remarkable scene in which the fraudulent Cabinet Minister reproached his wife with idealizing and worshipping his moral virtues instead of loving his very self as he loved her. This so exactly suits Mr Jerome's sentimental pessimism that he flourishes it in a crude state all over his love scenes. The lady reproves Dick for loving her in spite of her demerits: he replies by laboriously explaining Mr Oscar Wilde's point to her, thereby very effectually reducing it to absurdity. Fortunately for the play, Mr Jerome has a vein of shrewd fun, and has discovered that in working the familiar but safe stage trick of *dénouement* by coincidence, the long arm cannot be too long, in spite of the certainty that the critics will immediately fill up their notices with futile complaints of improbability. So what with Mr Jerome's jokes, and his manipulation of a camera and a microscope, the play passes the time. But it is as much inferior to The Prude's Progress as that play, I hope, will prove to Mr Jerome's next.

In order to fully realize how bad a popular play can be, it is necessary to see it twice. Messrs Morell and Waller gave me that opportunity by reopening the Shaftesbury last Monday with Mr Carton's Home Secretary. Mr Waller, unfortunately, had such a devastating cold that I forgot to criticize his acting in my anxiety about his health. Highly as I have always appreciated Mr Charles Wyndham's power as an actor, I doubt if I ever did him complete justice until I saw him replaced as Duncan Trendel by Mr Fred Terry. Yet I cannot help rather liking Mr Terry and Miss Neilson: after all, perhaps acting would spoil them. Miss Lottie Venne's bag of tricks, though infallibly effective, did not console me for the acting of Miss Mary Moore; and Mrs Arthur Ayres might almost as well have been Miss Fanny Coleman in Dick Halward, for all the success she had in persuading me that elderly ladies in society (or out of it) ever talked and comported themselves in her fashion anywhere but on the stage. Mr Kemble was a decided acquisition as the Solicitor-General; and Miss Millett, Mr Sidney Brough, and Mr Brookfield, were as amusing as before. But the performance, for some reason, was a perfunctory one; and the scruples of the Home Secretary's wife were more ridiculous on a second hearing than anyone could have believed. At the Criterion there was an atmosphere of conviction about the piece: here, it seemed to me, there was an atmosphere of incredulity. At all events, at the end of the second act I tried the atmosphere outside, and did not change it again that evening.

THE NEW MAGDALEN AND THE OLD

THE NEW MAGDALEN. By Wilkie Collins. (Revival). Theatre
Metropole, 28 October 1895.   [2 *November* 1895]

THE rise of the suburban theatre into artistic importance is a phenomenon which I have been expecting for many years. If the suburban population went to the theatre with anything like the assiduity with which it goes to church and chapel, I should not have had so long to wait. Even now there are districts of London, larger than many German towns which have their theatre and their grand ducal opera-house, where the inhabitants must come to the Strand district to find a theatre tolerable by people of the most moderate culture. But the signs of change in this respect are thickening. Whilst west end management is getting more and more desperately precarious, theatres like the Grand at Islington, the Lyric at Ealing, and the Metropole at Camberwell apparently prosper steadily. Still, until this week, I had never been invited by a suburban manager to a first night, because the suburban manager has usually nothing to shew except a piece already produced and criticized at a west end theatre. Now, however, Mr Mulholland, the manager of the Metropole, has taken a step forward by producing a play on his own account, the said play being no less a work than Wilkie Collins's New Magdalen, in which the late Ada Cavendish became famous twenty years ago. "It is a curious fact in connection with the recent craze for problem and sex plays," says Mr Mulholland, in a little manifesto circulated last Monday night in his theatre, "that the bold initiation of Wilkie Collins in this respect has been practically ignored. The existence alike of such a work as The New Magdalen, and the creation of Mercy Merrick in this relation, has never been adequately acknowledged. It is in some sense with a view to shewing the influence of this work on the so-called 'new movement' in dramatic literature, and placing dramatic facts in their true perspective, that the present revival has been undertaken."

On that let me say, respectfully but firmly, that The New Magdalen is no more a modern "sex play" than Mercy Merrick is a real Magdalen, or, for the matter of that, a real woman. Mercy is the old-fashioned man made angel-woman. She is only technically a liar, an impostor, and a prostitute; for the loss of her reputation occurs through no fault of her own; and the fraud by which she attempts to recover her place in society is so contrived as to seem quite harmless when she enters on it. Mercy is interesting, not because she is specifically feminine, or what Lombroso calls "sexually psychopathic," but because certain ideally and nobly human impulses are personified in her; so that she gains our sympathies in spite of inconsistent and improbable circumstances. To invent such an ideal figure; to thrust her into a refuge by a string of novelist-manufactured accidents, and then bring on a

Christian Socialist clergyman to raise her up and hail her as "the noblest of God's creatures" before an audience perfectly well aware that the typical women in our refuges are not in the least like her except in point of the susceptibility to sentimental sermons and the superficially amiable emotional facility which are only the symptoms of their weakness of character—to do all this was not to anticipate "the new movement," but to provoke it. Where Wilkie Collins really struck the new movement was in his sketch of the Reverend Julian Grey, who might have been a stagey forecast of the Reverend Stewart Headlam, though he was probably a reminiscence of some earlier pioneer of Christian Socialism. You will find hundreds of such parsons now: in fact, the Guild of St Matthew is a Guild of St Julian Grey. The scene in which Julian Grey describes all the little sallies by which he horrifies his bishop already falls flat because by this time the bishop himself might perpetrate them all, and worse, without scandalizing anybody.

The stage has moved as well as the world since Ada Cavendish created Mercy Merrick. Then The New Magdalen was a fashionable and well-made piece: today its innumerable asides and soliloquies, each more absurd and impossible than the last, are quite out of the question. In other respects it is still a strong play as plays go, hugely superior to the modern work of Messrs Carton, Frith, and Jerome, but presenting the fatal disqualification from the point of view of the west end manager of today that it requires acting, and powerful acting too. It is a significant fact that the return of The New Magdalen to the London stage has involved the return of Miss Janet Achurch, the only tragic actress of genius we now possess. After seeing Miss Achurch in the third act of The New Magdalen, I quite understand why she has not recently been let loose in modern plays. The other evening even the comparatively quiet and adaptable talent of Miss Marion Terry, in spite of all her tact and charm, nearly knocked Dick Halward to pieces; and I hardly expect to see Miss Terry on the stage again except on occasions when the supply of ladies who can be depended on not to act runs short. Miss Winifred Fraser, the English creator of

Ibsen's Hedwig Ekdal, was cautiously admitted on that occasion as a Temple laundress, in which capacity she could hardly do much harm. What would happen to a play of the Dick Halward class with Miss Achurch in it is hardly to be imagined—it is like trying to conceive a successful gunpowder plot. The supreme test of tragic acting is that indescribable disturbance of soul in which the spectator finds himself when the curtain comes down, a sensation from which I have usually found myself perfectly safe in London theatres except when Duse is at large here. How Miss Achurch managed to produce it with the execrable support she had, I do not know—it is hardly too much to say that in the most difficult scenes every speech of hers was followed by some ineptitude or obvious blunder which reduced the whole play to absurdity until she rescued it again—but she certainly did produce it. Three magnificent strokes in particular remain vividly in my memory: the gleam of rage through the hungry tenderness of her demand to Horace Holmcroft whether his love for her would stand the test of the loss of her social position; her annihilation of Grace Roseberry with the contemptuous "mad, youre mad," the words striking the woman in the face like a hammer; and the superb movement with which she swept herself to the feet of Julian Grey as the penitent Magdalen. This last would have been a fine piece of art even if there had been anything resembling a Julian Grey on the stage. As there was nothing but an unfortunate gentleman who was not within a fortnight of knowing his part, and not within five years of being able for it, the feat was all but miraculous. Miss Achurch actually persuaded the audience, between her efforts to prompt him, that he was acting rather well; and after one memorable scene, during which she had borne him with a strong hand through a troubled ocean of forgetfulness, unpreparedness, inexpertness, and general ignominy and confusion, he received a hearty round of applause from an audience which rightly felt that he had been taking part in a very powerfully acted scene. Comparing Miss Achurch's play in this third act, and in the first act at the point where the possibility of impersonating Grace Roseberry first strikes her, with the few squalls of temper which made Mrs Tanqueray's reputation, I am compelled to admit that our playgoing digestion has been rather weak of late.

For all that, The New Magdalen is not her old self at the Metropole, and never can, perhaps, be her old self again. When Ada Cavendish made her great success in it, she did no violence to the author. She gathered sympathy, first as the good hospital nurse on the battlefield, and then as the nice young lady at Mablethorpe House, quite as Wilkie Collins meant her to. Even the memorable fit of hysterics which swept away the audiences of the seventies with the undercurrent of rich, passionate, indignant emotion which was Ada Cavendish's chief gift, was ladylike in its form and conventional in its symptoms. But Miss Achurch belongs to an age which has little sympathy with the doves, soiled or unsoiled, of the age of Wilkie Collins. Mercy Merrick and Tom Hood's drowned young lady "fashioned so slenderly; young; and so fair" were not rebels against society: they were its victims, always conveying a faint suggestion that they were probably the daughters of distressed clergymen. And as victims, they were pitied. What has happened since is that we have changed sides to a great extent; and though we may not all care to say so, yet it is the rebel against society who interests us; and we want to see the rebel triumphant rather than crushed or reconciled, conventional society being just now in the pillory as a collective fool with whom we have lost patience. Miss Achurch, as might be expected from an actress who became famous as Nora Helmer in A Doll's House, presents Mercy Merrick as rebel rather than victim. Middle-aged playgoers will still remember the deep conviction and pathos of Ada Cavendish's "I cant get back: I cant get back" (into society), when she told her story at the beginning of the play. Miss Achurch made no such effect in this line: the effort of trying to imagine a woman in the honorable employment and heroic activity of Florence Nightingale, yearning like the Peri at the gate of paradise for a permanent situation as parlormaid in a respectably prejudiced family, was too much for her; and the once famous line came out almost with suppressed impatience and contempt. I can as easily conceive a tigress settling down in a dairy as

Miss Achurch's Mercy Merrick domesticating herself with Lady Janet Roy, and receiving an offer of marriage from such a sample of good form as Mr Horace Holmcroft. She has dignity and charm, but not the dignity and charm that Lady Janet would have recognized or liked: she has tenderness, but not quite the tenderness that soothes the fevered brow of the wounded soldier of the stage. She reproduced for me an old experience of the days when, as a musical critic, I gained from contact with great works and a living art the knowledge I am now losing and the finely trained sense I am now blunting in our silly and vulgar theatres. Just as Giula Ravogli first, and then Calvé, in the exuberance of their dramatic talent, wrecked an innocently pretty opera by suddenly springing upon the delicate romance of Bizet's and Prosper Merimée's fancy the worthless, fierce, sensual, reckless, rapscallionly Carmen of real life, so, precisely, has Miss Achurch taken this innocent old figment of Wilkie Collins's benevolent and chivalrous imagination, and played into it a grim truth that it was never meant to bear—played it against the audience, so that the curious atmosphere of reluctance and remonstrance from which Calvé used to wring the applause of the huge audiences at Covent Garden when the curtain fell on her Carmen, arose more than once when Miss Achurch disturbed and appalled us at moments when Ada Cavendish, looking at the part from an older point of view, would have soothed and pleased us. Only, Miss Achurch, unlike Calvé in Carmen, preserved the heroic element in Mercy's character. The clergyman's line, when her betrothed repudiates her, "Horace, I pity you," had its full value.

This incongruity between the New Woman and the Old was accentuated in an irresistibly comic way by the representative of Grace Roseberry, an actress with apparently no idea of any part but that of the heroine of a popular melodrama. Grace Roseberry is, from the professional point of view, an excellent part. Detestable as she is made to appear by her utter lack of charity, this odious defect of hers is dramatically so important at the crisis of the play, that an actress who plays the part forcibly and faithfully can make herself remembered as surely as Mercy Merrick herself can. Unfortunately the Grace Roseberry at the Metropole, a young lady with a promising appearance and temperament, to which she has added nothing except a presentable diction and a meaningless mannerism or two, proved so deficient in dramatic intelligence as actually to play for the sympathy of the audience, thereby not only destroying her own opportunity, but disabling the play at its most critical points to an extent which would have ensured a disastrous failure if Miss Achurch had not been sufficiently powerful to create the illusion which her incompetent colleague was feebly contradicting. The effect at the end of the second act (counting the prologue as the first), when Miss Achurch was not on the stage, nearly upset the whole performance. Grace Roseberry, instead of entering so as to make everyone hate her instinctively at once, thereby excusing her cool reception by Lady Janet, came in pale, slow, and pathetic, only needing a patch of snow on her cloak, and a sentimental strain from the band, to draw tears from the gallery as the long-lost, cruelly wronged heroine. As it was, they waxed indignant at Lady Janet's inhuman coldness to this sweet young creature. The curtain descended on Grace Roseberry, the one unsympathetic female character in the play, as its heroine, and all the sympathetic characters as brutal and uppish conspirators against an innocent maiden's happiness. She was loudly applauded amid the suppressed convulsions of the critics who knew the play, and what was coming in the next act. But it must have been extremely poor fun for Miss Achurch, who had to fight her way all through her great act against this silly blunder, instead of having its most powerful situation perfectly prepared for her, and needing only the touch of the match to the gunpowder, as Ada Cavendish always had.

Miss Ada Neilson as Lady Janet, and Mr Herbert Pearson as Horace Holmcroft, knew their parts, and got steadily and competently, if not very brilliantly, through them. But the play was in a desperately unprepared condition. In spite of a busy prompter, and considerable activity in that direction by Miss Achurch, appalling and irretrievable omissions occurred. A stupid cut in the first act, spoiling the introduction of Mercy's narrative, was, I am afraid, intentional. The stage-manager managed to get the curtain up and down punctually; but that was all. Grace Roseberry had to wait a long and weary time for the shell that was to strike her down; and when, after loud and long remonstrances by the authorities behind the scenes, the catastrophe at last came tardy off, the window was blown in first, and the shell exploded afterwards. I hope I have made it clear that my disposition towards the suburban theatre is altogether friendly. It seems to me a delightful thing that I should be able to reach, by reasonable tram or bus ride, a perfectly comfortable theatre where I can get a stall for four shillings and a program for a penny, with all other fees abolished, and as civil and efficient attendance as any west end theatre offers. It does not occur to me to question the right of such a theatre to as much critical attention for its original productions as the Haymarket or the St James's. But if such productions are to be rehearsed for three days instead of three weeks, and if the engagement of an eminent actress is to include an obligation on her part to do without any serious support, and risk leaving half her reputation behind her in consequence, then the suburban theatre must inevitably relapse into the provincial position of entertainer of companies on tour. I offer these hints to Mr Mulholland with due allowance for the difficulties of a first experiment, and will add just one more with reference to his orchestra. The members of that body play everything straight through at an unvarying and most unsympathetic forte. I presume this is because they do not know how to play piano, pianissimo, fortissimo, mezzoforte, or any other of the nuances. Therefore I suggest that they should be enclosed, like the swell organ, in a box with Venetian shutters, which could be opened and closed according to the gradations of tone required. Then, possibly, the audience would not be driven to desperation by the not exceptionally long waits between the acts, as they are at present.

Trilby—but no: I have neither time nor space this week for Trilby. Trilby can wait—for six months if necessary, I imagine— though I shall not keep her waiting longer than until next Saturday.

TRILBY AND L'AMI DES FEMMES

TRILBY. An entertainment in four acts based by Paul Potter on Du Maurier's novel. Haymarket Theatre, 30 October 1895.

THE SQUIRE OF DAMES. Adapted from L'Ami des Femmes of Dumas *fils* by R. C. Carton. Criterion Theatre, 5 November 1895. [9 *November* 1895]

I OBSERVE that some of my honored colleagues in dramatic criticism, not having read Trilby, explain that they were not lazy, but that they felt bound to present their minds in the condition of a *tabula rasa* to the Haymarket performance. Now I *am* lazy; and I never read anything; yet I have read Trilby and enjoyed it greatly. It is a no mere novel with illustrations, it is a homogeneous work of art in which the master, like a composer who sets his own poem to music, shews us his people by the art of the draughtsman, and tells us their story by the art of the fabulist. What Thackeray, with his enslaved mind and clumsy hand, tried to do in vain, is here brought happily off by the pleasantest of freethinkers and the most charming of artists. Oddly enough, the successful artist has taken the unsuccessful one for his model, greatly improving on him in every respect save one: to wit, honesty. Thackeray saved his reputation and forced his oppressive books like sentences of penal servitude on the reading public by telling the truth in spite of himself. He may protest against it, special-plead against it, exaggerate the extenuating circumstances, be driven into pessimism by it; but it comes raging and snivelling out of him, all the same, within the limit of his sense of decency. He exhausts all his feeble pathos in trying to make you sorry for the death of Colonel Newcome, imploring you to regard him as a noble-hearted gentleman instead of an insufferable old fool, developing into a mischievous old swindler; but he gives you the facts about him faithfully. Nothing can be more pitiable than Thackeray chuckling over his poor little stroke of genius in making Becky Sharp admire Rawdon Crawley when he assaults Lord Steyne, in which stroke he shews about as much knowledge of

Becky-Sharpness as Prosper Merimée's dragoon did when he went to Carmen to boast how he killed her hateful old husband-proprietor in single combat by a clever knife thrust. "You fool," said Carmen: "your thrust is all stuff. Why couldnt you buy me honestly? He'd have sold me for fifteen shillings." Rawdon Crawley's figure would have been higher; but he would have sold Becky for all that. Still worse is Thackeray's exultation over the success with which Major Pendennis quells the rebellion of his wretched valet; and there is something pathetically foolish in his attempt to convince himself that his pulses stirred at the thought of Waterloo, and in his absolutely sincere sense of the international gravity of a newspaper paragraph stating that a certain letter written from abroad was, "strange to say, on club paper" (implying the unspeakably awful accusation against a west end clubman of putting a quire of that commodity into his portmanteau). But he tells you no lies; and if you want to know Rawdon Crawley and Major Pendennis as they appeared to their own set, and their servants as they appeared to their masters, there they are, as no artist-author could ever give them to you.

Mr du Maurier, on the other hand, has all the artist's charm, and all his dishonesty. His Taffy is an attempt at the Colonel-Newcome-Dobbin sympathy catcher; but Mr du Maurier does not tell you the truth about Taffy, except for a moment when his professional point of honor is touched, when he is constrained to confess that Taffy was an impostor in art. There is not a character in the book which is not obviously drawn to please the author's imagination. For all we know, George Eliot may have been the original of Trilby: at all events, if she really had been, he would have altered her age and her face and her circumstances and profession in just the same way to please himself and please us. If I want to respect Thackeray, I must think of his veracity and forget his workmanship: if I would respect Mr du Maurier, I must think of his workmanship and forget his veracity. I know well that there never was any such person as Trilby—that she is a man's dream; but I am a man myself, and delight in her. Happily, truth and good-nature do not always clash. I am convinced as well as touched by Little Billee with the dead heart, going about and making himself affectionately agreeable in his remorse for being secretly unable to care for anybody. And I like an imagination without gall, to which poor Svengali is *not* a villain, but only a poor egotistical wretch who provokes people to pull his nose, although he has better grounds for egotism than anyone else in the book except Little Billee and Trilby (I must except the adorable Trilby). Besides, the philosophy of the book is humane and enlightened: Mr du Maurier is not afraid to write of religion and morals and the nude in art just as he would speak of them in the society of people whom he respects.

Trilby is the very thing for the English stage at present. No need to act or create character: nothing to do but make up after Mr du Maurier's familiar and largely popular drawings, and be applauded before uttering a word as dear old Taffy, or the Laird, or darling Trilby, or horrid Svengali. Mr Paul Potter has done his business with considerable knowledge of what was wanted of him, especially by the actor-manager. Nearly all the favorite pictures and passages from the book are worked in, without violence if possible, but at all events worked in. Thus, though the play ends with Trilby's death, Gecko is allowed to have his "Ich habe geliebet und gelebt" in the third act. Still, let nobody suppose that the play gives any idea of the book. Imagine Trilby, the incarnation of womanly sympathy, with Baratier and Besson and old Monsieur Penque cut out of her record for the sake of making a correct young English girl of her! Imagine Little Billee pared down and painted up into the most futile of "juvenile leads"! Imagine, above all, Svengali taken seriously at his own foolish valuation, blazed upon with limelights, spreading himself intolerably over the whole play with nothing fresh to add to the first five minutes of him—Svengali defying heaven, declaring that henceforth he is his own God, and then tumbling down in a paroxysm of heart disease (the blasphemer rebuked, you see), and having to be revived by draughts of brandy. I derived much cynical amusement from this most absurd scene; but if I were Mr du Maurier, I should ask whether the theatre is really in such an abject condition that all daintiness and seriousness of thought and feeling must be struck out of a book, and replaced by vulgar nonsense before it can be accepted on the stage. I grant that the public deserves nothing better from Mr Tree. It has done its silly best to teach him that it wants none of his repeated and honorable attempts to cater for people with some brains. But surely even the public would just as soon—nay, rather—have the original Svengali, the luckless artist-cad (a very deplorable type of cad, whom Mr du Maurier has hit off to the life), understanding neither good manners nor cleanliness, always presuming, and generally getting snubbed and nose-pulled and bullied, but taking Trilby's headache into his own elbows and making a great artist of her. Mr Tree began excellently with this: why, then, should he absurdly decline into the stagey, the malignant, the diabolic, the Wandering-Jewish, and vainly endeavor to make our flesh creep, besides making the play one act too long? No doubt Mr Potter, familiar with the ways of the American actor-manager, wrote the part for Mr Tree as he thought Mr Tree would like it. But he spoiled the book and very nearly spoiled the play in doing it.

With the exception of the sham serious episodes, Trilby is very bright and pleasant. There is no acting in it to speak of: Miss Rosina Filippi alone gets in a stroke of genuine art in the *ouvreuse* scene. Miss Baird's Trilby is a very pretty performance by a very pretty girl; but it is no more possible to base an estimate of her future on it than it was on the early performances of Miss Mary Anderson or Miss Dorothy Dene. The older ladies in the audience, dating from the age of reclining boards and straight backs, were of opinion that Miss Baird carried herself too creepily; and I will not deny that there may be some truth in this. As to Mr Tree, I should no more dream of complimenting him on the Svengali business than Sir Henry Irving on A Hero of Waterloo. The studio, the quadrille, Zouzou and Dodor, and all the rest of it, are great fun; and although the whole affair not only adds nothing to the merit of Mr du Maurier's original production of the book and the drawings, but steals a good deal from it, I imagine that everyone will enjoy a visit to the Haymarket just now. Let me, however, warn musicians that they will find Schubert represented by the notoriously spurious Addio.

At the Criterion Mr Wyndham has resumed his exhibitions of acting, an art now become so rare that people flock to see him, no matter what the play may be. This time, however, he has a tolerably good part—that of De Ryons in L'Ami des Femmes, transmuted by Mr Carton into Mr Kilroy in The Squire of Dames. L'Ami des Femmes is a bad play with good material in it. The material is what we now call Ibsenite: the technique is that of Scribe. In it, accordingly, we have serious characters philosophically discussing themselves and one another quite undramatically in long speeches, and at the same time senselessly carrying on an irrelevant comedy of intrigue of the old kind in five "well-made" acts. The dialogue and characterization of Emperor or Galilean tacked on to the action of Cheer, Boys, Cheer! would not be a whit more incongruous. De Ryons is a high-minded, chivalrous, delicate gentleman-philosopher in theory, in practice a busybody and go-between—Benedick and Figaro in one. De Montégre talks like Hernani, and behaves like the weak, vain fop in Thackeray's Vanity Fair (Osborne, if I recollect aright), who was shot at Waterloo. And so on. Mr Carton had therefore not merely to adapt the piece from French to English life, but to get rid of its incongruities and make a fairly homogeneous, compact drama of it. Necessarily, he has done this by discarding the serious side of the characterization, and retaining only that which is proper to the ignoble and commonplace action, since if he had taken the alternative course, he must have provided the piece with a different action—in short, written a new play, which was not what he was commissioned to do. He has not done his work consistently—Mr Carton never does anything consistently: a certain pleasant scatterbrainedness is of the very essence of his talent. He has retained a good deal that belongs to the side of the play which he has discarded, and has discarded some things (in Leverdet's part, for example) which would strengthen the side which he has retained. This in consequence has landed him in four acts where three would have sufficed; in dull and vague parts for Miss Mary

Moore and Mr Bernard Gould; and here and there in a speech
producing an effect belonging to the original play and not to the
adaptation. Occasionally he does not take the trouble to adapt:
he translates literally. In the original, Jane tells De Ryons that she
detests him, to which he replies coolly "Ça passera," the equivalent of which, I take it, is "Ah, you will get over that." Mr Carton
has made Mr Wyndham say "That will pass," a perfectly impossible speech for an Englishman, except when giving his
opinion of a doubtful coin. Another speech of Mr Wyndham, in
his great scene with Zoë Nuggetson, "What game are we playing
at?" is an excellent schoolgirl translation of "Quel jeu jouons-
nous, mademoiselle?" but it is not what an Englishman would
say under such circumstances.

The acting is a good deal better than most theatres provide at
present. Mr Wyndham's success as De Ryons Kilroy is genuine
and unprepared. No books have been written about his part; no
pictures of his make-up and attitudes have been circulated; no
preliminary conversations between the other characters give the
audience's imagination its cue. Mr Wyndham goes to work as the
curtain rises, and creates his character by pure acting. There was
no leaning on stage tricks and effects which any experienced actor
could produce, nor any of that feeble need of being constantly
played to by the rest, which is so often put down to the vanity of
the actor-manager, though it is really due to his incompetence.
Mr Wyndham is always playing to somebody, and getting double
value out of it, for himself as actor and artist, by making the most
of his own part, and for himself as manager by getting the most
out of the fellow-artist whose salary he pays. Everybody acts
better at the Criterion than at most other theatres; and yet Mr
Wyndham, whether he has the worst part in the piece, as in The
Home Secretary, or the best, as in the present instance, comes out
further ahead than the actor-managers who obviously dread com-
petition. Miss Mary Moore, though much on the stage, has no
part and no chance. The proud, half Greek Jane de Simerose, so
ill prepared for marriage that she is shocked by it into driving her
husband into the arms of another woman, and so fine witted that

she is able to deal her jealous Hernani lover such strokes as, "I suppose, when I have answered all your questions—when I have proved to you that I am an honest woman, you will then demand that I shall cease to be one to prove that I love you"—this distinguished person becomes the merest cipher in The Squire of Dames. Fräulein Hackendorf survives very healthily in an American millionairess, played by Miss Fay Davis, who made an unmistakeable hit in the part. The part of the lovesick schoolgirl Balbine, originally played by Chaumont, becomes a mere piece of tomfoolery in English. Miss Beatrice Ferrars amuses herself with it laughably enough. Chantrin, the hero of the beard, is more fortunate. He has survived the Channel passage without alteration; so that the part is as dangerous in English as in French: that is, it remains the part of a bore who actually is a bore, and not an unconscious humorist. Mr De Lange, however, averted the peril with great art, and was very funny and very finished at the same time, a combination rather scarce on our stage. Mr Bernard Gould was in the same difficulty as Miss Moore: his part was not very intelligible, and led to nothing but a paltry piece of spite, unrelieved by the tragic pretension with which, in the original, it is contrasted, Ibsen fashion, by Dumas *fils*. Nevertheless Mr Gould, always *persona grata*, but hitherto one of the most experimental of amateurs, begins to shew signs of serious formation as an artist with a definite style. As Sir Douglas Thorburn (Montégre) all he could do was to tow the wreck of his part into harbor without a catastrophe. Mr Frank Fenton did precisely what was wanted as the husband. A man so abjectly in love with his wife is hardly a decent spectacle; but it is the actor's business to supply sentiment when the drama demands it, and Mr Fenton certainly rose to the occasion, under no easy conditions, with remarkable efficiency. Mr Alfred Bishop and Miss Granville are also in the cast; but their parts have been adapted into unredeemed commonplace.

THE CASE FOR THE CRITIC-DRAMATIST

MERRIFIELD'S GHOST. An original comedietta in one act. By
H. M. Paull. Vaudeville Theatre, 13 November 1895.

[16 *November* 1895]

A DISCUSSION has arisen recently as to whether a dramatic critic
can also be a dramatic author without injury to his integrity and
impartiality. The feebleness with which the point has been de-
bated may be guessed from the fact that the favorite opinion
seems to be that a critic is either an honest man or he is not. If
honest, then dramatic authorship can make no difference to him.
If not, he will be dishonest whether he writes plays or not. This
childish evasion cannot, for the honor of the craft, be allowed to
stand. If I wanted to ascertain the melting-point of a certain metal,
and how far it would be altered by an alloy of some other metal,
and an expert were to tell me that a metal is either fusible or it is
not—that if not, no temperature will melt it; and if so, it will
melt anyhow—I am afraid I should ask that expert whether he
was a fool himself or took me for one. Absolute honesty is as
absurd an abstraction as absolute temperature or absolute value.
A dramatic critic who would die rather than read an American
pirated edition of a copyright English book might be considered
an absolutely honest man for all practical purposes on that particular subject—I say on that one, because very few men have
more than one point of honor; but as far as I am aware, no such
dramatic critic exists. If he did, I should regard him as a highly
dangerous monomaniac. That honesty varies inversely with
temptation is proved by the fact that every additional penny on
the income-tax yields a less return than the penny before it, shewing that men state their incomes less honestly for the purposes
of taxation at sevenpence in the pound than sixpence. The matter
may be tested by a simple experiment. Go to one of the gentlemen whose theory is that a man is either honest or he is not, and
obtain from him the loan of half a crown on some plausible pretext of a lost purse or some such petty emergency. He will not

ask you for a written acknowledgment of the debt. Return next day and ask for a loan of £500 without a promissory note, on the ground that you are either honest or not honest, and that a man who will pay back half a crown without compulsion will also pay back £500. You will find that the theory of absolute honesty will collapse at once.

Are we then to believe that the critic-dramatist who stands to make anything from five hundred to ten thousand pounds by persuading a manager to produce his plays, will be prevented by his honesty from writing about that manager otherwise than he would if he had never written a play and were quite certain that he never should write one? I can only say that people who believe such a thing would believe anything. I am myself a particularly flagrant example of the critic-dramatist. It is not with me a mere case of an adaptation or two raked up against me as incidents in my past. I have written half a dozen "original" plays, four of which have never been performed; and I shall presently write half a dozen more. The production of one of them, even if it attained the merest success of esteem, would be more remunerative to me than a couple of years of criticism. Clearly, since I am no honester than other people, I should be the most corrupt flatterer in London if there were nothing but honesty to restrain me. How is it, then, that the most severe criticisms of managers come from me and from my fellow critic-dramatists, and that the most servile puffery comes from writers whose every sentence proves that they have nothing to hope or fear from any manager? There are a good many answers to this question, one of the most obvious being that as the respect inspired by a good criticism is permanent, whilst the irritation it causes is temporary, and as, on the other hand, the pleasure given by a venal criticism is temporary and the contempt it inspires permanent, no man really secures his advancement as a dramatist by making himself despised as a critic. The thing has been tried extensively during the last twenty years; and it has failed. For example, the late Frank Marshall, a dramatist and an extravagantly enthusiastic admirer of Sir Henry Irving's genius, followed a fashion which at one time made the Lyceum Theatre a sort of court formed by a retinue of literary gentlemen. I need not question either their sincerity or the superiority of Canute to their idolatry; for Canute never produced their plays: Robert Emmett and the rest of their masterpieces remain unacted to this day. It may be said that this brings us back to honesty as the best policy; but honesty has nothing to do with it: plenty of the men who know that they can get along faster fighting than crawling, are no more honest than the first Napoleon was. No virtue, least of all courage, implies any other virtue. The cardinal guarantee for a critic's integrity is simply the force of the critical instinct itself. To try to prevent me from criticizing by pointing out to me the superior pecuniary advantages of puffing is like trying to keep a young Irving from going on the stage by pointing out the superior pecuniary advantages of stockbroking. If my own father were an actor-manager, and his life depended on his getting favorable notices of his performance, I should orphan myself without an instant's hesitation if he acted badly. I am by no means the willing victim of this instinct. I am keenly susceptible to contrary influences—to flattery, which I swallow greedily if the quality is sufficiently good; to the need of money, to private friendship or even acquaintanceship, to the pleasure of giving pleasure and the pain of giving pain, to consideration for people's circumstances and prospects, to personal likes and dislikes, to sentimentality, pity, chivalry, pugnacity and mischief, laziness and cowardice, and a dozen other human conditions which make the critic vulnerable; but the critical instinct gets the better of them all. I spare no effort to mitigate its inhumanity, trying to detect and strike out of my articles anything that would give pain without doing any good. Those who think the things I say severe, or even malicious, should just see the things I do *not* say. I do my best to be partial, to hit out at remediable abuses rather than at accidental shortcomings, and at strong and responsible people rather than weak and helpless ones. And yet all my efforts do not alter the result very much. So stubborn is the critic within me, that with every disposition to be as goodnatured and as popular an authority as the worst enemy of art could desire, I am to all intents and purposes incorruptible. And that is how the dramatist-critic, if only he is critic enough, "slates" the actor-manager in defiance of the interest he has in conciliating him. He cannot help himself, any more than the ancient mariner could help telling his story. And the actor-manager can no more help listening than the wedding guest could. In short, the better formula would have been, that a man is either a critic or not a critic; that to the extent to which he is one he will criticize the managers in spite of heaven or earth; and that to the extent to which he is not, he will flatter them anyhow, to save himself trouble.

The advantage of having a play criticized by a critic who is also a playwright is as obvious as the advantage of having a ship criticized by a critic who is also a master shipwright. Pray observe that I do not speak of the criticism of dramas and ships by dramatists and shipwrights who are not also critics; for that would be no more convincing than the criticism of acting by actors. Dramatic authorship no more constitutes a man a critic than actorship constitutes him a dramatic author; but a dramatic critic learns as much from having been a dramatic author as Shakespear or Mr Pinero from having been actors. The average London critic, for want of practical experience, has no real confidence in himself: he is always searching for an imaginary "right" opinion, with which he never dares to identify his own. Consequently every public man finds that as far as the press is concerned his career divides itself into two parts: the first, during which the critics are afraid to praise him; and the second, during which they are afraid to do anything else. In the first, the critic is uncomfortably trying to find faults enough to make out a case for his timid coldness: in the second, he is eagerly picking out excellences to justify his eulogies. And of course he blunders equally in both phases. The faults he finds are either inessential or are positive reforms, or he blames the wrong people for them: the triumphs of acting which he announces are stage tricks that any old hand could play. In criticizing actresses he is an open and shameless voluptuary. If a woman is pretty, well dressed, and

self-satisfied enough to be at her ease on the stage, he is delighted; and if she is a walking monument of handsome incompetence, so much the better, as your voluptuary rarely likes a
woman to be cleverer than himself, or to force him to feel deeply
and think energetically when he only wants to wallow in her
good looks. Confront him with an actress who will not condescend to attack him on this side—who takes her work with
thorough seriousness and self-respect—and his resentment, his
humiliation, his sense of being snubbed, break out ludicrously in
his writing, even when he dare not write otherwise than favorably.
A great deal of this nonsense would be taken out of him if he
could only write a play and have it produced. No dramatist begins by writing plays merely as excuses for the exhibition of pretty
women on the stage. He comes to that ultimately perhaps; but
at first he does his best to create real characters and make them
pass through three acts of real experiences. Bring a critic who
has done this face to face with the practical question of selecting
an actress for his heroine, and he suddenly realizes for the first
time that there is not such a galaxy of talent on the London stage
as he thought, and that the handsome walking ladies whom he
always thought good enough for other people's plays are not
good enough for his own. That is already an immense step in his
education. There are other steps, too, which he will have taken
before the curtain falls on the first public representation of his
play; but they may be summed up in the fact that the author of a
play is the only person who really wants to have it well done in
every respect, and who therefore has every drawback brought
fully home to him. The man who has had that awakening about
one play will thenceforth have his eyes open at all other plays;
and there you have at once the first moral with the first technical
qualification of the critic—the determination to have every play
as well done as possible, and the knowledge of what is standing
in the way of that consummation. Those of our critics who, either
as original dramatists or adapters and translators, have superin-
tended the production of plays with paternal anxiety, are never
guilty of the wittily disguised indifference of clever critics who

have never seen a drama through from its first beginnings behind the scenes. Compare the genuine excitement of Mr Clement Scott, or the almost Calvinistic seriousness of Mr William Archer, with the gaily easy what-does-it-matterness of Mr Walkley, and you see at once how the two critic-dramatists influence the drama, whilst the critic-playgoer only makes it a pretext for entertaining his readers. On the whole there is only as much validity in the theory that a critic should not be a dramatist, as in the theory that a judge should not be a lawyer nor a general a soldier. You cannot have qualifications without experience; and you cannot have experience without personal interest and bias. That may not be an ideal arrangement; but it is the way the world is built; and we must make the best of it.

Poor Mr Potton, at the Vaudeville, is now preceded by a little play by Mr H. V. Paull, entitled Merrifield's Ghost, which I cannot honestly pretend to have enjoyed. Mere custom has inured me to the stage hero who is impossibly virtuous; but the modern gentleman who appeals for my sympathy solely on the ground that he has forged or stolen just as any ordinary criminal does, gets beyond my patience. Merrifield's ghost had not the ghost of an excuse for forging his friend's name or inflicting his confession on me. He does not interest me; and I do not see why I should be put to a great deal of trouble simply to form a low opinion of him.

The revival of Liberty Hall at the St James's was chiefly remarkable for the happy termination of an absurd incident by Mr Alexander's reception, which attained the proportions of a public demonstration, and was so tremendously enthusiastic that he must have felt almost glad that the occasion of it, intensely disagreeable as it must have been, had happened to him. Liberty Hall is too long; and the scene in which the heroine overhears the hero saying to her sister "Nobody need ever know," and misunderstands it, is unpardonable; but otherwise it is a good-natured and amusing play. Miss Furtado Clarke played the part of the sister seriously and well; but probably the audience regretted Miss Maude Millet, because she is more interesting than the part, and would have taken care not to sacrifice herself to it. Serious acting is all very well for Ibsen and people of that kind; but with popular west end authors it is a most dangerous habit for a young actress to indulge.

MANXSOME AND TRADITIONAL

THE MANXMAN. In four acts. Adapted from Hall Caine's celebrated novel. Shaftesbury Theatre, 18 November 1895.
THE RIVALS. A revival of Sheridan's comedy. Court Theatre, 11 November 1895.   [23 *November* 1895]

IN the bill The Manxman is described as "adapted from HALL CAINE'S celebrated novel." Who is Hall Caine? How did he become celebrated? At what period did he flourish? Are there any other Manx authors of his calibre? If there are, the matter will soon become serious; for if that gift of intolerably copious and intolerably common imagination is a national characteristic in the Isle of Man, it will swamp the stage with Manx melodramas the moment the islanders pick up the trick of writing for the stage.

Whether the speeches in The Manxman are interpolated Wilson Barrett or aboriginal Hall Caine I cannot say, as I have not read the celebrated novel, and am prepared to go to the stake rather than face the least chapter of it. But if they correctly represent the colloquial habits of the island, the Manx race are without a vernacular, and only communicate with one another by extracts from Cassell's National Library, the Chandos Classics, and the like. In the Isle of Man you do not use the word "always": you say "Come weal come woe, come life come death." The most useful phrases for the tourist are "Dust and ashes, dust and ashes," "Dead sea fruit," "The lone watches of the night," "What a hell is conscience!" "The storm clouds are descending and the tempest is at hand," and so on. The Manx do not speak of a little baby, but of a baby "fresh from God." Their philosophy is that "love is best—is everything—is the cream of life—better than worldly success"; and they conceive woman—or, as they probably call her, "the fair sex"—as a creature "giving herself body and soul, and never thinking what she gets by it. Thats the glory of Woman!" And the Manx woman rather deserves this. Her idea of pleasantry is to sit on a plank over a stream dangling her legs; to call her young swain's attention to her reflection in the water; and then, lest he should miss the coquetry of the exhibition, to cut off the reflected view of her knees by wrapping her skirt round her ankles in a paroxysm of affected bashfulness. And when she sprains her ankle, and the gentleman tenders some surgical aid, she requests him to turn his head the other way. In short, the keynote of your perfect Manxman is tawdry vulgarity aping the heroic, the hearty, the primevally passionate, and sometimes, though here the show of vigor in the affectation tumbles into lame ineptitude, the gallant and humorous.

Even when I put my personal distaste for The Manxman as far as possible on one side, I cannot persuade myself that it is likely to live very long, although no device is spared to move the audience, from a cascade of real water to a poor little baby, which is exploited as shamelessly as if it had been let out on hire to an organ-grinder or a beggar. Thirty years hence, no doubt, we shall have some newly risen star telling the interviewers of a first appearance as the baby in The Manxman; but that interesting possibility cannot reconcile me to the meanness of such ways of fishing for sympathy. In the great Doll's House itself, where children are introduced with so serious a purpose that no one can have any sense of their being unworthily used, I always feel that I should prefer the baby to be an amateur. At the Shaftesbury melodrama, where there was no serious purpose, but only an ostentatious cradling and cuddling and dandling and bless-its-little-hearting in order to work up the greatest possible quantity of sentiment on the cheapest possible terms, I felt thoroughly ashamed of the business. What with the real water, the infant, and the well-worn incident of the fond and simple-hearted husband returning home to find his wife gone, the drama passes the time tolerably up to the end of the second act. The rest of it is as null and dull as the most cautious manager could desire. The third act is nothing but a "front scene" bulked out to fill up the evening; and the fourth act, with its offensively noisy street music, does not produce a moment's illusion. The play, originally designed for an actor-manager who played Quilliam, has evidently been a good deal botched in altering it to fit another actor-manager who plays Christian; but it never can have been a good play, because it is not really a drama at all, but an acted narrative. Any competent playwright could make the third act effectively dramatic if only he were released from all obligation to consult "the celebrated novel." As it is, it is a chapter in a story, not an act in a drama.

As to the acting, most of the sixteen parts are so indefinite in spite of their portentous names—Black Tom, Ross Christian, Jemmy y Lord, and so on—that there is nothing to act in them. Mr Cockburn is just the man for Pete Quilliam, a rather fortunate circumstance for him, as there is little art and no husbandry in his acting, though his natural equipment is first-rate of its kind. Miss Kate Phillips, with much greater skill, divided the honors with him. There were no other personal successes. Mr Fernandez, in one of those characters which the celebrated Hall Caine apparently copies very vilely from Sir Walter Scott, mouthed texts of Scripture in a manner which exposed him to the most serious risk of being described as "a sound actor." Professional methods were also illustrated by Mr Hamilton Knight as the Manxsome governor. He, having to leave the stage with the innocent words, "Come and see us as soon as you can," shewed us how the experienced hand can manufacture an effective exit. He went to the door with the words "Come and see us as soon." Then he nerved himself; opened the door; turned dauntlessly; and with raised voice and sparkling eyes hurled the significant words "as you can" in the teeth of the gallery. Naturally we were all struck with admiration, because it was just the thing that none of us would have thought of or known how to do.

Mr Lewis Waller managed to get a moment of real acting into the end of the first act, and then relapsed into nonsensical solemnity for the rest of the evening. I do not know what he was thinking of; but it can hardly have been of the play. He delivered his lines with the automatic gravity of a Brompton Cemetery clergyman repeating the burial service for the thousandth time. He uttered endless strings of syllables; but he did not divide them into words, much less phrases. "IcannotIwillnotlistentothisIwont-hearofit," was the sort of thing he inflicted on us for three mortal acts. As to Miss Florence West, if she persists in using her privilege as the manager's wife to play melodramatic heroines, she will ruin the enterprise. Some years' hard and continuous work might make her an accomplished performer in artificial comedy or in the Sardou-Bernhardt line of sensational drama. At present she is obviously a highly civilized modern London lady, whose natural attitude towards melodramatic sentiment is one of supercilious incredulity. There is about as much sense in casting her for Kate Cregeen as there would be in casting Mr Waller himself for Tony Lumpkin.

Of The Rivals at the Court Theatre, I can only say that Mrs John Wood's Mrs Malaprop is so good that it almost atones for the atrocity of the rest of the performance. I am sorry to say that the shortcomings are not all due to "the traditions," insufferable as they are. In more than one instance, a leading part has been deliberately given to a mere pupil, coached up to the requisite business gesture by gesture and phrase by phrase. Most of the rest of the acting is forced, noisy, and tiresome beyond description. The cackling, boisterous, mirthless laughter; the racketing and swaggering; the ostentatious consciousness of Sheridan's reputation; the tomfoolish stage business, which might have been invented by Pierce Egan, and would not now be tolerated in a modern play at any leading theatre: all this wearies me, disgusts me, jars on me unbearably. I will do Mr Sidney Brough the justice to admit that he tries to dehumanize himself, in the manner unhappily expected of him, without being offensive, and succeeds as far as that is possible; and that Mr Brandon Thomas plays Sir Lucius agreeably and even with dignity, mainly by not doing what is expected of him. But the others fall an unresisting prey to the traditions, which, as far as the stage business is concerned, are simply the coarse methods and Mohawk manners of Sheridan's day thrust on to our stage. Mr Farren, as Sir Anthony Absolute, is one of the worst offenders. He does not succeed in making the part live for a moment. Mr Farren can play Sir Peter Teazle adequately, because any polished elderly actor of comedy has only to repeat Sheridan's lines intelligently to be Sir Peter. But Sir Anthony, a well-marked choleric character type, demands a genuine feat of impersonation; and this Mr Farren does not give us. Of course, he is applauded in the part—I am convinced that if he had substituted the lines and costume of the ghost in Hamlet for Sir Anthony's, everybody would have gone into the customary raptures sooner than venture to use their own judgment when Mr Farren and Sheridan were in question—but to me there was no Sir Anthony there, nothing but an obsolete formula for old comedy worked out with plenty of technical address, but without verisimilitude or relevance to the peculiar temperament indicated in the play. Mrs John Wood's sincerity, and the genuine comic effect it produced, ought to have convinced the rest that her policy of never laughing at herself, or at Sheridan, or to persuade the audience that old comedy is immensely funny, was the right policy; but the lesson was quite lost on them.

The band played a maddening string of old English airs all the evening. If Mr Edward Jones will cut them all out except his variation on The Banks of Allan Water, which is effective and ingenious, all musicians will be grateful to him. Old English airs are all very well; but a couple of hundred of them on end is more than any reasonable person can be expected to endure at one sitting.

THE DIVIDED WAY

THE DIVIDED WAY. An original play in three acts. By H. V. Esmond. THE MISOGYNIST. An original one-act play. By G. W. Godfrey. St James's Theatre, 23 November 1895.

[30 *November* 1895]

"AT last a noble deed," says Hedda Gabler. "At last a charming play," I was able to exclaim at the St James's, last Saturday, after weeks of splenetic denunciation of the theatre and everything connected with it. The Divided Way is a romantically tragic love drama, written with a delicate freshness of feeling, and here and there a pardonable and even pleasant touch of exaggeration and indiscretion, which gives the work an air of boyish genius and surrounds it with an atmosphere of hope. That the author, Mr Esmond, is youthful in appearance, we all know. Whether he is a young man really, I have no idea. I have known men just like Mr Esmond, and treated them as children of genius—Chattertons, in fact—for fifteen years, during which period their appearance has not altered in the least, only to be finally invited by them to celebrate the tenth birthday of their second eldest grandchild. Consequently until I see Mr Esmond's certificate of birth, I shall suspend my judgment as to whether his years are those of Cayley Drummle or Little Billee. Fortunately age is not a matter of years only, but of evolution. A man of forty-eight is younger in body than a dog of twelve; and in the same way one man at sixty is sometimes younger in mind than another at twenty: at all events it is certain that anyone who chooses his friends from among the brightest spirits of his time will soon become familiar with fathers who are younger than their sons and mothers who are younger than their daughters. Therefore when I say that Mr Esmond's charm is a youthful one, I imply neither patronage nor disparagement: I am perfectly prepared to learn that he is old enough to be my father, and to venerate him in private life whilst envying him in his public aspect.

I call The Divided Way tragically romantic because it ends with death, in unquestioning obedience to the law of the realm of romance, that love is strong as death and jealousy cruel as the grave. In real life this law does not hold. As I have already had to point out in criticizing romantic dramas, love can be more easily baffled and jealousy more safely braved than any of the other passions, in spite of the fact that both social discipline and criminal law are sentimentally relaxed to an alarming degree in favor of people who act on the romantic theory, even to the extent of committing murder. In Mr Esmond's play a young lady falls in love with a young gentleman named Gaunt Humeden, who goes to Africa and gets killed. Thereupon the lady, acting on the celebrated view of the Grand Duchess of Gerolstein, that if you cannot have the man you love you must love the man you have, marries Jack, brother to the deceased. This is no sooner settled than the deceased comes back from Africa to contradict the news of his death, and settles down at Humeden Grange with the rest of the family. He allows the old flirtation to pass as a joke; and so does the lady, each believing that the other no longer cares. Enter to them one day Jay Grist, not, as one would expect, an unscrupulous American financier, but an African traveller. To the lady he reveals the fact that Gaunt, whilst dying in the African desert, raved continually of her: to Gaunt, who explains that the lady no longer cares for him, and that he is pretending not to care for her, he puts the question, "How do you know that she is not pretending also?" Then all the fat is in the fire. The lady takes a practical view of the case, the gentleman an idealistic one. She says, "I agreed to spend my life with Jack under the impression that you were not available. Now that it appears that you *are* available, I propose to spend my life with you. If I stay with Jack I shall make him miserable, make you miserable, and be miserable myself. Clearly it is better economy to make Jack miserable and make you and myself happy." Gaunt is too conventional to be able to explain to her that this is the logic of romance, not of life, and that a broken heart is a much more healthy complaint than she imagines. He threatens to run away to the East again. She trumps that card by threatening to follow him. He then says, "Very good: I shall poison myself; and you can follow me there if you like." This is the logic of romance with a vengeance. Vanquished, she declines the ordeal; and it is agreed that he is to return to the East and that she is not to follow him, but to go home like a good wife. At this point Jack comes in; and for some reason which escaped me at the performance, and which I confess I can trace neither in the logic of romance nor life, is informed of the whole situation. The lady, seeing that this makes the future, romantically speaking, impossible for her, suddenly drinks the poison and ends the play. The moral, apparently, is that which the French assassin offered on the scaffold as the lesson of his experience: "Never confess." But of course the ending, being a romantic ending, exists for its own sake, and not as a peg to hang a moral on.

Like all romantic plays which create a strong illusion, this one irresistibly raises the question how its final situation would do for the starting-point of a realistic play. All Ibsen's later plays, from Pillars of Society to Little Eyolf, are continuations of this kind, a fact which wrought so powerfully with Mr Austin Friars that he actually wrote and put on the stage the drama which lies implicit in the exposition of Rosmersholm, perhaps the most singular dramatic exploit of modern times, and one which, whether it was intended merely to teach Ibsen the right place to begin, or, as I believe, out of a perfectly genuine impulse to put the pathos of the story of Mrs Rosmer on the stage without the merciless philosophy of Ibsen behind it, had its value as an object lesson. It seems to me that if Mr Esmond would reverse the procedure of Mr Austin Friars, and, having already brought Gaunt Humeden to life after killing him, were to bring Mrs Gaunt to life also, we should have a remarkably interesting play on top of the romantic one. Anyone who has attentively watched the world for some years past must by this time be aware that conventional solutions of such situations are growing extremely dangerous and unstable in practice, and that unconventional ones are growing more practicable than they used to be. What exceptional people do in one generation, average people are generally found doing in the next. About twenty-six years ago a somewhat similar dilemma to that in Mr Esmond's play arose between three persons no less famous than Wagner, Hans von Bulow, and Liszt's daughter, Cosima von Bulow. Madame von Bulow preferred to spend her life with Wagner, just as Mrs Humeden in the play preferred to spend her life with Gaunt. The change was effected with the happiest results: at least I am not aware that anybody was a penny the worse—certainly not Madame Wagner, who holds her court at Bayreuth with a dignity which many actual princesses might, and probably do, envy. Far be it from me to suggest anarchical violations of our marriage laws rather than an orderly agitation for constitutional reform of them in harmony with the higher morality of our own times; but I do venture to remark that people who decline to carry obedience to that law too far are at least as interesting dramatically as people who forge and murder, and that the notion that the consequences of such disobedience, when carried out in good faith by respectable people (George Eliot, for example) are necessarily so awful that suicide is the more reasonable alternative, is a piece of nonsense that might as well be dropped on the stage. No human institution could stand the strain of the monstrous assumptions on which our existing marriage laws proceed if we were really sincere about them; and though there is much to be said for our English method of maintaining social order by collectively maintaining the sacredness of our moral ideals whilst we individually mitigate their severity by evasion, collusion, and never seeing anything until our attention is compelled by legal proceedings, yet the abuse of this system of toleration by people whose conduct we are not prepared to excuse, but who cannot very well be exposed if the excusable people are to be spared, is landing us in looser views than we ever bargained for. Already we have an aimlessly rebellious crusade against marriage altogether, and a curious habit of circumspection on the part of the experienced man of the world who, when newly introduced to an English household, picks his way very cautiously until he has ascertained whether the husband and wife really would be husband and wife in France or Germany or South Dakota, and, if his conclusion is unfavorable, which friend of the family is Mr Gaunt Humeden, so to speak. Not that the domestic situations which are not white are all necessarily jet black or even disagreeably grey; but the fact that under the English law a mistake in marriage cannot be effectively remedied except by the disgrace of either party—that is to say, cannot be remedied at all by decent people, divorce being thus a boon reserved to reward the dissolute—is continually producing a supply of cases not at all dissimilar to that which is the subject of

Mr Esmond's play. Most of them are settled, not by suicide, nor by flights into Egypt, but by the parties drifting along, nobody doing anything wrong, and nobody doing anything right, all seeing enough of one another to make them contented *faute de mieux*, whilst maintaining their honor intact. Whether this customary and convenable solution is really better—say in its effect on the children who grow up observing it—than the violent method of open scandal and collusory divorce, involving the public announcement of cruelties and adulteries which have never been committed, is an open question, not admitting of a general answer. Obviously, the ideal husband and wife who give all their affection to one another, and maintain a state of cold indifference to everyone else, should be executed without benefit of clergy as a couple of heartless monopolists; for the idealist may be safely challenged to produce a single instance of a thoroughly happy marriage in which the affection which makes the marriage happy does not extend to a wide circle of friends. Just as good mothers and fathers love all lovable children, so good wives and husbands love all lovable husbands and wives. People with this gift of heart are not prevented from marrying by Don Juan's difficulty: they can be faithful to one without being unfaithful to all the rest. Unfortunately, they are no more common than the domestic terrors who are utterly incapable of living with anybody on tolerable terms. Family life may mean anything between these two extremes, from that of the southern countries where the guide-book warns the English tourist that if he asks a man after his wife's health he will probably be challenged to fight a duel, or that of the English stage, where the same evil construction is maintained on the same pretence of jealousy of private morality and the honor of womanhood, to the most cultivated section of English and American society, where people think of our existing marriage law as Matthew Arnold thought about Tennyson, and unfortunately keep their opinion to themselves with equal "good taste." The practical result is, superhuman pretension, extravagant hypocrisy, tolerance of every sort of misconduct provided it is clandestine, and, of course, a conspiracy of silence. On the whole I think Mr Esmond might do worse than treat his theme over again, this time as a realist instead of a romanticist.

Even in the romantic version it strikes one as odd that it does not occur to the husband that if there is to be any poison taken, he is the man to take it. It seems to me that the natural attitude for a husband whose wife prefers another man is a purely apologetic one; though I observe that on the stage he seems to take it for granted that he is an injured person as well as an unfortunate one. No doubt my moral sense has not been properly trained on such points; so possibly I shall alter my opinion when I get married, though I confess I regard that as an additional reason for not getting married. Howbeit, taking the play as it is, I find it continuously engaging and pleasant, shewing us a humane and villainless society in which naturally sympathetic intercourse replaces the ostentatiously motived communications and revelations of the ordinary play (as if people never told their sorrows to one another spontaneously), and with parts in it that the actors can really feel and study. Miss Millard as Lois is not the somewhat romantic figure, passionate and tragic, that Mr Esmond conceived: she has made Lois a real woman, more fascinating and interesting than any man-made woman could possibly be. Her serious, thoughtful charm, so beautifully sober and dignified, has at last found a part in which it is not disastrously wasted. The moment she enters it is evident that she has created Lois, who lives all through the play, silent or speaking, and makes it her own story. One or two of Mr Esmond's more strained passages—notably the "Ring out the old, ring in the new" business at the end of the second act—were out of the character as she created it; but that was so much the worse for the passages. None of the others achieved anything like the same success, though Mr Vernon would perhaps have got upon the same artistic level if his part had given him the chance. He played admirably as far as his opportunity went. For the rest, Mr Alexander gave us a finished impersonation of Mr George Alexander; Mr Aynesworth was as popular as ever as Mr Allan Aynesworth; and Mr Waring played Mr

Herbert Waring to perfection. Mr Vincent disguised himself to some extent as an Irish doctor, educated at Rugby, where he had acquired an accent something between that of a Ringsend coal-heaver and a Sligo drover, as an Irish gentleman naturally would at an English public school. The play is handsomely staged; and though two unfortunate gentlemen in the gallery rent the air with comfortless lamentations at being defrauded of a happy ending, the rest of the house was enthusiastic in its appreciation.

The Misogynist, by Mr G. W. Godfrey, precedes The Divided Way. It is an elaborately serious background for a joke about a duke and a music-hall singer, which was so amazingly unexpected that it swept the house away. I grieve to say that Mr Alexander, fired by the vogue of the Hero of Waterloo, dodders through the piece as an old man, croaking and piping and exhibiting his tongue so as to produce an effect of having false teeth. The sole merit of the performance is that it deceives nobody. Mr Alexander, fortunately for himself and us, does not belong to the race of Small-weeds, who, born decrepit, can play old men at nineteen. However, we owe Mr Alexander much; and if it pleases him once in a way to paint his face and talk like that under the impression that he is giving a lifelike illustration of one of the Seven Ages, he can depend on us all to keep our countenances and praise him to the skies. Miss Ellice Jeffries, as Kitty Denison, played with a very marked increase of sincerity and artistic courage. If she maintains that rate of improvement her position will finally justify Mr Pinero's choice of her for a leading part in Mrs Ebbsmith.

TOLD YOU SO

Mrs Ponderbury's Past. A farcical comedy in three acts, adapted by F. C. Burnand from Madame Mongodin. By Ernest Blum and Raoul Toche. A Dangerous Ruffian. Comedy in one act. By W. D. Howells. Avenue Theatre.

[7 *December* 1895]

No truly magnanimous soul ever indulges in the mean triumph of "I told you so." Exhibitions of magnanimity, however, are not the business of a critic any more than of a general in the field: for both alike the pursuit is as important as the victory, though it may be a barbarous, murderous, demoralizing cavalry business of cutting down helpless fugitives. It was Lessing, the most eminent of dramatic critics (so I am told by persons who have read him), who was reproached by Heine for not only cutting off his victims' heads but holding them up afterwards to shew that there were no brains in them. The critical profession, in fact, is cruel in its nature, and demands for its efficient discharge an inhuman person like myself. Therefore nobody need be surprised if I raise an exultant and derisive laugh at the clouds of defeat, disappointment, failure, perhaps ruin, which overhang the theatre at present. Where is your Manxman now, with his hired baby and his real water? Has the desperate expedient of fitting Her Advocate with a new act and a new hero saved it from destruction? What of the adipose humors of Poor Mr Potton?—do its authors still believe that the cheaper the article the wider the consumption; or are they mourning with Mr Jerome K. Jerome and Mr Willard over the ingratitude of an imaginary public of idiots to whose level they have condescended in vain? I am not, I hope, an exacting critic: I have been reproached from my own side for approving of Miss Brown and disapproving of Mrs Ebbsmith; and although I should have advised, and been right in advising, Mr Lewis Waller to produce Ibsen's hitherto unacted and impossible Emperor or Galilean rather than The Manxman, since it would have secured him at least a fortnight's business, not to mention a lifetime of artistic credit, yet something as enjoyable as The Passport or The Prude's Progress would have quite satisfied me. I graciously tolerated these plays; and they flourished: I frowned on the others; and they withered from the stage. In this I acted as most sages do, making an easy guess at what was going to happen, and taking care to prophesy it. Dick Hallward, Her Advocate, and The Manxman were nothing but lame attempts to compete with the conventicle by exploiting the rooted love of the public for moralizing and homiletics. Nobody, I hope, will at this time of day raise a senseless braying against preaching in the theatre. The work of insisting that the church is the house of God and the theatre the house of Satan may be left to those poor North Sea islanders who have been brought up to believe that it is wrong to enter a playhouse. The theatre is really the week-day church; and a good play is essentially identical with a church service as a combination of artistic ritual, profession of faith, and sermon. Wherever the theatre is alive, there the church is alive also: Italy, with its huge, magnificent, empty churches, and slovenly, insincere services, has also its huge, magnificent, empty theatres, with slovenly, insincere plays. The countries which we call Scandinavian (to the exasperation of all true Norwegians, somehow) produce saints and preachers, dramatists and actors, who influence all Europe. The fundamental unity of Church and Theatre —a necessary corollary of the orthodox doctrine of omnipresence —is actually celebrated on the stage in such dramas as Brand, and in the Parsifal performance at Bayreuth, which is nothing less than the Communion presented in theatrical instead of ecclesiastical form. Indeed, the matter comes out in a simpler way. Some time ago I had occasion to deliver a public address on the Problems of Poverty in Bristol. Following the custom of those who understand such problems, I put up at the most expensive hotel in the town, where I arrived the night before that appointed for my own performance. After dinner I went into the hall of the hotel to study the theatrical announcements exhibited for the convenience of playgoing visitors. There, among bills of pantomimes and melodramas, I found, in carved wooden frames of "ecclesiastical" gothic design, and with capital letters suggestive of the ten commandments, the announcements of the churches, with the hours of service, and details of the musical arrangements, as to which "special attention" was guaranteed. Leaving all theological and sectarian considerations out of account, I have no doubt whatever that the Bristol churchgoer has a better time of it in point of comfort, decency, cheapness, music, interest, edification, rest and recreation than the Bristol playgoer. I sometimes believe that our playgoers in London are simply stupid people who have not found out those great "draws," the services in St Paul's and Westminster Abbey. Certainly, when I recall some of the evening services I have attended in cathedrals, and compare them with the dull drudgery of sitting out The Manxman, even in a complimentary stall (what must it be in the shilling gallery?) I begin to understand why it is that only the weaklings, the sentimentalists, the unbusinesslike people go to the theatre, whilst the solid, acquisitive, industrous, safely selfish Englishman who *will* have the best value for his money, sticks to the church.

In the face of these facts it cannot be pretended that either our late experiments in melodrama or any other enterprises of the kind in England have ever failed through preaching and sermonizing. The British public likes a sermon, and resents an exhibition of human nature. If you bring on the stage the Englishman who lives in a single-room tenement, as many Englishmen do, and who beats his wife, as all Englishmen do under such circumstances except when their wives beat them, you will be denounced as the author of "a problem play." If you substitute an actor-preacher who declares that "the man who would lift his hand to a woman save in the way of kindness, etc.," it will be admitted on all hands that your feelings do you credit. Your popular Adelphi actor may lack every qualification save one—pious unction. And his most popular act is contrite confession, just as the most popular "evangelist" is the converted collier or prizefighter, who can delight his hearers with the atrocities he committed before his second birth, whilst sanctifying the wicked story with penitent tears and sighs of gratitude for his redemption. I have followed the revivalist preacher through many an incarnation; and now he cannot elude my recognition by merely taking refuge in a theatre. In vain does he mount the stage in a barrister's wig and gown and call his familiar emotional display acting. I am not to be deceived: in his struggles with his mock passion for the leading lady I recognize the old wrestle with the devil: in his muddy joy and relief at having won a verdict of acquittal for her I detect the rapture of the sinner saved. I see him at a glance in Dick Hallward, in Pete Quilliam, in Governor Christian. Mr Cartwright, well schooled at the Adelphi, has his trick to the life; Mr Willard spoils him by trying to act; Mr Lewis Waller utterly destroys him by treating him in the High Church manner; but, spoiled or unspoiled, there he is, all over the stage; and there, too, in the auditorium, is the hysterical groan and sniff which passes with simple souls as evidence of grace abounding. Why, then, has he been so unsuccessful of late? The answer is easy: he has failed to carry conviction. The congregation has said to itself, "This is not Spurgeon, it is Stiggins; and his lying lips are an abomination. The whole thing is put on to make money out of us. Does he take us for fools, with his babies and cradles, his policemen and criminal trials, his bottles of poison and slow music?" That attitude is fatal. Any gospel or anti-gospel will succeed as long as the author and the audience are making for the same end, whether by affirmation and praise, or by satire and negation. But when an author is openly insulting his patrons in the gallery by flattering their conscious hypocrisy, and complimenting them on what he conceives to be their weaknesses and superstitions, and what they themselves equally conceive to be their weaknesses and superstitions, he is predestined to damnation. To be publicly and obviously played down to is more than human nature can bear.

The New Boy and The Strange Adventures of Miss Brown, on the other hand, are genuine appeals to our sense of fun. The authors frankly do their best to tickle us; and we are under no obligation to laugh if they fail, as we are to say Amen to the hypocrisies of the melodramatist. When they do not fail, they prove that they possess some humorous faculty, however schoolboyish it may be; and they seldom pretend to anything more. The danger of the Miss Brown business is that it leads actor-managers—Mr Kerr, for instance, if I may judge from a report of his speech at the Playgoers' Club—into the wild error that people want to be amused and pleased, and go to the theatre with that object. As a matter of fact, they want nothing of the sort. They want to be excited, and upset, and made miserable, to have their flesh set creeping, to gloat and quake over scenes of misfortune, injustice, violence, and cruelty, with the discomfiture and punishment of somebody to make the ending "happy." The only sort of horror they dislike is the horror that they cannot fasten on some individual whom they can hate, dread, and finally torture after revelling in his crimes. For instance, if Ibsen were to rewrite Ghosts, and make Mrs Alving murder her husband, flog Regina, burn down the orphanage purposely, and be killed with a hatchet by Eng-strand just a moment too late to save Oswald from filially taking her guilt on himself and then, after drinking poison to escape the scaffold, dying to slow music in the act of being united to Regina by Pastor Manders, the play would have an immense vogue, and be declared full of power and pity. Ibsen, being apparently of opinion that there is quite enough horror in the ordinary routine of re-spectable life without piling Pelion on Ossa, sends away his audi-ence with their thirst for blood and revenge unsatisfied and their self-complacency deeply wounded. Hence their murmurs against him. What is the secret of the overwhelming reputation of Edmund Kean among the English actors of this century? Hazlitt reveals it thus: "Mr Kean's imagination appears not to have the principles of joy or hope or love in it. He seems chiefly sensible to pain or to the passions that spring from it, and to the terrible energies of mind or body which are necessary to grapple with it." I know that some of our theatrical experts believe that the truly popular trait for a stage hero nowadays is the sort of maudlin goodnature that is an essential part of the worthlessness of the average Strand bar-loafer. But I have never seen much evidence in favor of this idea; and my faith in it is not increased by the en-tire concurrence of the public in my view of Dick Hallward and the barrister in Her Advocate. What the public likes is a villain to torment and persecute the heroine, and a hero to thrash and baffle the villain. Not that it matters much, since what the public likes is entirely beside the question of what it can get. When the popular tribune demands "good words" from Coriolanus, he replies, "He that will give good words to thee will flatter beneath abhorring"; and no great play can ever be written by a man who will allow the public to dictate to him. Even if the public really knew what it likes and what it dislikes—a consummation of wisdom which it is as far from as any child—the true master-dramatist would still give it, not what it likes, but what is good for it.

This brings me to the announcement of the last nights of The Benefit of the Doubt. A run of two months, though not brilliant in comparison with that of Charley's Aunt, is not bad for an entirely serious work of art, especially when it is considered that some of the most important parts are so badly acted that I had to point out after the first night that they might possibly lead to the failure of the piece. The sympathetic part of the play is original and unconventional, so that the sympathy does not flow in the old ready-made channels. Now it is only by a poignant beauty of execution that new channels can be cut in the obdurate rock of the public's hardened heart; and the best stage execution that Mr Pinero could command was for the most part ugly and clumsy. We shall presently have him sharing the fate of Ibsen, and having his plays shirked with wise shakes of the head by actor-managers who have neither the talent to act them nor the brains to understand them. Why was I born into such a generation of duffers!

By the way, I have discovered, quite by accident, an amusing farcical comedy. Somebody told me that there was a farce by Mr W. D. Howells at the Avenue Theatre. I looked in the daily paper, but could find no mention of the name of Mr Howells. However, it was evidently quite possible that the management had never heard of Mr Howells, just as they had apparently never heard of me. So I went, and duly found the name "Howels" on the program. The little piece shewed, as might have been expected, that with three weeks practice the American novelist could write the heads off the poor bunglers to whom our managers generally appeal when they want a small bit of work to amuse the people who come at eight. But no doubt it is pleasanter to be a novelist, to have an intelligent circle of readers comfortably seated by their firesides or swinging sunnily in hammocks in their gardens, to be pleasantly diffuse, to play with your work, to be independent of time and space, than to conform to the stern conditions of the stage and fight with stupidity before and behind the curtain. Mr Howells' piece was followed by a harmlessly naughty and highly entertaining adaptation by Mr Burnand of a certain French play

unknown to me, entitled Madame Mongodin, by Ernest Blum
and Raoul Toche. In it Mr Charles Hawtrey is irresistibly droll;
and Miss Lottie Venne does some clever and funny acting in addition to her old repertory of laughtraps and the inevitable though
obsolescent comic song. A Miss Oliffe, whom I do not remember
to have seen before, comes very near making an artistic success in
the title part, only missing it by a few unhappy lapses into clowning at the crucial passages, according to the tradition of the English stage, where people are always so carefully taught by the
stage-manager to force the fun and spoil it. If Miss Oliffe would
only try the effect of playing the part with absolute sincerity
throughout, and, without slackening her grip, absolutely refuse
to give away her handsome style at any moment for the sake of
raising a silly heehaw by a grimace or an ugly sound or gesture,
she would distinguish herself considerably. Miss Ada Mallon and
Mr W. F. Hawtrey help the performance materially; and the rest,
though they act very indifferently, do not hinder it.

At the Vaudeville The New Boy is at large again. The effective-
ness of this piece of buffoonery appears to be undiminished; but
I cannot help suspecting that the comparative lack of interest in
its successors means that the public have had enough of its vein.

THE OLD ACTING AND THE NEW

The Comedy of Errors. Performance by the Elizabethan Stage
Society in Gray's Inn Hall, 7 December 1895.

[14 *December* 1895]

For a delightful, as distinguished from a commercially promising
first night, the palm must be given this season to the Elizabethan
Stage Society's performance of The Comedy of Errors in Gray's
Inn Hall this day week. Usually I enjoy a first night as a surgeon
enjoys an operation: this time I enjoyed it as a playgoer enjoys a
pleasant performance. I have never, I hope, underrated the importance of the amateur; but I am now beginning to cling to him
as the savior of theatrical art. He alone among the younger generation seems to have any experience of acting. Nothing is more ap-

palling to the dramatic author than the discovery that professional actors of ten years standing have acquired nothing but a habit of brazening out their own incompetence. What is an actor nowadays, or an actress? In nine cases out of ten, simply a person who has been "on tour" with half a dozen "London successes," playing parts that involve nothing but a little business thoughtlessly copied from the performances of their London "creators," with long intervals spent between each tour in the ranks of the unemployed. At the end of a lifetime so spent, the "actor" will no doubt be a genuine expert at railway travelling, at taking lodgings, and at cajoling and bullying landladies; but a decent amateur of two years standing, and of the true irrepressible sort, will beat him hopelessly at his art. What a fate is that of these unhappy young professionals, sick to desperation of a provincial routine compared to which that of a commercial traveller is a dream of romance, longing for a chance which they have not skill enough to turn to account even if some accident thrust it upon them, and becoming less interesting and attractive year by year at a profession in which the steady increase of personal fascination should have no limit but positive senility and decrepitude! I remember, years ago, when the Playgoers' Club was in its infancy, hearing Mr Pinero, in the course of an address to that body, break into an enthusiastic eulogium on the actor of the past, produced by the old stock-company system, versatile, a singer, a dancer, a fencer, an elocutionist, ready to play any part at a day's notice, and equally expert in comedy, drama, melodrama, Christmas pantomime, and the "legitimate." There is some German novel in which a crowd of medieval warriors, fired by the eloquence of Peter the Hermit, burns with a Christian longing to rush to the Holy Land and charge in serried ranks on the Paynim hosts—all except one man, who is obviously not impressed. Indignant at his coldness, they demand what he means by it. "Ive been there," is his sufficient explanation. That is how I felt when I was listening to Mr Pinero. Having been brought up on the old stock-company actor, I knew that he was the least versatile of beings— that he was nailed helplessly to his own line of heavy or light, young or old, and played all the parts that fell to him as the representative of that line in exactly the same way. I knew that his power of hastily "swallowing" the words of a part and disgorging them at short notice more or less inaccurately and quite unimprovably (three months rehearsal would have left him more at sea than three hours) was incompatible with his ever knowing his part in any serious sense at all. I remembered his one absurd "combat" that passed for fencing, the paltry stepdance between the verses of his song in the pantomime that constituted him a dancer, the obnoxiousness of utterance which he called elocution and would impart to pupils for a consideration, the universal readiness which only meant that in his incorrigible remoteness from nature and art it mattered nothing what he did. Mr Pinero madly cited Sir Henry Irving as an example of the product of the stock-company training; but the fact is, when Sir Henry first attempted classical acting at the Lyceum, he did not know the A B C of it, and only succeeded by his original and sympathetic notions of the X Y Z. Nobody who is familiar with the best technical work of the Irving of today, its finish, dignity, and grace, and the exactitude of its expression of his thought and feeling, can (unless he remembers) form any idea of what our chief actor had to teach himself before he could carry veteran playgoers with him in his breach with the tradition of superhuman acting of which Barry Sullivan was, as far as I know, the last English exponent (need I say that the great Irish actor was born in Birmingham?). Barry Sullivan was a splendidly monstrous performer in his prime: there was hardly any part sufficiently heroic for him to be natural in it. He had deficiencies in his nature, or rather blanks, but no weaknesses, because he had what people call no heart. Being a fine man, as proud as Lucifer, and gifted with an intense energy which had enabled him to cultivate himself physically to a superb degree, he was the very incarnation of the old individualistic, tyrannical conception of a great actor. By magnifying that conception to sublimity, he reduced it to absurdity. There were just two serious parts which he could play—Hamlet and Richelieu—the two loveless parts in the grand repertory. I know that some people do not like to think of

Hamlet as loveless, and that the Irving Hamlet has his heart in the right place, and almost breaks it in the scene with Ophelia; but this I take to be the actor's rebuke to Shakespear rather than an attempt to fulfil his intentions. Sir Henry Irving has never thought much of the immortal William, and has given him more than one notable lesson—for instance, in The Merchant of Venice, where he gave us, not "the Jew that Shakespear drew," but the one he ought to have drawn if he had been up to the Lyceum mark. Barry Sullivan, with his gift of lovelessness, *was* Hamlet, and consequently used to put his Ophelias out of countenance more than it is easy to describe. In Hamlet, as in Richelieu, it was right to create a figure whose utter aloofness from his fellows gave him an almost supernatural distinction, and cut him off from all such trifling intimacy with them as love implies. And it was his success in producing this very curious and very imposing effect that made for Barry Sullivan, in his best days (I am not now speaking of the period after 1870 or thereabout), a unique provincial and Australian reputation which carried him over parts he could not play at all, such as Othello, through which he walked as if the only line in the play that conveyed any idea to him was the description of Othello as "perplexed in the extreme," or Macbeth, who was simply Cibber's Richard (a favorite part of his) in mutton-chop whiskers. No doubt his temperament, with its exceptional combination of imaginative energy with coldness and proud timidity of the sympathetic passions, accentuated the super-human pretension in the style of acting which he practised; but his predecessor, Macready (if I may judge from that extremely depressing document, his diary), must have been much more like him than like Sir Henry Irving. At all events, both Macready and Sullivan had abominable tempers, and relied for their stage climaxes on effects of violence and impetuosity, and for their ordinary impressiveness on grandiose assumption of style. Once, when my father mentioned to me that he had seen Macready play Coriolanus, and I asked him what it was like, he replied that it was like a mad bull. I do not offer this as evidence that my critical faculty is an inherited one—clearly there must have been some

artistic method in the bull's madness to have gained such a reputation—but I feel quite sure that when Sir Henry Irving fulfils his
promise to appear as Coriolanus, no father will describe him to
his son as my father described Macready to me. Barry Sullivan,
then, represented the grandiose and the violent on its last legs,
and could do nothing for the young Irving but mislead him.
Irving's mission was to re-establish on the stage the touching,
appealing nobility of sentiment and affection—the dignity which
only asserts itself when it is wounded; and his early attempts to
express these by the traditional methods of the old domineering,
self-assertive, ambitious, thundering, superb school led him for a
time into a grotesque confusion of style. In playing villains, too,
his vein of callous, humorous impishness, with its occasional
glimpses of a latent bestial dangerousness, utterly defied the
methods of expression proper to the heaven-defying, man-quell-
ing tyrant, usurper, and murderer, who was the typical villain of
the old school, and whose flavorless quintessence will be found by
the curious distilled into that instructive Shakespearean forgery,
Ireland's Vortigern. In short, Irving had to find the right expression for a perfectly new dignity and a perfectly new indignity;
and it was not until he had done this that he really accomplished
his destiny, broke the old tradition, and left Barry Sullivan and
Macready half a century behind. I will not say that he also left
Shakespear behind: there is too much of the "not for an age but
for all time" about our bard for that; but it is a pity that the new
acting was not applied to a new author. For though Sir Henry
Irving's acting is no longer a falsification of the old style, his
acting versions are falsifications of the old plays. His Hamlet, his
Shylock, his Lear, though interesting in their own way, are spurious as representations of Shakespear. His Othello I have never
seen: his Macbeth I thought fine and genuine, indicating that his
business is with Shakespear's later plays and not with his earlier
ones. But he owes it to literature to connect his name with some
greater modern dramatist than the late Wills, or Tennyson, who
was not really a dramatist at all. There is a nice bishop's part in
Ibsen's—— but I digress.

My point is that Sir Henry Irving's so-called training under the old stock-company system not only did not give him the individuality of his style—for to that it did not pretend—but that it failed to give him even those generalities of stage deportment which are common to all styles. The stock actor, when the first travelling companies came along, vanished before them, unwept, unhonored, and unsung, because the only sentiment he had inspired in the public was an intense desire for some means of doing without him. He was such an unpresentable impostor that the smart London person, well dressed and well spoken, figuring in plays ingeniously contrived so as to dispense with any greater powers of acting than every adroit man of the world picks up, came as an inexpressible relief. Dare I now confess that I am beginning to have moments of regret for him. The smart nullity of the London person is becoming intolerably tedious; and the exhaustion of the novelty of the plays constructed for him has stripped them of their illusion and left their jingling, rickety mechanism patent to a disgusted public. The latest generation of "leading ladies" and their heroes simply terrify me: Mr Bourchier, who had the good fortune to learn his business as an amateur, towers above them as an actor. And the latest crop of plays has been for the most part deliberately selected for production because of the very abjectness and venality which withered them, harvestless, almost as soon as they were above ground.

And yet there is more talent now than ever—more skill now than ever—more artistic culture—better taste, better acting, better theatres, better dramatic literature. Mr Tree, Mr Alexander, Mr Hare, have made honorable experiments; Mr Forbes Robertson's enterprise at the Lyceum is not a sordid one; Mr Henry Arthur Jones and Mr Pinero are doing better work than ever before, and doing it without any craven concession to the follies of "the British public." But it is still necessary, if you want to feel quite reassured, to turn your back on the ordinary commercial west end theatre, with its ignoble gambling for "a catch-on," and its eagerly envious whisperings of how much Mr Penley has made by Charley's Aunt, to watch the forlorn hopes that are led from time to time by artists and amateurs driven into action by the starvation of their artistic instincts. The latest of these is the Elizabethan Stage Society; and I am delighted to be able to taunt those who missed the performance in Gray's Inn Hall with being most pitiably out of the movement. The Lyceum itself could not have drawn a more distinguished audience; and the pleasant effect of the play, as performed on the floor of the hall without proscenium or fittings of any kind, and played straight through in less than an hour and a half without any division into acts, cannot be as much as imagined by any frequenter of our ordinary theatres. The illusion, which generally lapses during performances in our style whenever the principal performers are off the stage, was maintained throughout: neither the torchbearers on the stage nor the very effective oddity of the Dromio costumes interfering with it in the least. Only, the modern dresses of the audience, the gasaliers, and the portrait of Manisty next that of Bacon, were anachronisms which one had to ignore. The stage management was good as regards the exits, entrances, and groupings—not so good in the business of the speeches, which might have been made more helpful to the actors, especially to Adriana, whose best speeches were underdone. On the whole the acting was fair—much better than it would have been at an average professional performance. Egeon, one of the Dromios, and the courtezan distinguished themselves most. The evening wound up with a Dolmetsch concert of lute and viol, virginal and voice, a delectable entertainment which defies all description by the pen.

MR JOHN HARE

JOHN HARE, COMEDIAN. A biography by T. Edgar Pemberton. London and New York: George Routledge & Sons. 1895.

[21 *December* 1895]

IN view of the fact that Mr Hare is one of the best actors of my time, nothing has surprised me more in reading this book than the number of impersonations of his which I have seen and totally forgotten. A real part well acted is to me more easily and perfectly memorable than most things; so, considering how well I remember the good parts I have seen Mr Hare play, and that all his parts may safely be taken to have been well acted, I cannot help feeling that every part I forget raises a question as to whether it was a real part or not. Further, I am reminded that Mr Hare made a great success as a manager—that the mounting and acting, the elaborate rehearsing and thoughtfully minute preparation of plays at his theatre were the admiration of the critics to whom Robertson was as much the pioneer of a new order as Ibsen is to the present generation. In the days of Mr Hare's reign at the old Court Theatre, and of the St James's under the Hare-Kendal management, I quite agreed in this opinion. But the Garrick period is another affair. There was no carelessness, no slackening at the new house; and yet it seemed to me that Mr Forbes Robertson and Miss Kate Rorke acted worse and worse throughout their long engagement there; whilst as for the stage management, a climax of something like unsympathetic ineptitude was reached in Mrs Lessingham. No mortal playgoer, however credulous, could have believed in the third act of that play as it was put on the Garrick stage. Poor Mrs Lessingham, fainting with the shock of catching her husband embracing another lady on the summit of an eminence visible from seven counties, or dying by her own hand, after a prolonged scene of deepening despair, in a room like Maple's shop window, had no more chance than A Scrap of Paper would have had if mounted in the style of Pelléas et Mélisande. The fact is, that in the seventies and eighties, the art of stage management meant the art of making the stage look like a real room in a richly and handsomely furnished London house; and this Mr Hare did to perfection, with every nicety of discrimination between Russell Square and Park Lane. A well-kept gentleman's garden in Surrey, or even a pretty old vicarage, he could turn out also. There was another thing that he understood. Mr Pemberton quotes Mr Clement Scott on Mr Bancroft in the early Robertson days. "Think what it was to see a bright, cheery, pleasant young fellow playing the lover to a pretty girl at the time when stage lovers were nearly all sixty, and dressed like waiters at a penny-ice shop." Now these cheery, pleasant fellows, so smartly tailored and exactly true to nature in the young male as we see him at suburban garden parties or in the first-class carriage of the city train, would have made wings, flats, canvas doors and carpetless boards as ridiculous as pasteboard fowls, or white chairs with red damask seats and a strip of gold tinsel down the leg. They needed Mr Hare's interiors to move in. And they were indeed delightful when they got them. Young persons who saw the revival of Caste at the Garrick in 1894 may imagine that they enjoyed it as their fathers enjoyed it. They are wrong. They can never know what it was to see on the stage a gentleman who looked like a gentleman walking into a drawing room that looked like a drawing room after a lifetime spent in contemplating performances compared to which an average representation of La Traviata at Covent Garden might pass as photographically realistic. It was Mr Hare who carried this art to its summit; and since the youngest generation of London playgoers, taking such staging as a matter of course, may be unable to conceive the pleasure it gave when it was new, it is only fair to tell them how much they owe him for a reform which was of high artistic importance in bringing the stage into closer connection with contemporary life. I do not say that the stage drawing rooms of the old Court and the St James's were better than "four boards and a passion"; but they were worlds above flats, wings, sky borders and no passion, which was the practical alternative.

Now in art, as in politics, there is no such thing as gratitude. It is one thing to banish vulgarity and monstrosity from the stage and replace them by conventional refinement and scrupulous verisimilitude. It is quite another to surround a real drama with its appropriate atmosphere, and provide a poetic background or an ironically prosaic setting for a tragic scene. There are some rooms in which no reasonable person could possibly commit suicide; and when Mr Hare provided just such a one for Mrs Lessingham, he shewed that he was not a stage manager in the same sense as Sir Henry Irving, for instance. Even in the matter of refinement he is no longer in the front rank. When Mr Henry Arthur Jones produced The Crusaders at the Avenue Theatre under his own management, as a sort of polite hint to whomsoever it might concern that an author could do without an actor-manager better than an actor-manager could do without an author, he, being a disciple of Ruskin, repudiated the once admired gentlemanly apartment, and went off to Mr William Morris in search of a beautiful room. The scene in that play called The Parsley Garland, was the first piece of artistic as distinguished from commercial decoration I remember to have seen on the stage as a representation of a modern room. There must be some young people in the world whose first visit to a theatre was to The Crusaders, and who afterwards went to see Slaves of the Ring at the Garrick. I am afraid, after the Parsley Garland, they will open their eyes very wide indeed at the suggestion implied in Mr Pemberton's book that the ugly plutocratic interior in the first act of Mr Grundy's play, and the appalling conservatory in the last act, where Miss Kate Rorke jumped through the fir-tree, may be taken as samples of the taste of the acknowledged chief of stage managers in that class of work. It is but fair to explain to them that the work of making the stage clean, handsome, fashionable, correct, costly, and thoroughly gentlemanly, was an indispensable preliminary to any movement towards beauty, individuality, and imaginative setting.

If Mr Hare's scenic foundations are by this time built upon and hidden, what shall be said of the "bright, cheery, pleasant young fellows" who belonged to them? For thirty years we have sat at the play feeding our romantic imaginations on the "good form" of young stockbrokers and civil servants. Mr Hare was always an excellent host; and when he invited us to meet those nice people the Kendals, we knew that we could count upon amusement, instruction in manners, dress, and furnishing, and the contemplation of an edifying example of stainless domestic virtue. Still, so unregenerate is human nature, that the main part of the attraction was the amusement; and the amusement depended on the circumstance that Mrs Kendal could act and so could

Mr Hare. Even Mr Kendal was a bit of a comedian, and was always agreeable and sincere. They represented a generation of actors who had toned their acting down and their dress and manners up to stockbroker-civil-servant pitch. This was all very well whilst it lasted; but unfortunately the drawing room drama, being artistically a sterile hybrid, could not renew the generation of actors; and now the Kendals are replaced by couples equal to them in dress, manners, good looks, and domestic morality, but subject to the disadvantage of not possessing in their two united persons as much power of acting as there was in the tip of Mrs Kendal's little finger-nail. Besides, there has come along the terrible Ibsen. The stockbrokerly young gentleman, standing on the stage with his manners carefully turned to the audience like the painted side of an old stage banner, has suddenly been taken by the scruff of the neck by the grim Norwegian giant, and, with one ruthless twist, whisked round with his seamy side to the footlights, to stare in helpless bewilderment at the atmo-sphere of poetry, imagination, tragedy, irony, pity, terror, and all the rest of it, suddenly rising in the theatre from which they had been swept, he had hoped, for ever, along with the "stage lovers nearly all sixty and dressed like waiters at a penny-ice shop." And now he may shriek, with Judge Brack, that "people dont do such things"; he may plunge back to Whitechapel Road melodrama or forward to the best imitation "problem plays"; but he will struggle in vain against the fact that the surest way of boring yourself to death of an evening now is to go to the theatre. The drawing room comedy of furniture and manners, with a tastefully conducted intrigue as a pretext, is as dead as Donizetti and deader. The novelty of the change from the penny-ice shopman to the gentleman is exhausted; and now the people want a change from the gentleman to the actor.

Certain fine actors of the Robertsonian epoch can still attract us with the art of that period, and are even taken as models with success by younger artists, just as Patti keeps Una Voce and Bel raggio alive, and is followed to some extent by Melba, in spite of Wagner and Calvé. Mr Hare is just such a survival. As an

actor he has had to work in a drama so superficial that his fame
rests largely upon that most unreal of all stage pretences, a young
man pretending to be a very old one. Mr Hare, in these parts,
used to make himself up cleverly; and he is the sort of man whose
voice, figure, and manner, vary comparatively little from twenty-
five to seventy. But that any playgoer who had ever seen Chippen-
dale could have mistaken Mr Hare's business for the real thing
is beyond my belief. As a matter of fact we did not make any
such mistake: the fun of Mr Hare's old men was the cleverness
of the imitation, which was amusing even when his part was
utterly uninteresting in itself. Now that he is between fifty and
sixty, his acting of elderly parts is no longer a pretence; consequently we no longer chuckle at it: we are touched—which is
much better—if the part is a touching one. Fortunately for me,
the first part I ever saw Mr Hare play (my first ten years' experience as a playgoer was not gained in London) was that of the boy
Archie in A Scrap of Paper. I remember Archie perfectly—should
know him if I met him tomorrow. But Mr Hare's made-up old
men I forget as individuals, though I can recall certain stage
moments in which they figured. For example, I can see him in
The Queen's Shilling gripping Mr Kendal's wounded arm; and
the picture recalls the make-up, uniform, and general aspect of
the Colonel; but this recollection of a painful scene, which would
be equally vivid had the officer been the young man and the
soldier the old one, is quite a different affair from recollection
of a character. Again, I recollect his Jack Pontifex in Mamma
(Duval in Les Surprises de Divorce) as his masterpiece in farcical
comedy; and Jack Pontifex was younger, not older, than Mr Hare.
His Baron Croodle in The Money Spinner was a genuine impersonation: I shall never forget that old blackguard. His unvener-
able years, however, were the merest accident. Jack Pontifex was
especially interesting to the critic because Mr Hare has very seldom played what may be called a standard part: that is, one in
which his performance can be compared with that of other eminent performers in his line. Luckily, Les Surprises de Divorce
had been made famous by Coquelin, the greatest comedian known

to us. Mr Hare had by no means the worst of the comparison in
point of execution. In the great scene in the second act, where
the wretched musician, having escaped by divorce from an un-
bearable mother-in-law, and settled down on his remarriage into
tranquil domestic felicity, sees the terrible old woman re-enter,
imposed on him again in the old relation by a fresh turn of the
matrimonial courts, Mr Hare surpassed Coquelin. Coquelin
clowned it, even to the length of bounding into the air and throwing forward his arms and legs as if to frighten off some dangerous
animal. But he did not produce the electric effect of Mr Hare's
white, tense face and appalled stare, conveying somehow a mad
speed of emotion and a frightful suspense of action never to
be forgotten by any playgoer with the true dramatic memory.
Coquelin's compensation in the comparison lay in the greater
fullness of his contributions to the drama. He played between
the lines, and quadrupled the value of the part: Mr Hare, with
his swift, crisp method, and his habit of picking up a cue as if
it were a cricket ball to be smartly fielded, only made the most
of the play as it was. No doubt Mr Hare's method is the right
method for a man who forms his conclusions rapidly and gives
them instantaneous and incisive expression; but Duval, in Les
Surprises, was certainly not that sort of man. Nothing could
have been truer or more entertaining than Coquelin's play in
the first act, where he shews out the gentleman and his daughter
who have come to look at the rooms he wishes to let. It was not
from anything that Duval said that you saw that the daughter
had made an impression on him. As he slowly came back with
preoccupied gait from the door, you could read a whole chapter
of unconscious autobiography in the changes of his face; and
when at last, after a long but most eloquent and interesting
silence, the words "Elle est charmante!" slipped from him, he
had in effect left the technical cue for that speech half a dozen
well-filled pages behind. Mr Hare's method is too impatient, and
his imagination too dry and sane for this; consequently he adds
little or nothing to the written part, whereas with Coquelin the
written part is always the merest skeleton of his creation. What

Mr Hare does do he does as well, and here and there better than the French comedian. It is unreasonable to say to an artist who has done so much so finely that he might have done more; and I only say it myself to encourage the others. In so rapidly progressive a business as fine art now is in England, no mortal man can lead more than one generation. No doubt Mr Hare ought to have done for Ibsen what he did for Robertson: for example, he might have created old Ekdal in The Wild Duck, instead of leaving that immortalizing chance to an amateur. But in his early days the standard classic was London Assurance; and throughout his management at the old Court and the St James's, the plays he produced were, after all, the best to be had. Some, like The Hobby Horse, were too good for the public; and many were excellent plays of their kind, superexcellently done. All one can say is that the poetry of the Ellen Terry days, of New Men and Old Acres (a piffling play, only I can still see and hear Lilian Vavasour crying like mad in it) and of Olivia, stands the test of time better than the clever prose of the Kendal period. Miss Terry had at that time hidden somewhere about her a certain perverse devil, since exorcised by the elevating influence of the Lyceum Theatre and that actress-devouring ogre William Shakespear, which gave the most curious naughty-child charm to Lilian and Olivia. Nowadays you can only admire or adore: then she gave you something to forgive and coaxed you to forgive it. The coaxing was a surprisingly pleasant process; and as I was one of those who experienced it, I should advise the public not to pay too much attention to my criticisms of Miss Terry, as they are sure to be grossly partial. And that partiality I owe among other things to Mr Hare.

I leave the subject only half exhausted for lack of space. I can only add that the book ends with a testimonial to Mr Hare's professional competency, and a recommendation of him to the encouraging notice of the American nation from the Siddonian hand of Mary Anderson de Navarro. How proud Mr Hare must feel! It is just like our Mary's—I mean it does credit to Madame de Navarro's feelings.

ONE OF THE WORST

ONE OF THE BEST. A drama in four acts. By Seymour Hicks and
George Edwardes. Adelphi Theatre, 21 December 1895.

[28 *December* 1895]

THE new entertainment at the Adelphi has for its object the
reproduction on the stage of the dramatic effect of the military
ceremony of degradation undergone not long ago in France by
Captain Dreyfus. The idea is not a bad one from the Adelphi
point of view; but the work of setting it into a dramatic frame
has fallen into the wrong hands, the two authors' familiarity with
the stage and its requirements only giving an absurdly cheerful
and confident air to their feeble and slippery grip of a subject
much too big for them.

The Dreyfus affair was interesting in many ways. It was
French—French in the most un-English way, because it was not
only theatrical, but theatrical at the expense of common sense
and public policy. At the Adelphi Mr Terriss is able to exclaim
at the end of the piece that no English officer has ever betrayed
his country; and this understanding, the value of which we are
all sensible enough to appreciate, we keep up by breaking and
getting rid of our Dreyfuses in the quietest possible manner,
instead of advertising them by regimental *coups de théâtre*, which,
in addition to being as demoralizing as public executions, would
shatter that national confidence in the absolute integrity of our
public services and institutions which we all keep up with such
admirable *esprit de corps*, not that any of us believes in it, but
because each of us thinks that it is good for all the rest to believe
in it. Our plan is to govern by humbug, and to let everybody
into the secret. The French govern by melodrama, and give
everybody a part in the piece. The superiority of our system
lies in the fact that nobody dislikes his share in it, whereas the
French are badly hampered because you cannot have broadly
popular melodrama without a villain, and nobody wants to be
cast for the villain's part. Consequently a delinquent like Dreyfus

is a perfect godsend to the French authorities, and instantly has all the national limelights flashed on him, whereas here he would be quietly extinguished in support of the theory that such conduct as his could not possibly occur in the British army.

There is another weakness in the French method. Even when you have got your villain, how are you going to make him do his best for the effect of the sensation scene? At the Adelphi it is easy enough, since the villain, though he might often make a whole play ridiculous by a single disloyal intonation, can be depended on to omit no stroke of art that will intensify the loathing or louden the execrations of the gallery. It is his point of honor as an artist to blacken himself: he is paid to do it, proud to do it, and depends on doing it for his livelihood. But Dreyfus was not in this position. He had every possible motive to "queer the pitch" of the military melodrama of which he was the villain and victim; and he did it most effectually. He declined to be impressed by the ceremony or to pretend that the parade of degradation was worse than death to him as a French soldier. He displayed a sardonic consciousness of the infinite tomfoolery of the whole proceeding, and succeeded in leaving all Europe able to think of nothing in connection with it except the ludicrous fact that the uniform which had been stripped and defaced had been carefully prepared for that stage trick the night before by having its facings and buttons ripped off in private and basted on again with light cotton. When the farce was over, he took the stage, shouted, "Vive la République," and marched off, having made the hit of the piece, and leaving the Republic and its army looking like the merest crowd of "extras." This was perhaps a mistake; for the shout of "Vive la République" was, at least to English ways of thinking, out of the wronged and innocent character which Dreyfus was assuming: at least, it is certain that an English officer, if innocent, would under such circumstances either keep his feelings to himself, or else, if unable to contain them, roundly and heartily damn his country, his colonel, the court-martial, the army, the sergeant, and everybody else on whom he could with any sort of relevance bring his tongue and temper to bear.

A Dreyfus case is the less likely to arise here because we are not only free from the fear of invasion from armed neighbors which makes Continental nations so sensitive on the subject of spies, but also less childishly addicted to keeping secrets that are no secrets. Campaigns depend on strategy, fighting, and money, not on patents; and a nation which had no better idea of preparation for war than hiding a secret explosive or a new weapon or an undisclosed plan of fortification up its sleeve—an idea which appears particularly plausible to the civilian imagination—would richly deserve what it would probably get in the field. We have many ways of making idiots of ourselves; but the Continental way of arresting artists on sketching tours, and confiscating drawings which give no information that cannot be obtained at any stationer's shop where they sell maps, photographs, and railway timetables, is one which we have so far spared ourselves.

These observations are not very recondite; but they appear to have completely escaped the perspicacity of the authors of One of the Best. In the second act an impossible K.C.B., A.D.C., declaims against the folly of England in allowing strangers to roam the land with kodaks, photographing her forts and worming out the secrets of the Tower of London, Woolwich Arsenal, Dover Castle, and other strongholds of our national independence, instead of imitating the heroic example of the foreigner by turning out the garrison and searching the pretended tourist, artist, and holiday-maker for concealed copies of the Monroe Doctrine. A gratuitously asinine opinion, I thought, which was received by the gallery with obediently asinine applause. The degradation scene shewed an equal want of grasp of military life and English character. The one sentence that was taken from life as exemplified by Dreyfus was just the one sentence that stamped that gentleman as probably guilty. Lieutenant Dudley Keppel is made to finish his ordeal by shouting "God save the Queen" (the equivalent of "Vive la République"), which at such a time can only mean either that the creature is tamed by discipline to the point of being an absolute spaniel, or else that he is a genuine criminal, asserting his highmindedness in a fine stock phrase, as all rascals do whenever they get a chance. On the points of Dreyfus's bearing which seem worthy of imitation by officers in trouble, Dudley Keppel was resolutely original. He did his utmost to make the barbarous and silly spectacle a success by displaying frightful emotion. Before parting with his claymore he kissed it and then broke it across his knee, a proceeding which even the greenest country cousin in the pit must have known to be quite acutely the reverse of anything that a British officer could be conceived as doing upon any provocation or in any extremity. And yet the scene, properly re-written, could be made highly entertaining with Mr Fred Kerr instead of Mr Terriss in the principal part.

It is interesting to observe that Messrs Hicks and Edwardes seem as incapable of realizing the reality and humanity of a woman as of a soldier. I am not now alluding to the maiden of Keppel's heart. Like most such maidens she is a nonentity; and the unlucky lieutenant is driven to the most abject expedients to work up the sentiment in his love scene with her, shaking blossoms from a tree over her, and helplessly repeating a catalogue of the most affecting objects and circumstances of the scene (provided on purpose), as, for instance, "The old Abbey, the organ, the setting sun," and so on. But there is another young and beauteous female in the piece, a Miss Esther Coventry, who in the most pathetically sentimental way commits a series of crimes which Jonathan Wild himself would hardly have gone through without moments of compunction. Political treachery, theft, burglary, perjury, all involving the most cruel consequences to her father and his amiable young lieutenant, are perpetrated by her without hesitation or apology to get money for a man with whom she is carrying on an intrigue out of pure love of deceit, there being no mortal reason why he should not woo her in honorable form. Throughout all her nefarious proceedings I failed to detect any sign of its having occurred to the authors that any moral responsibility attached to this young woman. In fulfilment of their design she went about with an interesting air of having sinned and suffered, cheating, lying, stealing, burgling, and bearing false witness exactly as if she were the heroine of the play, until, in the last scene in the barrack square, the rehabilitated Keppel suddenly said, "Allow me," and gallantly ordered his general to take that wounded dove to his manly bosom and be more a father to her than ever. As in real life the young lady could not, even by the most violent stretch of judicial leniency, have got off with less than ten years penal servitude, it was difficult, in spite of the magnificent air with which Mr Terriss proclaimed the amnesty, to quite believe that the civil authorites would submit to be set aside in this manner; but apparently they did: at all events she was still in the peace of complete absolution when the curtain descended.

On the whole, the play, even judged by melodramatic standards, is a bad one. The degradation scene is effective in a way; but what that way is may best be shewn by pointing out that if a military flogging had been substituted, the effect would have been still greater, though the tax on Mr Terriss's fortitude would no doubt have been unreasonable. The court-martial is also effective, but not more so than any trial scene must necessarily be. A trial is the last resource of a barren melodramatist: it is so safe an expedient that improvised amateur attempts at it amused even the doomed aristocrats in the Paris prisons during the Terror. The scene of the attempt to rob the safe produces a certain curiosity as to how the authors will bring about the foregone conclusion of fixing the guilt on the innocent Keppel; but the clumsiness of the solution soon melts this curiosity into a sensation like that of watching a bad chess-player. Then there is the scene in which the villain is thrown like a welsher on a racecourse to a savage crowd, who delight the audience by making as plausible a pretence of tearing him to pieces as is consistent with the integrity of Mr Abingdon's person. The comic scenes may be divided into three parts: first, puerile jokes about the deficiencies in a Highlander's uniform and the situation of the "pistol pocket" in the bicycling suit worn by Miss Vane Featherstone; second, speeches not in the least funny which are nevertheless funnily delivered by Mr Harry Nicholls; and third, a certain quantity of tolerable fun mixed with a few puns and personalities, evidently the invention of that gifted comedian. The rest hardly rises sufficiently above nothingness to be as much as dull; and I see no reason to anticipate an exceptionally prosperous career for the play. Mr George Edwardes was immensely congratulated on his appearance as an author, the audience seeming to regard it as an irresistible joke; and I am rather inclined to take that lenient view myself. If I am to take it seriously I can only say that however successful Mr Edwardes may be as a manager, he must work a good deal harder if he wishes to succeed in a really difficult profession like that of dramatic authorship.

The acting is, of course, consistently outrageous, though by no means unskilfully so. Mr Terriss contrives to retain his fascination even in tartan trousers; and he rises fully to such heights as there are in the trial scene and the degradation scene. It is always a pleasure to hear his voice now that we have on the stage so many made-up voices which ring with monotonous sonority in the speakers' noses. With the single exception of Mr Bernard Gould, Mr Terriss appears to be the only serious actor in his line from whom we hear a cultivated natural voice instead of an acquired artificial one. Of Miss Millward's capacity I have no idea beyond the fact that she has clearly more than sufficient for such parts as are to be had at the Adelphi. Mr Nicholls is an excellent actor: it is a thousand pities that his talent is only employed to put us into good humor with bad plays.

I observe that Mr Dana, at the Duke of York's Theatre, has also fallen back on military melodrama. But the enterprise, not having expressly courted my notice, escaped it until too late; and I can only admire Mr Dana's daring in making yet another effort to convert the west end to melodrama after the extremely poor luck which has attended that aspiration so far.

END OF VOL. I